The Historical Mosques of Saudi Arabia

The HISTORICAL MOSQUES *of* SAUDI ARABIA

G R D King

Longman
London and New York

Longman Group UK Limited,
Longman House, Burnt Mill, Harlow,
Essex CM20 2JE, England
and Associated Companies throughout the world.

© Longman Group UK Limited 1986
All rights reserved; no part of this publication may be reproduced, stored in a retrieval system, or transmitted in any form or by any means, electronic, mechanical, photocopying, recording, or otherwise, without the prior written permission of the Publishers.

953.8
King

First published 1986

King, Geoffrey R.D.
The historical mosques of Saudi Arabia.
1. Mosques—Saudi Arabia—History
I. Title
953.8 BP187.65.S2

ISBN 0-582-78392-5

Set in 10/11pt Linotron 202 Garamond Light

Printed in Spain
by Graficas Estella, S.A.

Contents

Special acknowledgment 7
Acknowledgment 8
Note on transliteration 9
Foreword 10
Introduction 11
Historical background 13

I Western Saudi Arabia 17
The Hejaz and the Red Sea coast 18
Makkah al-Mukarramah: The Honourable Ka^c^ba and the Holy Mosque 19
Other mosques of Makkah al-Mukarramah 26
al-Madina al-Monawarah: Masjid Qubā' 27
The Mosque of the Prophet (Ṣ) 27
Other mosques of al-Madina al-Monawarah 34
Jidda 34
al-Ṭā'if 41
al-Wajh 42
Tabūk 47
al-^c^Ulā 50
Khaybar 51
al-Thamad 54
The Tihāma 55
al-Qunfudha 55
Tihāmat ^c^Asīr 56
Ṣabyā 56
Abū ^c^Arīsh 60
Muḥāyil 65
Farasān 65
The Tihāma mountains 75
Banī Mālik 75
Fayfā' 79
The southern Hejaz and ^c^Asīr 82
Bilād Zahrān 83
al-Suqā' 83
Jamal 87
Sharama 89
Ṭabab 91
Masqī 93
Aḥad Rufayda 98
Wādī Najrān 99
Dahdha al-Ṣuqūr 99
Sha^c^b Burān al-Ḥārith 108
Bilād Banī Salman, Banī ^c^Alī 110
al-Aswār 113
II Central Saudi Arabia 115
Northern Nejd 117
Dūmat al-Jandal 117
Ḥā'il 120
al-Qaṣīm 122
^c^Unayza 122
Burayda 125
Western Nejd 130
al-Batrā' and al-Rawḍa 130
Uqlat al-Ṣuqūr 132
Shaqrān 132
Central Nejd 133
Zilfī 133
Majma^c^a 134
Jalājil 136
al-Rawḍa 141
al-^c^Awda 142
Malham 143
Ḥuraymilā' 144
Sudūs 146
Ḥazwa 149
al-Dir^c^iyya and its environs 149
Wādī Ḥanīfa 152
al-Ghaṣība 153
^c^Arqa 154
Riyadh 156
Ghaṭ Ghaṭ 160
Southern Nejd 161
al-Kharj 162
al-Ṣaḥanā' 162
al-Ḥawṭa 165
Na^c^ām 166
al-Aflāj 166

III The Eastern Province 167
al-Hufūf 169
al-Mubarraz 176
al-Aḥsā' oasis 177
The coast 180
al-Qaṭīf 180
al-ᶜUqayr 182
al-Jubayl 184

Saudi Arabian mosques and the Islamic architectural tradition 189
Notes 192
Bibliography of Arabic sources 201
Bibliography of non-Arabic sources 202
Glossary of Arabic terms 205
Index 206

Special acknowledgment

The very considerable assistance and advice provided by the Ministry of Information of the Kingdom of Saudi Arabia at every stage in the research and preparation of this book is acknowledged with gratitude. Without this generous co-operation from the outset I could not have undertaken this project and I am deeply indebted to the Ministry.

The Ministry of Pilgrimage and Religious Endowments of the Kingdom of Saudi Arabia likewise has provided much assistance which is also greatly appreciated. I extend my sincere thanks to the officials of both Ministries for their continuous support throughout this research project.

GRDK

Acknowledgments

I am indebted to many people in the Kingdom of Saudi Arabia for their assistance during research for this account of the mosques of their country. From the outset I have received every possible assistance and facility thanks to the support of H.E. Dr Abdulaziz H. Alsowayegh, Assistant Deputy Minister for Foreign Information at the Ministry of Information. H.E. Mr Hussam Khashuqji, Assistant Deputy Minister at the Ministry of Pilgrimage and Religious Endowments has also given me the benefit of his advice and encouragement on many occasions. I express my profound gratitude to both Dr Alsowayegh and Mr Khashuqji for their sustained interest in this book and their enthusiasm. I also wish particularly to thank H.R.H. Amīr ʿAbd Allah b. Fayṣal b. Turkī Al ʿAbd Allah Al Saʿūd, whose advice and guidance has always been forthcoming and whose encouragement has had much to do with the completion of this book.

Since 1402/1982 I have been assisted by many Saudi officials in different parts of the Kingdom. I have met with courtesy, kindness and much hospitality, and without the help which has been given to me in so many ways, the research could never have been undertaken. I am greatly indebted to all who have given me their assistance and co-operation and I wish to thank the following:

ʿAsīr Province: H.E. Mr Muḥammad al-Sulaymān al-Suwaylim, Assistant Deputy Governor, ʿAsīr *amārā*; Dr Ibrāhīm al-Saʿīd, ʿAsīr *amāra*; Mr Muḥammad ʿAlī, ʿAsīr *amāra*.
Ṭabab: Shaykh Saʿūd; Mr ʿAbd Allah b. ʿAbd al-ʿAzīz.

Eastern Province: H.H. Amīr Muḥammad b. Fahad b. Jilūwī, Governor, al-Aḥsā' area; H.E. Mr ʿAbd al-Wahhāb al-Budai, Deputy *wakil*, al-Aḥsā'; H.E. Shaykh Muḥammad Mubārak, *imām, jāmiʿ* Imām Fayṣal b. Turkī, al-Hufūf; H.E. Mr ʿAbd al-ʿAzīz al-ʿIsā, Director, and Mr A. al-Thāni and Mr Adel al-Arfaj, Department of Pilgrimage and Religious Endowments, al-Aḥsā'.

Ḥā'il Province: H.R.H. Amīr Miqrin b. ʿAbd al-ʿAzīz Al Saʿūd, Governor, Ḥā'il Province; H.E. Shaykh Muqbil, Deputy Governor, Ḥā'il Province; Mr. Lafi Irshaid al-Ḥarbī, Ḥā'il *amāra*.
Jalājil: H.E. Mr Aḥmad b. ʿAbd Allah Suwir, Governor, Jalājil.

al-Jawf Province: H.H. Amīr ʿAbd al-Raḥmān b. Aḥmad al-Sudairy, Governor, al-Jawf; H.H. Amīr Sulṭān b. ʿAbd al-Raḥmān al-Sudairy; H.H. Amīr Ziād b. ʿAbd al-Raḥmān al-Sudairy.
Jidda: Mr Izzat Mufti, Director, Ministry of Information, Jidda; Mr Aḥmad Ṣāliḥ al-Ghamdī, Ministry of Information, Jidda.

Jīzān Province: H.H. Amīr Muḥammad Turkī al-Sudairy, Governor, Jīzān Province; H.H. Amīr Aḥmad Turkī al-Sudairy, Deputy Governor, Jīzān Province; Mr ʿAbd al-ʿAzīz al-Huwaidī, former Director of General Affairs, Jīzān *amāra*; Mr Fahad Muḥammad al-Fahaid, Director of General Affairs, Jīzān *amāra*; Mr Muḥammad Haiḍar al-Manṣūr, Jīzān *amāra*.
Abū ʿArīsh: H.E. Mr Yahya Ibrāhīm Quraibī, Governor, Abū ʿArīsh; Mr ʿAli Yahya ʿAsīr, Abū ʿArīsh *amāra*.
Banī Mālik: H.E. the Governor,Banī Mālik.
Ṣabyā: H.E. Mr Ṣāliḥ Sulaimān al-ʿAid, Governor, Ṣabyā; Mr Ibrāhīm ʿAbd Allah Mabrūk, Ṣabyā *amāra*.

Khaybar: H.E. Mr Muḥammad b. Misaymir al-ʿAtaybī, Governor, Khaybar.

Makkah al-Mukarramah Province: H.R.H. Amīr Majid b. ʿAbd al-ʿAzīz Al Saʿūd, Governor, Makkah al-Mukarramah Province.
al-Qunfudha: H.E. Mr ʿAbd Allah Muḥammad, Governor, al-Qunfudha; H.E. Mr Saʿīd ʿUmar Bā Ashwān, Deputy Governor, al-Qunfudha; Mr Nāṣir Muḥammad Bā Sindwa, al-Qunfudha *baladiyya*; Mr ʿAlawi ʿAbd al-Wāḥid, al-Qunfudha *baladiyya*.

Najrān Province: H.H. Amīr Fahad b. Khālid al-Sudairy, Governor, Najrān Province; H.H. Amīr Nāṣir b. Khālid al-Sudairy, Deputy Governor, Najrān Province; Mr Nāṣir al-Rāshid, General Director, Najrān *amāra*; Mr. Manṣūr Muḥammad al-Ṣuqūr, Najrān *amāra*.

al-Qaṣīm Province: H.E. Mr Muḥammad Al Suwaylim, Assistant Deputy Governor, al-Qaṣīm Province.

Burayda: Mr ʿAbdul ʿAzīz ʿAbd Allah al-ʿOmari, Director of General Affairs, al-Qaṣīm Province.

al-Qaṭīf: H.E. Mr Muḥammad ʿAbd al-Raḥmān al-Sharīf, Governor, al-Qaṭīf.

Riyadh Province: H.R.H. Amīr Salman b. ʿAbd al-ʿAzīz Al Saʿūd, Governor, Riyadh Province; H.R.H. Amīr Sulṭān b. Salmān b. ʿAbd al-ʿAzīz Al Saʿūd; H.E. Mr ʿAbd al-ʿAzīz Balaihid, *wakil,* Riyadh Province; Mr Saḥl b. ʿAbd Allah, Riyadh *amāra*.

Tabūk Province: H.R.H. Amīr ʿAbd al-Majid b. ʿAbd al-ʿAzīz Al Saʿūd, Governor, al-Madina al-Monawarah; Mr Muḥammad al-Tayar, Director, General Affairs, Tabūk Province.
al-Wajh: H.H. Amīr Nāṣir ʿAbd Allah al-Sudairy, Governor, al-Wajh; Mr Shuwaysh Ḥamūd, al-Wajh *amāra*.

I also gratefully acknowledge the kind assistance of H.R.H. Amīr Turkī b. Muḥammad b. Saʿūd al-Kabīr in Riyadh and in London.

At King Saud University, Riyadh, I express my thanks to H.E. Dr Manṣūr al-Turkī, President of the University, and to Professor ᶜAbd al-Raḥmān al-Anṣāry, Chairman, Department of Archaeology and Museology, for their support during the research for this book; and to Dr Saᶜd ᶜAbd al-ᶜAzīz al-Rāshid and Dr ᶜAbd Allah al-Ṣāliḥ al-ᶜUthaimin for their advice. I should also mention Mr Idris Miqa, Mr. Khālid al-Muwannis and Mr Khālid al-Ṣālih, students in the Department of Archaeology and Museology for their help in locating certain references.

I also express my thanks to Dr T. Prochazka Jr., and to Mr and Mrs G.F. Battle for their assistance in field research.

Finally, I thank my wife, Joan Wucher King, who has patiently helped me in the research for this book for the past three years and without whose encouragement and participation it would never have reached conclusion.

GRDK

Riyadh 1405/1984

Credits

All photographs are by the author, except where stated. The publishers would like to thank the following for permission to use material from their collections:

British Museum:
Page 19: ref.1781 B6 pl.I, 0571216. Page 20: ref.1781 B6 pl.II, 0571216. Page 21: ref.1781 B6 pl.III, 0571216.

Mr. Khālid Khidr, Kingdom of Saudi Arabia: Page 22.

Royal Geographical Society, London:
Page 27: neg. A863. Page 28: neg. C2785. Page 29: neg. A865. Page 30: neg. C2722. Page 48: neg. C3188. Page 55: neg. X228/021694.

A note on the transliteration of Arabic

The author and publishers have made every effort to transliterate names in a systematic way, allowing the original Arabic form to be accurately rendered. This system follows that used in the *Encyclopaedia of Islam,* second edition, London and Leyden (1960; hereafter referred to as EI^2) except for *jīm* (rendered as *j*) and *qāf* (rendered as *q*), but underlinings have not been adopted for double letter transliterations. For a tabulation of this amended version see R.S. Serjeant and R.L. Bidwell, eds, *Arabian Studies,* i, (1974), p. ix.

For names common in English usage we have retained the standard form (e.g. Oman, not ᶜUmān) except where directed otherwise by the Ministry of Information, Saudi Arabia. These exceptions are: Makkah al-Mukarramah, al-Madina al-Monawarah, Nejd, Hejaz and Riyadh, which are followed in the text, notes and bibliography.

A glossary of architectural and other terms used in the book will be found on page 205.

Foreword

Let me begin by asking myself why Dr Geoffrey King requested me to write a foreword for his invaluable work. Is it because I am the Head of the Department of Archaeology and Museology at King Saud University, where both of us have worked hitherto? Or is it due to our deep social relations and mutual respect? I have no doubt that the latter is the more appropriate reason, because of his esteemed and sincere character. Even so, I was rather hesitant as I do not know any Arab who has written a foreword for a western author in the academic field. Yet I could not resist the temptation, for this is a good opportunity to record my general impressions of a western scholar, and a truthful and sincere one, who has shared with me more than a decade of genuine work.

I have known Dr King since my Headship of the Department of History in 1394/1974, when he was an Assistant Lecturer in the Department of English, teaching historical texts in foreign languages to the students of my Department. At that time, I requested him to teach them about Arab and Islamic antiquities in the Arabian peninsula on the basis of western sources. He told me that the literary style of these works was not easy and was beyond the level of the students. I therefore suggested that he should read the texts and simplify them for the students. He welcomed my proposal with the agreement of my colleague, Dr Izzat Khattab, the then Head of the English Department. I assigned him the texts and he prepared the lessons in a manner that suited the students. The experiment succeeded; consequently the students started to read about Taymā', al-Hijr, Dūmat al-Jandal, Najrān and other Arabian antiquities in English, and they felt at ease with this method of study which culminated in excellent results. The honour goes to the help of God and the diligence of Dr King.

Thereafter, Dr King returned to London to prepare for his PhD in Islamic Archaeology at the University of London. After completion of his PhD he renewed his contract with King Saud University, this time lecturing in Arabic in the newly established Department of Archaeology and Museology. Furthermore, he has collaborated in the research of the Department as well as carrying on his own research on Islamic antiquities in the Kingdom and elsewhere. Among his studies are the mosque attributed to ᶜUmar b. al-Khaṭṭāb in Dūmat al-Jandal, the traditional mosques of Nejd and studies of mosques in other areas of the Kingdom, published in several academic journals. Apart from these, he has published research arising from his four seasons of field survey in the Hashemite Kingdom of Jordan, to which the Research Centre of the College of Arts of King Saud University contributed support. As a result of this distinguished scientific work, he was promoted to Associate Professor two years ago.

His past research on the mosques of the Kingdom has undoubtedly encouraged him to undertake this comprehensive book, *The Historical Mosques of Saudi Arabia*, and I am very pleased to say that I have followed this book from its inception as an idea until its publication.

Many Islamic historians have written about mosques, but few of them have paid much attention to those of the Kingdom of Saudi Arabia, apart from the two most sacred mosques. Moreover, those Orientalists who have written about mosques have followed the same tendency with few exceptions. Hence this book becomes the foremost of its kind in this field, especially because it has been written for a western readership by a western author dealing with our Islamic traditions, heritage and civilization. Many westerners have had the opportunity to undertake a similar task, but none of them could have superseded Dr King's work because of his objectivity and his honesty.

While leaving the plan and the scientific methodology of the book for the reader, I would like to highlight some points that distinguish this book. Firstly, the general survey of all the traditional mosque types in the Kingdom of Saudi Arabia and the accurate, detailed and first-hand description of each mosque. Only the two sacred mosques of Makkah al-Mukarramah and al-Madina al-Monawarah are described solely through the Arabic and other sources. Secondly, the references to Arabic sources which have described some of the mosques at various times. In this respect Dr King is one of the very few western scholars to have used earlier and more recent Arabic authorities; many have tended to neglect them for one reason or another. Thirdly, he has arranged the mosques according to regions, giving us the chance to compare and classify them, and to distinguish indigenous and foreign influences. Fourthly, his accuracy in description gives the reader a clear impression of the design of the mosques – as plans are not available, he has depended mainly on verbal description and illustrations. Fifthly, he has used nearly 300 photographs of his own, indicating the extent of the effort he has made to reach every relevant mosque. Furthermore, he has put each mosque into its geographical context and has thrown light on its recorded history such as it is, and has gathered together the relevant sources. Finally, he has included a rare group of photographs of the two sacred mosques of the *ḥaramayn*, which gives a sense of completeness to such an important and distinguished work.

In conclusion, it gives me great pleasure to congratulate Dr King on this memorable work which will make him a pioneer in the study of Islamic antiquities. I have no doubt that the book will become a basic reference for the study of Islamic architecture in the Arab and Islamic world and internationally. I hope that it will be translated into Arabic, especially for the benefit of students of Islamic archaeology.

Professor Abdul-Rahman Bin Mohammad al-Tayyib al-Ansāry, Chairman, Department of Archaeology and Museology, College of Arts, King Saud University.

Introduction

The major religious monuments of the Islamic world have become familiar to a wide audience in recent years, but, apart from the mosques of the Holy Cities, only limited research has been undertaken on the mosques of much of the Arabian peninsula[1], and the least known are those of Saudi Arabia. It is true that the development of the Holy Mosque (Ḥarām Mosque) in Makkah al-Mukarramah and the Mosque of the Prophet (*ṣalā Allah ᶜalayhi wa salam*) in al-Madina al-Monawarah has been quite precisely documented by both Muslim and western sources, but of the rest of the mosques of the country little has ever been written. In the past, Muslim and western travellers in Arabia occasionally mentioned mosques in the towns that they visited, and a very few were even photographed, but it was not often that a detailed account of any of these mosques was given. This lack of a record of the traditional mosque styles of Saudi Arabia has become more pressing in the face of the intense modernisation that has taken place in the Kingdom over the past few years, which has resulted in the replacement of many older mosques by modern ones. A decade ago, there were still numerous mosques built in traditional materials and styles in the towns and villages of Saudi Arabia, and today enough of these remain to give some idea of the regional mosque styles that constitute a part of the national cultural heritage.

It seems quite likely that the form of many of these mosques reflects a far older tradition of mosque design in the country, a relationship with the Arabian past which takes on particular importance in view of the scarcity so far of archaeological remains of mosques in Arabia that date from the earlier days of Islam. Recent excavations at al-Rabadha on the Darb Zubayda, directed by Dr S.A. al-Rāshid, of the Department of Archaeology and Museology, King Saud University, Riyadh, have revealed early Arabian mosques on the *hajj* route from Iraq to Makkah al-Mukarramah[2]. Nevertheless, the present state of archaeological study is such that much has still to be added to our rather meagre knowledge of a long period of Arabian architectural history. In this respect, by illuminating the past, the traditional mosque styles of the Kingdom take on an importance that goes beyond their own considerable intrinsic interest.

It is hoped that this attempt to put the mosques of the Kingdom into their historical and architectural context will contribute towards correcting the lack of attention shown to the country's indigenous religious building tradition by scholars in the past, when Arabia was less accessible. It is, after all, a most curious anomaly that so little should be known of the mosques that have arisen in Arabia itself, the birthplace of Islam.

Some of the photographs published here were taken between 1392/1972 and 1395/1975, while many more have been taken since 1402/1982. A few photographs and illustrations are also taken from the works of early travellers. Although my journeys in Saudi Arabia in recent years have shown that in some parts of the country the traditional architectural pattern remains intact, nevertheless the effects of modernisation and recent construction are obvious in most places. Occasionally I have had the fortune to have recorded a mosque a decade ago which has since been replaced by a new building, and sometimes I have included this juxtaposition of a vanished aspect of Arabia and its modern replacement. In other noteworthy instances, a concern to preserve and to conserve older buildings can be seen, with modern construction taking place, where appropriate, on sites nearby. This is an approach to development that has the advantage of meeting current needs without obliterating all trace and memory of the Islamic monuments of the Arabian past.

Map of Saudi Arabia

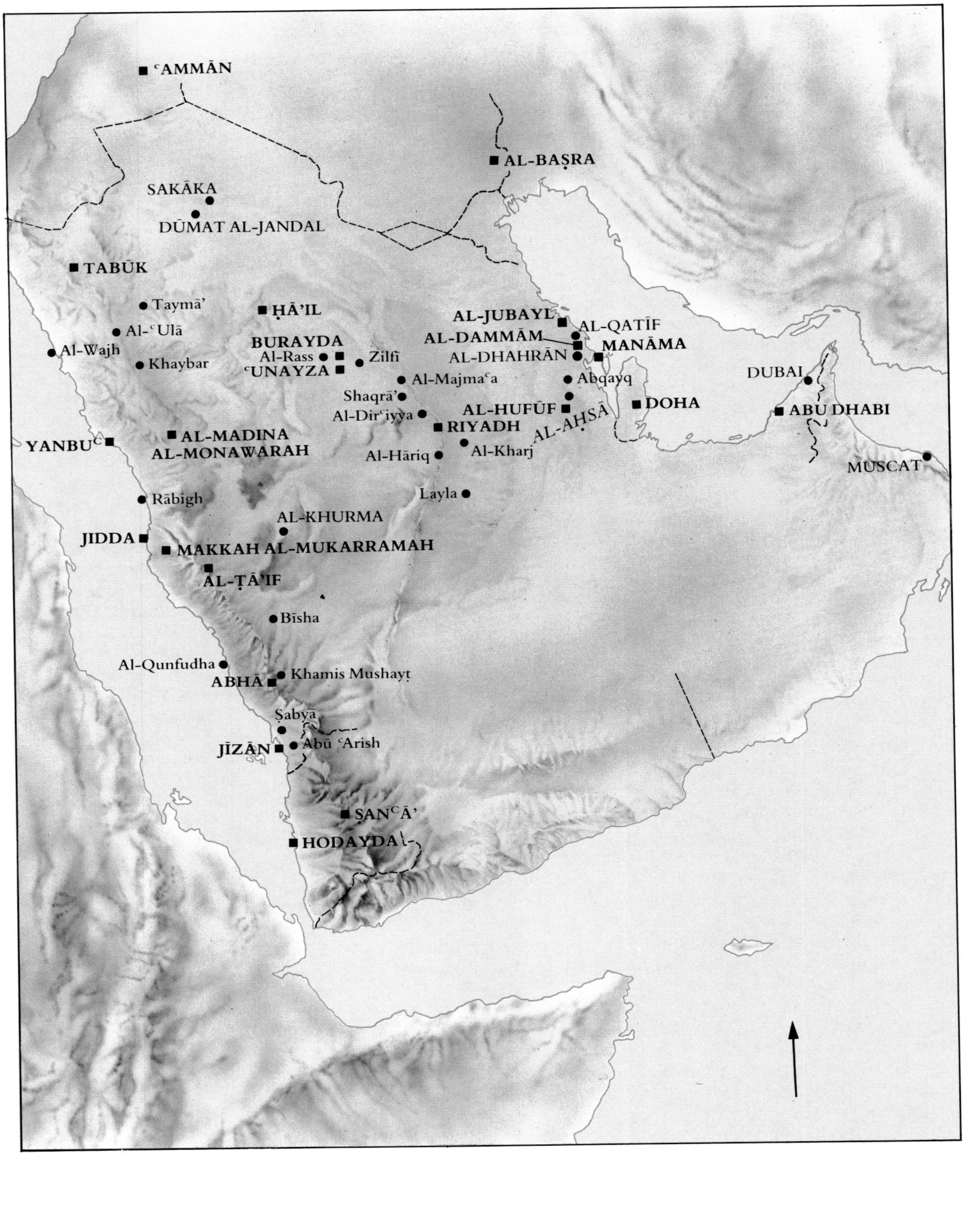

Historical background

The revelation of the Holy Qur'ān to the Prophet Muḥammad (ṣ)*, first in Makkah al-Mukarramah and thereafter in al-Madina al-Monawarah, the establishment of the *umma* in al-Madina al-Monawarah in the first year of the *hijra* (AD 622) and the subsequent expansion of Islam in the Arabian peninsula, led very early on to the foundation of a number of mosques. The earliest of these were founded by the Prophet (ṣ) himself in al-Madina al-Monawarah, although they have undergone much reconstruction and extension in later times. Apart from mosques in the Holy Cities (the *ḥaramayn*), several mosque sites in Arabia go back to the time of the Prophet (ṣ) or shortly afterwards, some being associated with the expeditions of the Prophet (ṣ) into various parts of Arabia, others being founded in the earliest days of Islam by those converted to the faith. Among these early mosques outside the Holy Cities themselves are the mosques of Tabūk, al-Ṭā'if and Jawātha in al-Aḥsā' (alternatively spelt al-Ḥasā). Other early mosques in the peninsula include the mosque attributed to ᶜUmar b. al-Khaṭṭāb in Dūmat al-Jandal, and a mosque in Khaybar that is attributed to very early times. However, these ancient mosques appear to have been reconstructed on more than one occasion, and, as they stand, some have been rebuilt quite recently. Although these early mosques are discussed here, the form which they presently take reflects later development in the tradition of mosque construction in Arabia.

Although the transformations of the Holy Mosque in Makkah al-Mukarramah and the Mosque of the Prophet (ṣ) in al-Madina al-Monawarah under the Rightly Guided Caliphs and later Islamic rulers are carefully chronicled by historians, nevertheless for much of the rest of the peninsula only a limited amount is known archaeologically of the design of mosques in early times. To bridge the great period of time during which we have no material evidence of mosque design in Arabia will require much more archaeological investigation like that at al-Rabadha by King Saud University, which has exposed two mosques dated by Dr Saᶜd al-Rāshid to the early Islamic period. In the meantime, study of standing mosques of later times serves to illuminate the Arabian mosque-building tradition for those periods when nothing is at present known.

Within Saudi Arabia, there is a diversity of mosque-building styles that reflects the different environmental circumstances of its regions and the varying degree of isolation or accessibility to the rest of Arabia and to the wider Islamic world. Some Arabian mosques incorporate elements from outside Arabia but many mosques in the peninsula appear to derive principally from local traditions of design. By contrast, the various extensions and reconstructions of the *ḥaramayn* mosques have led to the introduction of a variety of motifs of Islamic art and architecture from beyond Arabia. This process of course reflects the incomparable significance of these two mosques in Islam and the concern shown for them by Islamic rulers outside the peninsula. The pious interest of patrons in the *ḥaramayn* has also led to the refurbishing of other mosques in these cities in styles that reflect the architecture of the wider Islamic world and has also extended to the towns through which pilgrims passed on their way to the Hejaz. This process has been most noticeable in recent centuries as a result of the involvement of Egypt and the Ottoman state with the Hejaz, which has left a marked influence on certain mosques in western Arabia apart from those in the Holy Cities.

The concern of rulers in the Islamic world with the needs of the pilgrimage has led also to the provision of facilities in Arabia to ease the pilgrims' journey. The construction of water-tanks and other improvements along the *ḥajj* route from Iraq to Makkah al-Mukarramah by the Lady Zubayda, wife of the ᶜAbbāsid Caliph Hārūn al-Rashīd, in the 3rd/9th century represents a systematic effort at organising a pious and charitable work in the early Islamic period.(3) In the same vein in later times was the construction of the short-lived Hejaz railway in the closing years of the Ottoman period, linking north-western Arabia and al-Madina al-Monawarah with Syria and Asia Minor; similarly, the recently completed *ḥajj* terminal at King ᶜAbd al-ᶜAzīz International Airport at Jidda fulfils a similar role in modern terms for pilgrims arriving from throughout the Islamic world.

The conditions of security and order that appear to have existed in Islamic Arabia until the early ᶜAbbāsid period seem to have changed for the worse by the 4th/10th century, and the Arabian plateau as far as Makkah al-Mukarramah was subjected to great disruption by the incursions of the Qaramatians. By the 5th/11th century, the security of central Arabia had declined to such an extent that routes through the peninsula had become more difficult and were less frequented than in former times. The Persian traveller Nāṣir-i Khusraw provides a description of his attempts to return to Iran from Makkah al-Mukarramah via al-Ṭā'if in 443/1051, during which he found himself compelled to sojourn in al-Aflāj in central Arabia for four months before he could join a caravan to al-Yamāmah and al-Aḥsā'. His vast detour from Makkah al-Mukarramah to southern Nejd involved a journey through the mountains near al-Ṭā'if, where he found total political disunity, with independent chieftains and fortified castles everywhere. In the desert, travel was dangerous and required the services of a *ghafīr*, a tribal escort, through the separate areas of the tribes. Al-Aflāj itself was in ruin as a result of endemic internecine warfare and had fallen into deep poverty: the conditions that Nāsir-i Khusraw witnessed seem to have continued for many centuries thereafter in central Arabia.

The interest that Islamic rulers showed in the Holy Cities and the *ḥajj* routes did not affect most other parts of Arabia, least of all in these periods of disruption. The Ayyūbids, the Mamlūk Sultans of Egypt and thereafter the Ottoman Sultans in Istanbul, maintained a presence in certain coastal and inland towns and exercised control

**The full blessing will hereafter be shortened to (ṣ)*

over routes important to them. However, they lacked either the need or the means to extend their control beyond these limited areas. Such was very clearly the case for the Ottoman period in Arabia and the situation in Ottoman times was probably similar to that which had prevailed at an earlier date. The areas where Ottoman presence was strongest reveal themselves very readily through the architecture, and especially that of mosques, which reflect clearly the impact of Ottoman influence.

The Hejaz passed under Ottoman control in 923/1517 when they supplanted the Egyptian Mamlūk Sultans as the strongest power in the region. In Makkah al-Mukarramah a Sharīfian regime had been established by Ibn Qatāda in *c.* 598/1200, and the Ottomans reconfirmed these Sharīfs in their position. Indeed, the Sharīfs were to retain their authority under the Turks until temporarily eclipsed by the expansion of the first Saudi state into the Hejaz in the 13th/19th century. The initial expansion of the Ottomans into western Arabia in the 10th/16th century eventually brought them to south-western Arabia, where for a time their authority supplanted that of the indigenous dynasties. An Ottoman official was appointed to rule the Tihāma from Abū ᶜArīsh in 946/1539, but in this area as a whole their authority was tenuous and eventually they gave way once more to independent indigenous dynasties in Yemen and the south-west. The Arabian Gulf coast likewise fell to the Ottomans following their conquest of Iraq in 941/1534. As a result they established themselves in al-Qaṭīf and in 959/1552 they took the al-Aḥsā' oasis, where they remained until 1090/1668-9. On their withdrawal, they left eastern Arabia to the domination of the Banī Khālid tribe by whom it was ruled until the rise of the first Saudi state in the following century.

It was against this fragmented and unsettled background that the first Saudi state arose in Nejd in the 12th/18th century to transform the religious and political situation in Arabia. It is to the period of Saudi rule that many of the mosques in Nejd and elsewhere in the Kingdom that are discussed here should be dated, as far as can be judged, while other mosques of earlier date were also refurbished or reconstructed during this period. This concern with mosque building or repair reflects the religious priorities established by the first Saudi state and its successors, for the centuries of neglect and strife which had preceded the establishment of the first Saudi state had also brought about a severe deterioration in religious observance in Arabia. The historian of Nejd, ᶜUthmān b. Bishr, makes it clear that by the mid-12th/18th century, isolation and internecine war had allowed much of Arabia to fall away from the practice of Islam as prescribed in the Holy Qur'ān and the *ḥadīth* of the Prophet Muḥammad (ṣ).[4] The absence of stability in a politically fragmented country exacerbated this situation and led to a decline in personal security throughout the area. According to Ibn Bishr, it had become common for people to put their faith in trees, stones, prayer at tombs, protective amulets and sacrifices. All of this represented a profound departure from Islam and constituted the sin of *shirk* or the association of other objects with the worship of the One God, Allah; *shirk* is strictly forbidden in Islam.

Shaykh Muḥammad b. ᶜAbd al-Wahhāb, son of a *qāḍī* of al-ᶜUyayna in Nejd, reacted strongly to the violations of Islamic practice that he saw all around him as a youth. After a pilgrimage to Makkah al-Mukarramah he spent some time studying at al-Madina al-Monawarah where he came under the influence of the writings of the 8th/14th century Ḥanbalī legal jurist, Ibn Taymiyya, and of other authors associated with the Ḥanbalī legal school. This enabled him to develop his views on, and his opposition to, the manner in which the customs of the time deviated from Islam, as prescribed by the Holy Qur'ān and the *ḥadīth*. Following his studies in al-Madina al-Monawarah, Muḥammad b. ᶜAbd al-Wahhāb made further visits outside Nejd to Baṣra, Zubayr and al-Aḥsā' before he eventually returned to his native Nejd, and joined his father who was then residing at Ḥuraymilā'.

Unitarianism, the Islamic reform movement which Muḥammad b. ᶜAbd al-Wahhāb started, was to transform religious practice in Arabia and ultimately was to affect all aspects of its social and political character. This transformation created the circumstances in which many of the Arabian mosques illustrated here were constructed. Shaykh Muḥammad declared his mission publicly following his father's death in 1153/1740, and made clear his intention of trying to return the area to the practice of Islam as it had been in the time of the Prophet Muḥammad (ṣ). When his teaching encountered opposition in Ḥuraymilā', Shaykh Muḥammad moved to his home town of ᶜUyayna, some 35 kilometres to the south-east. There he was welcomed by the *amīr,* ᶜUthmān b. Ḥamad b. Muᶜammar, who gave the reform movement his active support. The Shaykh's desire to suppress *bidaᶜ* (innovation in religion) and *shirk* was expressed in direct terms. With his own hands, he helped his followers cut down a tree in al-ᶜUyayna which the local people had been wont to revere, contrary to Islam. He then organised the demolition of a dome at al-Jubayla which stood over the tomb of Zayd b. al-Khaṭṭāb, a Companion of the Prophet (ṣ) and brother of the second Caliph, ᶜUmar b. al-Khaṭṭāb; this tomb had become the object of visits and prayers not acceptable in Islam. The Shaykh also ensured the application of *sharīᶜa* law to social and moral issues.

The Shaykh's teachings and his success in attracting followers was viewed with disfavour by the *amīr* of the Banī Khālid, who was the most powerful ruler in eastern Arabia at that time. He applied pressure on the ruler of al-ᶜUyayna, and eventually Ibn Muᶜammar was forced to ask Shaykh Muḥammad to leave in 1158/1745. The Shaykh sought refuge in a town further down the Wādī Ḥanīfa, al-Dirᶜiyya, which was the family seat of the Al Saᶜūd. Shaykh Muḥammad was initially given shelter by one Muḥammad b. Suwailam al-ᶜArīnī, and then gained the support of the *amīr* Muḥammad b. Saᶜūd, thanks to the intercession of members of his family and in particular on the advice of his wife, Mūḍī bint Abī Waṭbān, a lady renowned for her perceptiveness. The *amīr* gave Shaykh Muḥammad sanctuary at al-Dirᶜiyya, and committed the town and its people to follow the Shaykh's teachings. In turn, the Shaykh gave his backing to the Saudi amirate, and this alliance flourished to become the foundation of the first Saudi state, gradually spreading its religious and political sway throughout Nejd.

The following decades saw the expansion of Saudi authority and Unitarian Islam over much of the Arabian peninsula. The alliance effected between the Al Saᶜūd and the Shaykh has maintained itself to this day, and is manifest in the Unitarian Islam which has remained the *raison d'être* of successive Saudi states in Arabia, while the descendents of Muḥammad b. ᶜAbd al-Wahhāb, the Al Shaykh, have remained prominent in religion and education throughout this time.

In the half century which followed the establishment of the first Saudi state, the hegemony built up by the Al Saᶜūd expanded steadily, and with it spread the proselytisation of Unitarian teaching. As early as 1175-7/1761-3, Carsten Niebuhr, the German-born Danish explorer of Yemen, had heard much about the religious reforms taking place in Nejd. Niebuhr's account, although incorrect and uncertain in some details and interpretation, is sympathetic to the movement. Indeed, he commented quite independently on the deterioration he perceived in Islamic practice, and he expressed his approval of Shaykh Muḥammad's efforts to return Arabia to Islam as practised at the time of the Prophet Muḥammad (s).[5] In Niebuhr's day, the Shaykh and the Al Saᶜūd had already enjoyed considerable success in uniting central Arabia, but it was not until somewhat later that the power of Dirᶜiyya extended beyond Nejd itself. In 1208/1793, advances were made as far north as Dūmat al-Jandal in the area of al-Jawf, while in the east al-Aḥsā' passed under Saudi rule, ending the Banī Khālid domination of eastern Arabia. A decade later, ᶜAsīr in the south-west and the ᶜAsīr Tihāma came under Saudi control and accepted the religious teaching that was introduced. A Saudi force made an expedition to Karbalā' in Iraq in 1216/1802. In 1217/1803 Saudi rule was established in the Hejaz at the expense of the Sharīfs and their Ottoman overlords, when Saudi forces peaceably entered Makkah al-Mukarramah in *hajj* dress to perform the pilgrimage. Finally, al-Madina al-Monawarah came under Saudi control in 1220/1805.

Although the Ottomans had been concerned at the earlier spread of Saudi power, the loss of the Holy Cities moved them to action against the Saudi state. Not only did Saudi power now stretch from the confines of Yemen and Oman to the threshold of Syria, but their control of the Holy Cities posed a direct challenge to the Ottoman Sultan in his position as guardian of the Holy Places. The Albanian governor of Egypt, Muḥammad ᶜAli Pasha, was appointed by the Sultan to act as his avenger in Arabia to reverse these Saudi successes. In 1226/1811 Muḥammad ᶜAlī despatched his son Aḥmad Ṭūsūn Pasha to the Hejaz with a large force of troops; but after desultory campaigning, another son, the far more effective Ibrāhīm Pasha, succeeded Ṭūsūn and led the Turco-Egyptian force on an eastwards advance across the vast plains that form the approaches to the main settlements of Nejd. His large army and heavy artillery permitted Ibrāhīm Pasha to take the towns and villages opposing him. He advanced steadily on each of the Nejdi strongholds in Qaṣīm and the Sudayr district; Shaqrā' and Ḍurmā fell to him and were sacked one by one. By 1233/1818, Ibrāhīm was beseiging Dirᶜiyya itself. After tenacious resistance and heavy bombardment by the Turco-Egyptian artillery, the town's defenders and the Saudi *imām*, ᶜAbd Allah b. Saᶜūd, had been confined to the citadel of al-Dirᶜiyya. ᶜAbd Allah surrendered after six months of this struggle, rather than inflict further suffering on his followers. He was taken to Cairo and then to Istanbul, where he was executed; Dirᶜiyya itself was razed in 1234/1819.

Ibrāhīm Pasha remained in Nejd for nearly a year following the fall of al-Dirᶜiyya. By the time he departed in 1234/1819, as much damage as possible had been done to the countryside, its society and its people. An English officer, Capt. G.F. Sadleir, arrived at al-Dirᶜiyya a month after Ibrāhīm Pasha had retreated to al-Madina al-Monawarah from the wreckage he had wrought in Nejd. Sadleir described the misery of the people of central Arabia, left as they were with daily insecurity and an abiding hatred of the Pasha.[6] It is quite clear from his persecution of the Al Shaykh as well as of the Al Saᶜūd that Ibrāhīm Pasha was attempting to eradicate the spiritual as well as the political foundation of the first Saudi state, for in his systematic ruin and impoverishment of Nejd, he was not only avenging the Ottoman Sultan but making every effort to ensure that Saudi power in central Arabia should never revive.

Despite this vigorous suppression, the overturning of Saudi power, and the Turco-Egyptian occupation of the Hejaz, the religious reforms introduced by the first Saudi state proved more tenacious and long-lasting than Ibrāhīm Pasha's power, and survived this period of repression. The reformist Islamic fervour which accompanied the expansion of the first Saudi state had led to missionary work by religious teachers in all parts of the Arabian peninsula. The depth and spread of the movement gave it a resilience which enabled it to survive the reverses of Ibrāhīm Pasha's campaign and subsequent attempts by Muḥammad ᶜAlī Pasha to reassert Egyptian control in central Arabia.

A reduced Saudi state was re-instituted in Nejd by Imām Turkī b. ᶜAbd Allah b. Muḥammad b. Saᶜūd once Turco-Egyptian interest in central Arabia had slackened. As Saudi autonomy was gradually re-established, religious activity continued on the foundations established during the first Saudi state. This renewal of religious activity seems to have been the background to a major period of mosque foundation in Nejd and eastern Arabia.

In the autumn of 1240/1824, Imām Turkī established a new capital at Riyadh, to the south-east of the ruined al-Dirᶜiyya. Aided by his son and successor Fayṣal, the *imām* expelled the remaining Turco-Egyptian forces from Nejd. However, the Egyptians maintained their control of the Hejaz for some time, although Muḥammad ᶜAlī's ambition to bring ᶜAsīr and Yemen under his control involved him in costly and inconclusive campaigns in the area. Resistance in the ᶜAsīr stemmed largely from the adherence of the mountain population to Unitarian Islam, which had spread in the region under the first Saudi state.

The Egyptians managed briefly to re-establish their power in Nejd in 1252/1837 when Muḥammad ᶜAlī once more sent an expedition to the area, this time to crush the resurgent second Saudi state. However, by 1256/1840 the Egyptian ruler had come under pressure from the European powers, concerned at his advances in the Near East and Arabia at the expense of the Ottoman Sultan, his nominal suzerain. As a result, the Egyptians were compelled to withdraw from most of Arabia. In the Hejaz, they handed over power to the Ottomans, although they maintained a presence in the coastal towns of northern Hejaz, albeit illegally, until 1304/1887.

Imām Fayṣal b. Turkī re-established Saudi power in Nejd following the Egyptian withdrawal, and the second Saudi state endured, with varying fortunes, until 1308/1891. Although the second Saudi state was more limited in its territorial spread than its predecessor, its rulers were no less concerned with religious instruction. Imām Fayṣal b. Turkī himself seems to have followed a programme of mosque construction in his territory, the evidence of which W.G. Palgrave saw during his visit to eastern Arabia *en route* from Riyadh to the Gulf in 1279/1862-3. Imām Fayṣal's mosques in al-Hufūf and al-Mubarraz̤ were both seen by Palgrave, who commented favourably on their design. Unfortunately the buildings Palgrave mentioned are no longer extant.

The completion of the Suez Canal in 1286/1869 greatly facilitated the attempts of the Ottomans to reassert their position in Arabia. Although they ruled the Hejaz through the Sharīfs of Makkah al-Mukarramah, it was not until the Canal was completed that they were able to expand their position in western Arabia, including the ᶜAsīr and Yemen. In 1288/1871, they occupied al-Aḥsā' which they held until the province was regained by the Al Saᶜūd in 1331/1913.

Egyptian and Ottoman influence on the coastal areas of Arabia was particularly marked in this period and its effect on the architectural forms of these regions is quite widespread. This is especially so in the case of the Holy Cities of Makkah al-Mukarramah and al-Madina al-Monawarah, but it was also true of towns connected with the pilgrimage such as Jidda, al-Ṭā'if, al-Wajh and other areas of this region which were on *ḥajj* routes. In both religious and domestic architecture in these towns and cities, a clear Egyptian and Ottoman element can be identified which has been grafted on to the indigenous Arabian architectural tradition.

In the latter part of the 13th/19th century, Ottoman power had nominally reasserted itself in broad areas of the Hejaz, ᶜAsīr, Yemen and the eastern part of Arabia; but in practice, many districts of these regions were outside their effective control. In the early years of the 14th/20th century, a number of movements seeking autonomy arose to challenge Ottoman power, such as the Idrīsiyya in the Tihāma, and, in addition, the Ottomans had to cope with the renewed expansion of the Al Saᶜūd. Ottoman power in Arabia was finally brought to an end with their defeat in the First World War.

The second Saudi state had been eclipsed in 1308/1891 by the former Al Saᶜūd governors of Ḥā'il, the Al Rashīd. A brief exile in Kuwait was ended in 1319/1902, when ᶜAbd al-ᶜAzīz b. ᶜAbd al-Raḥmān Al Saᶜūd won back al-Riyadh from the Al Rashīd and established the third, present, Saudi state. ᶜAbd al-ᶜAzīz began a political and military expansion which was ultimately to result in his regaining his family's Arabian domains. Side by side with his political and military advance there was a sustained programme of religious teaching. A new feature of the third Saudi state was Ibn Saᶜūd's decision to settle the beduin in farming communities or *ḥijras*. These communities were intended to replace the old ties of tribal loyalty with an identification with the religious teaching of Unitarian Islam. At the heart of the relationship was a sense of brotherhood and community based in Islamic faith, hence the movement's name, *ikhwān*, or "brotherhood". This process of settlement and religious instruction, which began in about 1330/1912, led to a new wave of mosque building throughout the countryside. The numerous *ḥijras* constructed at the height of the movement's expansion each had a mosque for prayers and religious instruction. This large-scale provision of mosques for the spiritual needs of the *ikhwān* is outmatched only by the mosque-building that has accompanied the current prosperity and expansion of cities and towns in the Kingdom of Saudi Arabia today. The introduction of modern building techniques into the Kingdom in recent times has meant that concrete has replaced traditional materials and many older style mosques have been replaced with modern mosques. Nevertheless, the older mosques of the Kingdom, as reflections of the religious and cultural tradition of Arabia, deserve record and discussion, in particular because they remain so little known and also for the light which they throw on the Islamic history of the Kingdom and the Arabian peninsula as a whole.(7)

I

Western Saudi Arabia

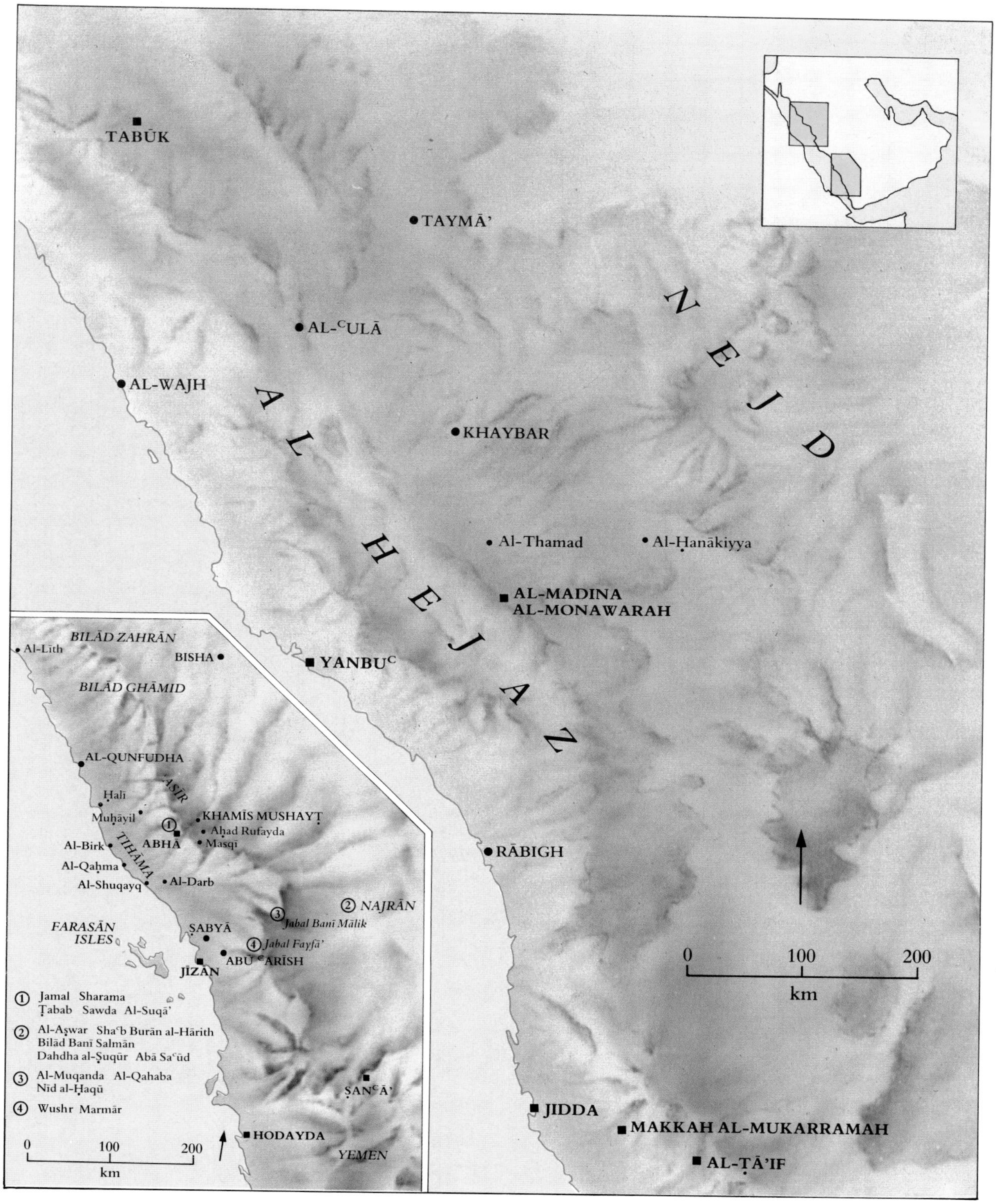
TABŪK
TAYMĀ'
AL-ᶜULĀ
AL-WAJH
KHAYBAR
AL HEJAZ
NEJD
Al-Thamad
Al-Ḥanākiyya
AL-MADINA
AL-MONAWARAH
YANBUᶜ
RĀBIGH
JIDDA
MAKKAH AL-MUKARRAMAH
AL-ṬĀ'IF
0 100 200
km
BILĀD ZAHRĀN
Al-Līth
BISHA
BILĀD GHĀMID
AL-QUNFUDHA
ʿASĪR
Ḥalī
Muḥāyil
KHAMĪS MUSHAYṬ
Aḥad Rufayda
Masqī
ABHĀ
Al-Birk
TIHĀMA
Al-Qaḥma
Al-Shuqayq
Al-Darb
NAJRĀN
Jabal Banī Mālik
FARASĀN ISLES
ṢABYĀ
Jabal Fayfā'
ABŪ ᶜARĪSH
JĪZĀN
① Jamal Sharama Ṭabab Sawda Al-Suqā'
② Al-Aṣwar Shaᶜb Burān al-Hārith Bilād Banī Salmān Dahdha al-Ṣuqūr Abā Saᶜūd
③ Al-Muqanda Al-Qahaba Nīd al-Ḥaqū
④ Wushr Marmār
ṢANᶜĀ'
HODAYDA
YEMEN
0 100 200
km

The Hejaz and the Red Sea coast

The geography of western Arabia is dominated by the Hejaz mountain chain which forms a barrier between the Red Sea and the high plateau of Nejd, inland to the east. The northern part of the Hejaz is rugged and generally barren, and the mountains do not rise to a great height. In this desert country there are scattered oases in an otherwise harsh landscape that varies between red sandstone mountain formations, rolling areas of sand and harsh black plains strewn with basalt, the *ḥarra*. Within Saudi Arabia the mountains of the Hejaz rise to their highest point in ᶜAsīr in the south, and they rise yet higher still in Yemen. On the western face, the Hejaz mountains fall in a steep escarpment to the Tihāma foothills and the coastal plain of the Red Sea. The southern highlands enjoy a far cooler climate than the rest of Saudi Arabia, and they receive frequent rainfall and mist even in summer. In the foothills, *wādīs* carry the flood waters from the Hejaz highlands westwards to the Tihāma's coastal plain where they peter out in the desert; although no perennial streams reach the Red Sea, flowing streams and pools can be seen in the foothills even in summer. In full flood, these *wādīs* become violent rivers, and of the major cities of Saudi Arabia, few have been so affected by the consequences of flooding in the past as Makkah al-Mukarramah in the foothills of the Hejaz. Since early times the Holy Mosque and the Honourable Kaᶜba itself have been occasionally engulfed by flood water and only in recent years has the problem been alleviated.

The southern Hejaz is a principal beneficiary of the rainfall of western Arabia. From the vicinity of al-Ṭā'if in the mountains above Makkah al-Mukarramah and southwards to the ᶜAsīr, the countryside is characterised by farmland rolling between mountain peaks; laboriously constructed terraces exploit the rainfall running off the hillsides, especially in the southern districts. Some of the most spectacular staircase-like terracing in Saudi Arabia is to be seen in the Tihāma mountains of Fayfā' and Banī Mālik. Throughout the mountain area, and especially between al-Ṭā'if and the southern frontier, the principal building material for houses and mosques alike has traditionally been stone, although there is some use of mud for construction, especially around Abhā. In the mountains, hard waterproof plaster is used to cover roofs in a direct response to the wet climate that prevails in these districts.

On the western side of Hejaz escarpment, beyond the foothills, the coastal plain is largely desert, traversed by the *wādīs* descending to the sea from the mountains. However, a number of towns and cultivated areas are found along the coast and inland, and there are several harbours on the Red Sea, of which Jidda, Yanbūᶜ and Jīzān are the main ones today. Others, including al-Wajh and al-Qunfudha, have also provided points of access to western Arabia for pilgrim traffic and commerce from Egypt, the Sudan and other parts of Africa. A particularly fertile region of the Tihāma is the level hinterland of Jīzān in the far south, around Abū ᶜArīsh and Ṣabyā, where modern development has improved the capacity of an area whose use for farming probably goes back to much earlier times.

The entire Red Sea coast is characterised by a climate of heavy humidity, made more bearable today by air-conditioning. In the past, buildings had to be designed in a manner able to provide at least some ventilation as a relief from the climate, and this manifests itself in traditional buildings along the coast, as well as in towns further inland on the plain, e.g. at al-Wajh, Jidda, al-Qunfudha, Jīzān, Abū ᶜArīsh, Ṣabyā and on the Farasān islands offshore from Jīzān. In the coastal towns, the building material is coral, taken from the reefs in the Red Sea, carved up and then employed as very hard building blocks. It is the main traditional material of construction in all the towns of the coast, and is used also on the Arabian Gulf. However, the humidity has a deleterious effect on these coral buildings, and this seems to have caused a process of frequent reconstruction, with the result that few buildings are of great age as they presently stand.

Inland towns on the Tihāma plain, where coral aggregate is not available, are constructed in various materials, with some of the finer buildings, especially mosques, made of baked brick and basalt. In the foothills and the mountains of the Tihāma, behind the coastal plain, there are numerous small settlements, often perched high on hillsides, and above the flood channels of *wādīs*. Here the building material is stone and in a style related to that of the southern Hejaz mountains, rather than the coastal plain. Some of these districts in the foothills are surprisingly fertile and rich agriculturally, especially around al-Muḥāyil and to the south, in the mountains of Banī Mālik and Fayfā'.

Routes between the highlands of the Hejaz and the coast are limited, but as a result of the construction of well engineered modern roads in recent years, the journey by car to the coast is now completed easily and quickly, whereas a decade ago it was accomplished only after many hours of arduous driving. Points of descent from the highlands to the coast, even for those on foot and for riders, have always been few because of the terrain, and traffic must have followed certain well established routes.

Commerce since ancient times has traversed the highland route from southern Arabia to the north and visitors to the Holy Cities have used the same route. Furthermore the pilgrim traffic by sea from Egypt and the other Islamic countries of Africa has long disembarked at the Arabian ports of the Red Sea. The consequence of this communication between the ports and towns of western Arabia with other Islamic countries can be seen in the cosmopolitan Islamic architecture of the region which is especially noticeable in the *ḥaramayn*, in Jidda, al-Wajh, al-Ṭā'if and elsewhere, and which shows itself so much in mosque architecture.

فَوَلِّ وَجْهَكَ شَطْرَ الْمَسْجِدِ الْحَرَامِ وَحَيْثُ مَا كُنْتُمْ فَوَلُّوا وُجُوهَكُمْ شَطْرَهُ

سورة البقرة ١٤٤

"Turn then thy face in the direction of the sacred Mosque: wherever ye are, turn your faces in that direction."

Holy Qur'ān, *sūra II, 144* (*sūrat al-baqara*)

The Honourable Ka^{c}ba and the Holy Mosque, Makkah al-Mukarramah

The Holy Mosque (*al-Masjid al-Ḥarām*) in Makkah al-Mukarramah with the Honourable Ka^{c}ba (*al-Ka^{c}ba al-Mushrifa*) at its centre is the holiest site in the world of Islam, towards which all Muslims turn in prayer. The Holy Qur'ān states that the first House of Worship appointed by Allah for mankind was Makkah al-Mukarramah (or Bakka), the site of the Honourable Ka^{c}ba and the Holy Mosque.[(1)] Through its history the Holy Mosque has undergone reconstructions and extensions on numerous occasions, the most recent by the Saudi government.

The first Ka^{c}ba was raised by Adam (ṣ) but the Prophet Ibrāhīm (ṣ) and his son, the Prophet Ismā^{c}īl (ṣ), were directed by Allah to rebuild it, the site having been obliterated by time. The site which was established by Allah is regarded as sacred and as a place where no tree can be cut, animal hunted or blood shed. The order to the Prophet Ibrāhīm (ṣ) to raise the Honourable Ka^{c}ba

View of Makkah al-Mukarramah with the Holy Mosque in 1302/1884-5. (S. Hurgronje)

The Holy Mosque and the Honourable Kaba in 1302/1884-5.
(S. Hurgronje)

was accompanied by Allah's instruction to proclaim the Pilgrimage (*ḥajj*) and to perform the prescribed rites at the appropriate time at the Ancient House, al-Bayt al-ᶜAtīq (one of the synonyms for the Honourable Kaᶜba). It was at this time that the sites of al-Ṣafā and al-Marwa were established, two hills in Makkah al-Mukarramah between which Hajar, the wife of the Prophet Ibrāhīm, ran to and fro seven times to find water for her child Ismāᶜīl, when they were in the barren and waterless desert. Water sprang forth to assuage their thirst, and this spring henceforth was the Well of Zamzam within the precincts of the Holy Mosque.

The Maqām Ibrāhīm is another site in the Mosque associated with the Prophet Ibrāhīm (ṣ), marking the position of the stone on which he stood to build the Honourable Kaᶜba. To the north-west end of the Honourable Kaᶜba is the *ḥujr* Ismāᶜīl, a low, semicircular walled enclosure known as the *ḥatīm*, which is regarded as the burial place of the Prophet Ismāᶜīl b. Ibrāhīm (ṣ).(2)

The Honourable Kaᶜba was rebuilt on several occasions in the period of the *jāhiliyya*, by Quṣayy b. Kilāb, an ancestor of the Prophet Muḥammad (ṣ), and again in the days of ᶜAbd al-Muṭṭalib, the grandfather of the Prophet (ṣ). Yet another rebuilding took place not long before the coming of Islam, as a result of flooding, a major problem of the city until very recent times. The ruling tribe of Quraysh repaired the building with wood taken from a wrecked Byzantine ship (3), apparently using it to reconstruct the Honourable Kaᶜba with alternating courses of wood and stone: the date for this work has been suggested as *c.* CE 608. The Honourable Kaᶜba at this time was 18 cubits high and the level roof rested on six columns. The Black Stone was replaced in the eastern corner of the Kaᶜba by the Prophet Muḥammad (s) himself, assisted by the chiefs of the tribes. The Stone is in the same position today, marking the starting point of the seven circuits (*ṭawāf*) of the Honourable Kaᶜba that all pilgrims are obliged to make. Only a limited space was available at this period for people to circumambulate the Honourable Kaᶜba, for the houses of the city came close to the sacred building.

The Honourable Kaᶜba maintained this form at the time when the Prophet Muhammed (ṣ) first began his mission in Makkah al-Mukarramah with the call to Islam. In the earliest times and indeed, until some 18 months after the *hijra* to al-Madina al-Monawarah, the Prophet Muḥammad (ṣ) and the Muslim community prayed northwards towards al-Quds al-Sharīf (Jerusalem). However, after the revelation of *Sūra II, 142-50,* the Muslims henceforth prayed in the direction of the Honourable Kaᶜba.(4) The revelation was sent down to the Prophet (ṣ) in the Masjid al-Qiblatayn in al-Madina al-Monawarah, named in commemoration of the change of the direction of prayer (*qibla*).

The Muslim community in al-Madina al-Monawarah

The Honourable Kaᶜba in 1302/1884-5. (S. Hurgronje)

View of Makkah al-Mukarramah in 1405/1984 (Ministry of Information, Saudi Arabia)

made the Islamic Pilgrimage (*hajj*) to Makkah al-Mukarramah in 7/628, and the next year the Prophet (ṣ) himself took control of Makkah al-Mukarramah from the Quraysh, eradicating all traces of polytheistic paganism from the Honourable Ka^cba, from the city itself and from its surroundings. Although the Prophet (ṣ) did not make the *hajj* himself in the next year, 9/630, he delegated the future Caliph, Abū Bakr al-Ṣiddīq, as leader of the Pilgrims. However, in 10/631 the Prophet (ṣ) led the Pilgrims himself in what is known as the Pilgrimage of Farewell (*ḥijjat al-wadā*ᶜ), establishing before his death the rituals of *hajj* followed ever since by the Muslim community on the basis of Qur'ānic revelation. The Prophet (ṣ) made no alteration to the structure of the Honourable Kaᶜba during his visits from al-Madina al-Monawarah, nor to its surroundings. It was not until the Caliph ᶜUmar b. al-Khaṭṭāb made the Pilgrimage in 17/638 that the Honourable Kaᶜba was surrounded by a wall, with an enlarged space for the *ṭawāf* because of the increased numbers of Muslims on the Pilgrimage.[5] It is also reported that the Maqām Ibrāhīm had been destroyed by flooding and had to be reconstructed.

An important feature of the Honourable Kaᶜba that has continued from ancient times is the covering of the

The new riwāqs *of the Holy Mosque in 1405/1984.* (Ministry of Information, Saudi Arabia)

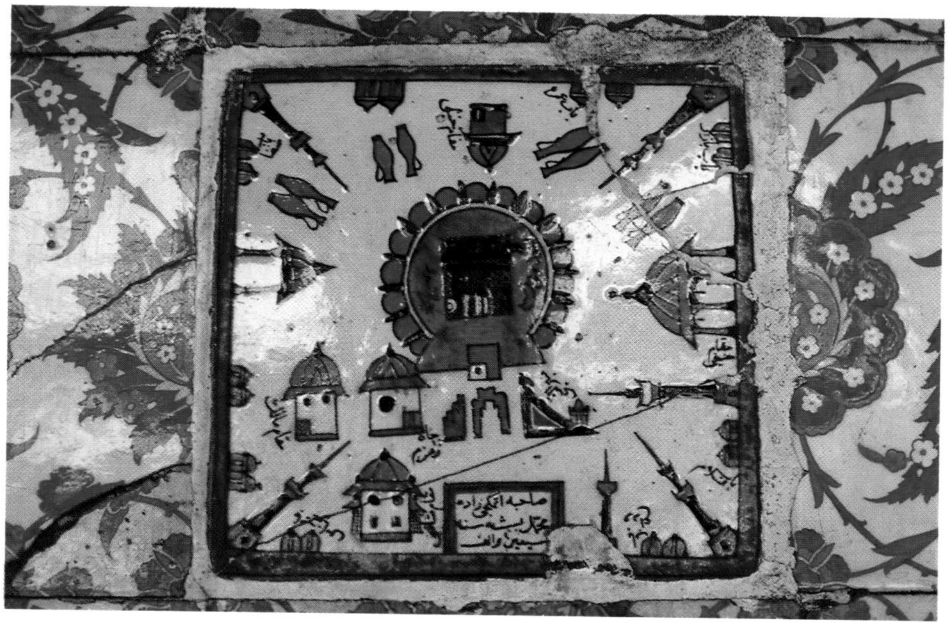

Glazed ceramic tile in Rustem Pasha jāmiᶜ, *Istanbul, showing the Honourable Kaᶜba and the Holy Mosque, 1070/1659-60.*

building with the great fabric, the *kiswa*.[6] The tradition is recorded as originating in the most ancient period of the Honourable Kaᶜba's history and the Prophet (ṣ) instructed that the *kiswa* covering the Honourable Kaᶜba should continue to be replaced. Subsequently the custom of providing the Kaᶜba with a new *kiswa* at the time of the *hajj* has been respected and followed by the Muslim community. Traditionally it has been replaced by the Muslim authority that protects the Holy Cities of Islam, and this practice has remained unchanged to the present day.

The size of the Holy Mosque was increased by the third Caliph, ᶜUthmān b. ᶜAffān, in 26/646 and arcades were built for the first time around the open area within which the *ṭawāf* is performed.[7] The Holy Mosque retained the form that it took at this date until the siege of Makkah al-Mukarramah during the contention over the Caliphate between ᶜAbd Allah b. al-Zubayr and the Umayyad candidate, ᶜAbd al-Malik b. Marwān.[8] In 64/683, during the ensuing conflict, the Honourable Kaᶜba and the Holy Mosque were both damaged and Ibn al-Zubayr was compelled to reconstruct the Honourable Kaᶜba and the Mosque in 65/684. The Black Stone was removed, and the Honourable Kaᶜba was rebuilt in stone in dimensions larger than it had been in the time of the Prophet (ṣ) It appears that the Mosque was enlarged and decorated at this time with mosaic and marble, this being the first recorded instance of mosaic decoration in Islam.[9] Further work on the Honourable Kaᶜba and the Holy Mosque was carried out by Hajjāj b. Yūsuf for the Umayyad Caliph ᶜAbd al-Malik b. Marwān.[10] The decoration in the Mosque by this Caliph should be seen in context of his activities in Palestine where he completed the Dome of the Rock in Jerusalem in 72/691.

The concern to improve or build religious monuments that ᶜAbd al-Malik displayed was continued by his son, the Caliph al-Walīd I, on a still greater scale. Al-Walīd pressed forward with the building programme initiated by his father in Arabia itself, in Palestine, Syria and Egypt, endowing the Islamic community with some of the finest buildings for worship that it possesses. He extended the Mosque of the Prophet (ṣ) in al-Madina al-Monawarah and the *jāmiᶜ* of Ṣanᶜā'; he reconstructed the al-Aqṣā Mosque in Jerusalem, the Jāmiᶜ al-Umawī in Damascus and the Mosque of ᶜAmr b. al-ᶜĀṣ in al-Fusṭāṭ, decorating most of these as well as the Mosque of the Prophet (ṣ) with mosaics and marble in the years between 85 and 96/705-15. Given this degree of Umayyad building activity, it is of little surprise that al-Walīd should have undertaken building work in the Holy Mosque in Makkah al-Mukarramah.[11] In 91/709 he had a roof in teak made, supported on marble columns, while in the Honourable Kaᶜba gold was used to decorate the door, the Mizāb al-Raḥma (the Water-Spout of Mercy) and the columns. Mosaic was used to decorate the walls of the Mosque, as in al-Walīd's other constructions in the Near East.

Under the ᶜAbbāsid Caliphs, the Holy Mosque underwent a succession of enlargements commencing with one by the Caliph Abū Jaᶜfar al-Manṣūr in 137-40/754-7. Having made the *hajj*, and seeing the confined space of the Holy Mosque and the number of the pilgrims to Makkah al-Mukarramah, al-Manṣūr undertook to enlarge the mosque once more to accommodate the pilgrims performing the *ṭawāf*. At the same time he built the first minaret in the north-west corner. Like the Umayyads before him, he decorated the mosque with marble and mosaic.[12]

Notwithstanding the constructions by al-Manṣūr, only some twenty years later the Caliph al-Mahdī saw fit to undertake yet more construction work in the Holy Mosque in 161/777 and in 164/780.[13] One of his major preoccupations was to protect the Holy Mosque from the consequences of flood. Marble columns were imported from Egypt and Bilād al-Shām, and the roof of the Mosque was made of teak, carved and inlaid with gold, mosaics and inscriptions from the Holy Qur'ān. According to recent accounts [14] there are inscriptions in low relief on columns inside the Mosque near the Bāb al-Ṣafā, in the name of the Caliph al-Mahdī; one is dated 167/783-4. Further reconstruction work took place in 271-2/884-5 under the Caliph al-Mu^ctamid, including rebuilding the roof in teak.[15] Further work took place in 281/894. However, the plan of the Holy Mosque was to remain unchanged from the time of al-Mahdī right up to the Ottoman period.[16]

Building took place at the Bāb Ibrāhīm in 306/918 although apparently this was of limited extent.[17] The city was assaulted by the Qaramatians in the 4th/10th century, but though the Black Stone was carried off for a space of some twenty years, no other damage was done to the Mosque.[18] From the following century there is a description of the Honourable Ka^cba and the Holy Mosque recorded by the pilgrim and traveller, Nāṣir-i Khusraw, of 442/1050.[19] There is also a remarkable illustration of the Holy Mosque on a marble panel dated to 486-93/1093-9, showing the plan of the building.[20] The marble in the Honourable Ka^cba was replaced in 550/1155 by Jamāl al-Dīn al-Iṣfahānī al-Jawād, *wazīr* of the prince of Mosul.[21] Nevertheless, the plan of the Holy Mosque remained just as al-Mahdī had rebuilt it when the traveller Ibn Jubayr visited Makkah al-Mukarramah in 579/1183. Ibn Jubayr gives the following description of the Holy Mosque and the Honourable Ka^cba as they appeared in his day, recording the building and the *hajj* in detail:[22]

"The venerable House has four corners and is almost square... its height, on the side which faces the Bab (Gate) al-Safa and which extends from the Black Stone to the Rukn al-Yamani (Yemen Corner), is twenty-nine cubits. The remaining sides are twenty-eight cubits because of the slope of the roof towards the water-spout.

"The principal corner is the one containing the Black Stone. There the circumambulation begins, the circumambulator drawing back (a little) from it so that all of his body might pass by it, the blessed House being on his left. The first thing that is met after that is the ^cIraq corner, which faces the north, then the Syrian corner which faces west, then the Yemen corner which faces south, and then back to the Black corner which faces east. That completes one shaut *(single course). The door of the blessed House is on the side between the ^cIraq corner and the Black Stone corner, and is close to the Stone at a distance of barely ten spans. That part of the side of the House which is between them is called the Multazam: a place where prayers are answered.*

"The venerable door is raised above the ground eleven and a half spans. It is of silver gilt and of exquisite workmanship and beautiful design, holding the eye for its excellence and in emotion for the awe God has clothed His House in. After the same fashion are the two posts, and the upper lintel over which is a slab of pure gold about two spans long. The door has two large silver staples on which is hung the lock. It faces to the east, and is eight spans wide and thirteen high. The thickness of the wall in which it turns is five spans. The inside of the blessed House is overlaid with variegated marbles, and the walls are all variegated marbles. (The ceiling) is sustained by three teak pillars of great height, four paces apart, and punctuating the length of the House, and down its middle. One of these columns, the first, faces the centre of the side enclosed by the two Yemen corners, and is three paces distant from it. The third column, the last, faces the side enclosed by the ^cIraq and Syrian corners.

"The whole circuit of the upper half of the House is plated with silver, thickly gilt, which the beholder would imagine, from its thickness, to be a sheet of gold. It encompasses the four sides and covers the upper half of the walls. The ceiling of the House is covered by a veil of coloured silk.

"The outside of the Ka^cbah, on all its four sides, is clothed in coverings of green silk with cotton warps; and on their upper parts is a band of red silk on which is written the verse, 'Verily the first House founded for mankind was that at Bakkah (Mecca)' (Koran III, 96). The name of the Imam al-Nasir li Din Ilah, in depth three cubits, encircles it all. On these coverings there has been shaped remarkable designs resembling handsome pulpits, and inscriptions entertaining the name of God Most High and calling blessings on Nasir, the aforementioned ^cAbbaside (Caliph) who had ordered its instalment. With all this, there was no clash of colour. The number of covers on all four sides is thirty-four, there being eighteen on the two long sides, and sixteen on the two short sides.

"The Ka^cbah has five windows of ^cIraq glass, richly stained. One of them is in the middle of the ceiling, and at each corner is a window... Between the pillars (hang) thirteen vessels, of silver save one that is gold."

Ibn Jubayr goes on to give a detailed account of the interior of the Honourable Ka^cba and of the Holy Mosque around it, which in his time consisted of roofed arcades on four sides of the open courtyard. The roof of the Mosque had large merlons forming a perimeter, and on the facade on all four sides was a stucco frieze. The minarets of the Holy Mosque he describes in the following terms: [23]

"The minarets also have singular forms, for the (lower) half is angulated at the four sides, by means of finely sculptured stones, remarkably set, and surrounded by a wooden lattice of rare workmanship. Above the lattice there rises into the air a spire that seems as the work of a turner, wholly dressed with baked bricks fitting the one into the other with an art that draws the gaze for its beauty. At the top of the spire is a globe also encircled by a wooden lattice of exactly the same pattern as the other. All these minarets have a distinct form, not one resembling the other; but all are of the type described, the lower half being angulated, and the upper columned."

Several subsequent restorations and repairs to the Honourable Kaba and the Holy Mosque are described by Ḥusayn Bā Salāma. The work affecting the Honourable Kaᶜba is recorded on seven marble panels set in its walls. One of these refers to construction work ordered by the ᶜAbbāsid Caliph Abū Jaᶜfar al-Mustanṣir Bi'llāh in 629/1230-1.[24] Another panel in the Honourable Kaᶜba refers to restoration of its marble by a Rasūlid ruler of Yemen, al-Malik al-Muẓaffar, in 680/1282.[25] Subsequent restorations in the Holy Mosque were undertaken by the Mamlūk Sultan, al-Nāṣir Muḥammad b. Qalā'ūn in 720/1320[26]; the Sultan al-Manṣūr ᶜAlī b. Shaᶜbān in 781/1379-80 carried out work on the Holy Mosque[27] but far more extensive reconstruction was commenced in 803/1400 and was completed in the time of the Mamlūk Sultan Faraj b. Barqūq in 807/1404-5.[28] The Honourable Kaᶜba had its marble renewed by the Sultan al-Ashraf Barsbay in 826/1422-3.[29]

Another Mamlūk Sultan, al-Malik al-Ẓāhir Jaqmaq, restored the Honourable Kaᶜba in 843/1439-40[30], while one of the greatest builders among the Mamlūk Sultans, Qayt Bay, carried out work in the Holy Mosque in 882/1477[31] and in the Honourable Kaᶜba in 884-8/1479-80-1483.[32] With the fall of the Circassian Mamlūk Sultanate in Egypt in 923/1517 the protection of the Holy Cities of Islam passed to the new power in the Near East, the Ottoman Sultanate, and henceforth it was primarily the Ottomans who took the responsibility for restoring the Honourable Kaᶜba and the Holy Mosque, until the early years of the present century. The accounts of the Mosque by the travellers ᶜAlī Bey and J. L. Burckhardt and the first photographs of the Holy Mosque preserve the record of what was essentially an Ottoman reconstruction of both the Holy Mosque and the Honourable Kaᶜba.

The transfer of the protection of the Holy Cities from Cairo to the Ottoman capital, Istanbul, led to the replacement of predominantly Egyptian Islamic architectural influence by Ottoman influence emanating from Istanbul. This was to have profound architectural consequences in several parts of the Hejaz, where the Ottoman style was to affect the design of mosques, and especially minarets, in al-Madina al-Monawarah, Jidda, al-Ṭā'if, al-Wajh and al-ᶜUlā. It may be that these elements of Ottoman architectural origin in western Arabia were filtered through the Holy Cities to the other Hejaz towns, rather than stemming from Istanbul or Cairo directly.

The Holy Mosque underwent very extensive reconstruction in the time of Sultan Sulaymān al-Qānūnī (known in the west as "the Magnificent"), who added a new marble *minbar* among other major works in 972/1564[33]; further reconstruction was undertaken by his successor, Sultan Salīm, in 979-1571-2.[34] In Shaᶜbān 1039/1630 a great flood occurred in Makkah al-Mukarramah and undermined much of the Honourable Kaᶜba, which had to be reconstructed.[35] The Ottoman Sultan, Murād IV, ordered a major rebuilding which is recorded by an inscription in the Honourable Kaᶜba, dated Ramaḍān 1040/1631.[36] It is the structure repaired by Sultan Murād that remains today, although the Holy Mosque around it has been rebuilt in modern times.[37]

In 1217/1803 Imām Saᶜūd b. ᶜAbd al-ᶜAzīz b. Muḥammad Saᶜūd led his forces into the Hejaz and entered Makkah al-Mukarramah, taking it for the first time from the Sharīfian ruler, Ghālib b. ᶜAwn, who held authority on behalf of the Ottoman Sultan.[38] The practices in the Holy City which contradicted Islam were eradicated by the Al Saᶜūd, with domed tombs and *mashhads* being demolished in accordance with the teaching of Islam regarding tombs, while other practices were also rectified.

During the rule of the first Saudi state in the Hejaz, the traveller ᶜAlī Bey visited Makkah al-Mukarramah for over a month from 14 Dhū'l-Qaᶜda 1221/23 January 1807.[39] He described the Honourable Kaᶜba and published a plan of the Holy Mosque, of which he provided the following account:[40]

"The great court is circumscribed by four wings or porticos supported by columns and pillars. It presents a parallelogram, the large sides of which in the direction of the E. 34½°N. to the W. 34½°S., are five hundred and thirty-six feet nine inches long; and the small ones, in the direction of the N. 34½°W. to the S. 34½°E., are three hundred and fifty-six feet broad.

"The fronts of each of the longest sides present thirty-six arches, and the shortest ones twenty-four arches, which are slightly pointed. They are supported by columns of greyish marble, of different proportions, but which in general appear to approach the Doric.

"Instead of a column between every fourth arch, there is an octangular pilaster of hewn stone, about three feet in diameter.

"Each side of the great gallery is composed of three naves, or rows of arches, which are, with the exception of some partial irregularities, all equally supported by columns; so that there may be counted more than five hundred columns and pilasters, which support the galleries or porticos of the temple.

"The capitals of the columns which form the four fronts of the court are very fine, although they do not belong to either of the five orders of architecture; but the capitals of the columns of the interior of the gallery are all either of the corinthian or composite. I observed some carved in the most exquisite manner.

"Their bases are almost all attic. There are some that have a little attic pedestal, others a false base, and some even, by an extravagant whim of the architect, a corinthian capital reversed.

"The arches that front the court are all crowned with little conical cupolas; but the interior ones have only low spherical vaults.

"The four fronts of the court are surmounted also with stone ornaments, that very much resemble fleurs-de-lys.

"All the galleries are paved like the ways, with hewn stones of quartz rock, with schorl and mica, which abound in the country. The walls of the temple are also built of it."

The Al Saᶜūd continued to act as the protectors of the Holy City until the Albanian Pasha of Egypt, Muḥammad ᶜAlī, took Makkah al-Mukarramah in 1228/1813 on behalf of the Ottoman Sultan. The following year, Burckhardt visited the Hejaz and described the Holy Mosque:[41]

"The Kaaba stands in an oblong square, two hundred and fifty paces long, and two hundred broad, none of the sides of which run quite in a straight line, though at first sight the whole appears to be of a regular shape. This open square is enclosed on the eastern side by a colonnade: the pillars stand in a quadruple row: they are three deep on the other sides, and united by pointed arches, every four of which support a small dome, plastered and whitened on the outside. These domes, according to Kotobeddyn, are one hundred and fifty-two in number. Along the whole colonnade, on the four sides, lamps are suspended from the arches. Some are lighted every night, and all during the nights of Ramadhan. The pillars are above twenty feet in height, and generally from one foot and a half to one foot and three quarters in diameter; but little regularity has been observed in regard to them. Some are of white marble, granite, or porphyry, but the greater number are of common stone of the Mekka mountains. El Fasy states the whole at five hundred and eighty-nine, and says they are all of marble, excepting one hundred and twenty-six, which are of common stone, and three of composition. Kotobeddyn reckons five hundred and fifty-five, of which, according to him, three hundred and eleven are of marble, and the rest of stone taken from the neighbouring mountains; but neither of these authors lived to see the latest repairs of the mosque, after the destruction occasioned by a torrent, in A.D. *1626. Between every three or four columns stands an octagonal one, about four feet in thickness. On the east side are two shafts of reddish gray granite, in one piece, and one fine gray porphyry column with slabs of white feldspath. On the north side is one red granite column, and one of fine-grained red porphyry: these are probably the columns which Kotobeddyn states to have been brought from Egypt, and principally from Akhmim (Panopolis), when the chief El Mohdy enlarged the mosque, in* AH *163."*

Further on he continues:

"Seven paved causeways lead from the colonnades towards the Kaaba, or holy house, in the centre. They are of sufficient breadth to admit four or five persons to walk abreast, and they are elevated about nine inches above the ground. Between these causeways, which are covered with fine gravel or sand, grass appears growing in several places, produced by the Zemzem water dozing [sic] out of the jars, which are placed in the ground in long rows during the day. The whole area of the mosque is upon a lower level than any of the streets surrounding it. There is a descent of eight or ten steps from the gates on the north side into the platform of the colonnade, and of three or four steps from the gates, on the south side.

"Towards the middle of this area stands the Kaaba; it is one hundred and fifteen paces from the north colonnade, and eighty-eight from the south. For this want of symmetry we may readily account, the Kaaba having existed prior to the mosque which was built around it, and enlarged at different periods."[42]

The Holy Mosque was still in much the same condition seventy years later when it was photographed by Snouck Hurgronje in the course of his residence in the Hejaz in 1302/1884-5 (Plates 1-3).

After Makkah al-Mukarramah had been recovered by Muḥammad ᶜAlī Pasha, it remained under the Egyptians, the Ottomans and finally, the Sharīfs of Makkah al-Mukarramah until Ṣafar 1343/September 1924. In this year, the forces of His Late Majesty King ᶜAbd al-ᶜAzīz Al Saᶜūd peacefully entered the Holy City wearing the *iḥrām* of pilgrims to the Holy Mosque. With the security and wealth that subsequently came to the Kingdom, the wherewithal was available to carry out large-scale extensions to the Holy Mosque which made it the largest on earth. On 4 Rabīᶜa II 1375/20 November 1955 the government of the Kingdom initiated a rebuilding of the Holy Mosque and endowed it with the form that it has today.[43] In recent years, the authorities have improved facilities to assist pilgrims to complete their *ḥajj*: a major contribution to the Honourable Kaᶜba has been the ordering of a new gold door by His Late Majesty King Khālid b. ᶜAbd al-ᶜAzīz Al Saᶜūd which was placed in the Honourable Kaᶜba on 22 Dhū'l-Qaᶜda 1399/14 October 1979.[44]

Other mosques of Makkah al-Mukarramah

There are a number of other mosques of early foundation in Makkah al-Mukarramah and its neighbourhood, most of which have been restored or reconstructed in recent times. These have recently been described and illustrated.[1]

Masjid Qubā', al-Madina al-Monawarah

When the Prophet Muḥammad (ṣ) made his *hijra* from Makkah al-Mukarramah to al-Madina al-Monawarah in 1/622 he stayed at Qubā' close to al-Madina al-Monawarah with the Banī ᶜAmr b. ᶜAwf from Monday until Thursday, until he continued on to al-Madina al-Monawarah itself.[1] In the course of his stay at Qubā', the Prophet (ṣ) prayed on the site of the mosque of Qubā'[2], which thus takes the honour of being the first site at which he prayed after his *hijra* from Makkah al-Mukarramah.[3]

The mosque of Qubā' is in the south-west part of the city of al-Madina al-Monawarah and its recent form dates from the restorations undertaken by His Late Majesty King Fayṣal b. ᶜAbd al-ᶜAzīz Al Saᶜūd in 1388/1969. These restorations were among a succession of reconstructions on the site where the Prophet (ṣ) had prayed.[4] The third Rightly Guided Caliph, ᶜUthmān b. ᶜAffān, added to the mosque between 23 and 35/644-656 and it continued in the condition in which he left it until the Caliphate of the Umayyad al-Walīd b. ᶜAbd al-Malik, who extended and reconstructed it between 87/706 and 93/712. Al-Walīd ordered his governor in al-Madina al-Monawarah, his cousin ᶜUmar b. ᶜAbd al-ᶜAzīz (the future Caliph ᶜUmar II), to undertake this building, which included the construction of a *raḥaba* and *riwāqs*, and, for the first time in this mosque, a minaret was built. The Umayyad work on the mosque at Qubā' should be seen in context of the large-scale mosque-building programme in the Hejaz, Yemen, Palestine, Syria and Egypt undertaken by al-Walīd and his father which has been referred to above.

In 435/1043-4 some renovation was carried out around the *miḥrāb* by Sharīf Abū Yaᶜlī al-Hussayni, while under the Ottomans further reconstructions or renovations were undertaken, the most recent of which was that of the Sultan Maḥmūd II in 1245/1829-30, according to ᶜAbd al-Quddūs al-Anṣāry. He adds that the work on the mosque of Qubā' which His Late Majesty King Fayṣal ordered was undertaken at a cost of 800,000 Saudi riyals.

At the time of writing, a new foundation stone has been laid by H.M. King Fahad b. ᶜAbd al-ᶜAzīz Al Saᶜūd for a new extension to the Qubā' mosque (8 Ṣafar 1405/1 November 1984).[5]

The Mosque of the Prophet (Ṣ), al-Madina al-Monawarah[1]

The Mosque of the Prophet (ṣ), al-Madina al-Monawarah, in 1326/1909. (Rifᶜ at Pasha)

In the first year of the *hijra*, after the Prophet Muḥammad (ṣ) had departed from Makkah al-Mukarramah to establish the Muslim community in al-Madina al-Monawarah, he was greeted by the people of the latter city with invitations to reside in various houses.(2) However, he declined these offers, allowing his camel to take him to wherever it stopped. Twice the camel lay down on a place for drying dates and it was here that the Prophet (ṣ) finally alighted. The land was the property of two orphans, Sahl and Suhayl, whose guardian, Muᶜādh b. ᶜAfrā', gave the land to the Prophet (ṣ), reimbursing the orphans himself. Meanwhile, Abū Ayyūb Khālid b. Zayd moved the Prophet's (ṣ) baggage into his house and the Prophet (ṣ) lodged with him until his own residence was built. On the land where his camel had halted, the Prophet (ṣ) set about building the mosque that remains to this day, albeit much altered, and against the exterior of the enclosure wall he built chambers for himself and his wives.

The *muhājirūn* (those Muslims who had joined the *hijra* from Makkah al-Mukarramah) and the *anṣār* (the Muslims of al-Madina al-Monawarah) assisted the Prophet (ṣ) in this work, constructing the mosque walls in the customary building material of central Arabia, *libin* (unfired mud-brick).(3) Against the north side of the courtyard of the mosque a covered area was built, with palm branches resting on palm-trunk columns, while on the southern side of the courtyard another roofed area was built against part of the south wall of the enclosure, known as a *ṣuffa*. Against the east side of the enclosure, on the exterior, were the chambers for the Prophet (ṣ) and his wives. At this stage, the Muslim community prayed northwards towards Jerusalem, but as a result of a revelation when the Prophet (ṣ) was leading prayers in the *muṣalla* of al-Madina al-Monawarah, the *qibla* was changed to the south, to Makkah al-Mukarramah.(4) The *muṣalla* was henceforth known as Masjid al-Qiblatayn (the "Mosque of the two *qiblas*"), while the arrangement of the Mosque of the Prophet (ṣ) was also changed: henceforth, the roofed area for shading the community at prayer was against the south (*qibla*) wall, and the *ṣuffa* was the portico against the north wall. The Mosque was entered by doors set in the west, the north and the east sides. That to the west was Bāb ᶜĀtika (Bāb al-Raḥma), and to the east, Bāb Jibrīl and Bāb al-Nisā', the entrance for women. According to ᶜAbd al-Quddūs al-Anṣāry(5), the Mosque was initially rectangular, measuring about 35 metres from north to south and 30 metres from east to west. In 7/628-9 the Mosque was made a regular square.

The Mosque of the Prophet (ṣ) in 1326/1909 (?)

The Mosque of the Prophet (ṣ) as established in the lifetime of the Prophet Muḥammad (ṣ) was the antecedent of the architectural form of mosques subsequently constructed throughout the Islamic world. Its structural details arose from the traditions of Arabian building, while its arrangement arose from the requirements of worship in Islam. The mosques of Arabia remain extremely close in plan to the initial mosque form established at al-Madina al-Monawarah by the Prophet (ṣ) and, indeed, the same building material, *libin*, can be found throughout central Arabia to this day.

The Mosque of the Prophet (s) in 1326/1909, showing the dome over the Noble Tomb and the minaret at the south-east corner, the mi'dhanat al-ra'īsiyya, *completed by Sultan Qayt Bay in 892/1487.* (Rifʿat Pasha)

In the early days, the Prophet (ṣ) would lean against one of the wooden pillars of the Mosque to address the Community[6], but subsequently a wooden *minbar* with three steps, constructed in tamarisk (*'athal*), was built for him. The Prophet (ṣ) would sit on this in the Mosque to speak to the people, and after his death, the first Caliph, Abū Bakr, would sit one step lower than the Prophet (ṣ) had sat; on his succession to the Caliphate, ᶜUmar b. al-Khaṭṭāb would sit a step below the place of Abū Bakr. From this *minbar* and its use to deliver the *khutba* in the Mosque of the Prophet (ṣ) derives the entire tradition of *minbars* and their general design in Islam.

The area of the Mosque of the Prophet (ṣ) which includes the site of the Prophet's (ṣ) *minbar* and his *miḥrab* is known as *al-rawḍa*, arising from a declaration by the Prophet (ṣ):

*"There is a garden (*rawḍa*) in Paradise for these prayers situated between my* minbar *and my house".*[7]

To the east of this area is the Noble *ḥujra*, known formerly as the *maqṣūra*.[8] Behind this screened enclosure is the tomb of the Prophet Muḥammad (ṣ) and those of the Caliphs Abū Bakr al-Ṣiddīq and ᶜUmar b. al-Khaṭṭāb. Today the Noble *ḥujra* is covered by the great green dome built by the Ottoman Sultan Maḥmūd in 1233/1818[9], but this part of the Mosque was not actually incorporated into the enclosure until the Umayyad period. This had been the site of the chambers of the Prophet (ṣ) and his wives, and it was beneath his residence that he was buried in 11/632.

The second Caliph, ᶜUmar b. al-Khaṭṭāb, extended the Mosque in 17/638[10], the first of numerous enlargements and reconstructions. His work involved extension on all sides except the east, where he left the chambers of the Prophet's (ṣ) wives undisturbed. A further rebuilding took place in the Caliphate of ᶜUthmān b. ᶜAffān, ᶜUmar's successor.[11] In 29/649-50, ᶜUthmān constructed *riwāqs* on all four sides of the *ṣaḥn*, using stone, plaster and columns secured with iron: the roofing of the colonnades was of teak. The south limit of the mosque to this day is that defined by the Caliph ᶜUthmān.[12] The mosque at this stage of its development had six entrances.

A fundamental rebuilding of the Mosque of the Prophet (ṣ) took place in the Umayyad period, when the Caliph al-Walīd b. ᶜAbd al-Malik greatly enlarged the Mosque, reconstructing it and lavishly embellishing it.[13] This building activity was part of an extensive campaign initiated by his father and continued by al-Walīd and which affected the major mosques of Arabia, Bilād al-Shām and Egypt. In 88/707 al-Walīd sent instructions to his cousin, ᶜUmar b. ᶜAbd al-ᶜAzīz, governor of al-Madina al-Monawarah and a future Caliph, to demolish the chambers of the wives of the Prophet (ṣ) and to include the land within the Mosque. As a result, the Mosque henceforth encompassed the burial place of the Prophet (ṣ) and of the Caliphs Abū Bakr and ᶜUmar b. al-Khaṭṭāb. Four minarets were also constructed. Al-Walīd ordered the decoration of the Mosque in mosaic and marble and built the roof in teak, ornamenting it with gold-leaf. Although nothing remains of the decora-

Qibla riwāqs *in the Mosque of the Prophet (ṣ), 1326/1909*

tion to the Mosque of the Prophet (S) by al-Walīd, there is a detailed description of it by Ibn Jubayr, quoted below. This makes it quite clear that the decoration was very similar to that which still remains in the Umayyad *jāmiᶜ* of Damascus, which al-Walīd also re-built. The mosaics surviving in Damascus give a reasonable idea of what the mosaics in al-Madina al-Monawarah must have been like (see illustration below).

The Mosque of the Prophet (S) underwent a further extension by the ᶜAbbāsid Caliph al-Mahdī in 161-5/777-81.[14] Yet more construction was carried out in 246-7/860-2 by the Caliph al-Mutawakkil[15]; this included decorating the Mosque with mosaics. Thereafter, the Mosque appears to have retained its plan unchanged until the 7th/13th century. It was the Mosque in this form that was described by the traveller Ibn Jubayr who visited al-Madina al-Monawarah in 580/1184. He provided an account of the Mosque of the Prophet (S) as it was in his day, which is of particular value as subsequently it was entirely rebuilt after a fire. Of the overall design of the Mosque, Ibn Jubayr says the following:

"The blessed Mosque is oblong in shape, and is surrounded on all four sides by porticoes. In its centre is a court covered with sand and gravel. The south side has five rows of porticoes running from west to east, and the north side also has five porticoes in the same style. The east side has three porticoes and the west four. The sacred Rawdah is at the eastern extremity of the south side. It extends over two rows of porticoes on the side of the court and projects about four spans into the third. It has five angles and five sides, and its form is so wondrous that one can barely portray or describe it. Four of its sides incline away from the direction of the qiblah *in an ingenious fashion, and because of this deviation from the* qiblah, *no one is able to face them in his prayers."*[16]

Umayyad mosaics in the Great Mosque, Damascus (86-96/705-15). Similar mosaics decorated the Mosque of the Prophet (S) during the same period.

Further on Ibn Jubayr gives more information on the form of the Mosque:

"The venerated Mosque is one hundred and ninety-six paces long and one hundred and twenty-six wide. It has two hundred and ninety columns that are like straight props, for they reach the ceiling and have no arches bending over them. They are composed of stone hewn into a number of round, bored blocks, mortised together and with melted lead poured between each pair so that they form a straight column. They are then covered with a coat of plaster, and rubbed and polished zealously until they appear as white marble. The portico to the south, which we have mentioned as having five rows of porticoes, is enfolded by a maqsurah *that flanks its length from west to east and in which there is a* mihrab. *The imam prays in the aforementioned little Rawdah beside the chest. Between this* maqsurah *and the Rawdah and the sacred tomb is a big painted reading-desk on which lies a large Koran locked in a case. It is one of the four copies sent by ᶜUthman ibn ᶜAffan – may God hold him in His favour – to the several cities."*[17]

Of the decoration of the Mosque of the Prophet, Ibn Jubayr recorded the following:

"The lower half of the south wall is cased with marble, tile on tile, of varying order and colour: a splendid marquetry. The upper half is wholly inlaid with pieces of gold called fusayfisa *[mosaic] in which the artist has displayed amazing skill, producing shapes of trees in divers forms, their branches laden with fruits. The whole Mosque is of this style, but the work in the south wall is more embellished. The wall looking on the court from the south side is of this manner, as also is that which does so from the north side. The west and east walls that overlook the court are wholly white and carved, and adorned with a band that contains various kinds of colours."*[18]

In Ibn Jubayr's time the *minbar* of the Prophet (ṣ) was still preserved, although not in use, being a protected object of sanctity in the Mosque. The number of gateways to the enclosure in his day had increased to nineteen, while there were three minarets, of which one was whitened and could be seen from afar.

The Mosque of the Prophet (ṣ) remained as Ibn Jubayr had seen it for less than a century. On the first night of Ramaḍān 654/1256 a great fire engulfed it, burning the *minbar* of the Prophet (ṣ), the Holy Qur'ān of ᶜUthmān, and everything else inflammable, including the roof. The mosaics were presumably lost in the same fire. The year afterwards, the ᶜAbbāsid Caliph al-Mustaᶜṣim took responsibility for repairing the Mosque, but with the fall of Baghdad to the Mongols and the death of the Caliph, it was the ruler of Yemen, al-Malik al-Muẓaffar[19], and the Mamlūk Sultan of Egypt, al-Ẓāhir Baybars al-Bunduqdārī, who actually completed the restoration. From this time onwards, the prominence of Egypt led to the frequent renovation of the Mosque by the Mamlūk Sultans and this ended only with the establishment of Ottoman hegemony in the 10th/16th century.

Among the more important works by the Mamlūk Sultans of Egypt was the construction of a wooden roof over the Noble Tomb of the Prophet (ṣ) by Sultan Qalā'ūn in 678/1279. A number of restorations to the roof and extensions were made by his son, the Sultan al-Nāṣir Muḥammad, in 705-6/1305-6 and in 729/1329[20]. According to Jean Sauvaget, the south-west minaret was rebuilt in 705-6/1305-7.[21] A series of repairs to the roof of the Noble Tomb and other work including a new *minbar* were carried out by Sultan Ḥasan b. Nāṣir Muḥammad in 765-7/1363-6. Another new *minbar* was placed in the mosque in 797/1394-5 and yet another in 820/1417. Major repairs to the *riwāqs* of the Mosque were carried out by the Sultan al-Ashraf Barsbay in 831/1427-8, and further construction was undertaken in 853/1449, which included fixing marble panels in the prayer-hall and around the Prophet's (ṣ) Noble Tomb. Qayt Bay, one of the most lavish builders among the Circassian Mamlūk Sultans, repaired the mosque for the first time in 879/1474-5 and again in 881/1476-7, when he built a stone dome over the Prophet's (ṣ) Noble Tomb, to replace the wooden roof of Sultan Qalā'ūn. However, very shortly afterwards, in 886/1481, the Mosque was again destroyed by fire and Qayt Bay once more undertook the complete restoration of the Mosque. The south-east minaret was rebuilt and survives still in what is essentially an Egyptian Islamic form. Al-Anṣāry also dates the *maqṣūra* of the Mosque in its essentials to the work of Qayt Bay, who completed his restoration in 892/1487.[22]

With the fall of the Mamlūk Sultans, the Ottomans assumed responsibility for the maintenance of the Mosque of the Prophet (ṣ). Extensive work was carried out by Sultan Sulaymān II, beginning in 938/1531-2 with the construction of the *miḥrāb* Sulaymānī. In 974/1566-7 the Sultan rebuilt the west wall of the Mosque from the Bāb al-Raḥma and the Minārat al-Sulaymāniyya at the north-east corner. Sultan Selīm II undertook further work on the Mosque in 980/1572. Under the Ottomans the present green dome was built over the Noble Tomb of the Prophet (ṣ) and of the first two Caliphs: al-Anṣāry attributes the dome to the Sultan Maḥmūd II (1233/1818).[23] Other late Ottoman work includes the insertion of the Bāb al-Majīdī by Sultan ᶜAbd al-Majīd I between 1265 and 1277/1848 and 1860-1, and, on the eve of the disintegration of Ottoman power in the Arabian peninsula, Fakhrī Pasha restored the *miḥrāb* of the Prophet (ṣ) and the Sulaymānī *miḥrāb* in 1336/1917-18.

The Swiss traveller, John Lewis Burckhardt, visited al-Madina al-Monawarah in 1230/1815 and published a description of the Mosque of the Prophet (ṣ) although, unfortunately, ill health prevented him from drawing a plan. The Mosque as he described it was essentially the building as Qayt Bay and Sulaymān II had left it:[24]

"Its dimensions [the Mosque of the Prophet (ṣ)] *are much smaller than those of the mosque at Mekka, being a hundred and sixty-five paces in length, and a hundred and thirty in breadth; but it is built much upon the same plan, forming an open square, surrounded on all sides by covered colonnades, with a small building in the centre of the square. These colonnades are much less regular than those at Mekka, where the rows of pillars stand at much the same depth on all sides. On the south side of this mosque, the colonnade is composed of ten rows of pillars behind each other; and on the west side are four rows; on the north, and part of the east side, only three rows. The columns themselves are of different sizes. On the south side, which contains the Prophet's tomb, and which forms the most holy part of the building, they are of larger dimensions than in the other parts, and about two feet and a half in diameter."*

The colonnades were of stone but coated in white plaster. Floral motifs and arabesques were painted on this plaster while the columns in the southern (*qibla*) colonnade in *al-rawḍa* were encased in glazed green tiles and ornamented in arabesques in different colours.

"The roof of the [southern] *colonnade consists of a number of small domes, white-washed on the outside, in the same manner as those of Mekka. The interior walls are also white-washed all round, except the*

southern one and part of the S.E. corner, which are cased with slabs of marble, nearly up to the top. Several rows of inscriptions, in large gilt letters, are conducted along this wall, one above the other, and have a very brilliant effect upon the white marble. The floor under the colonnades, on the west and east sides, and part of the north, is laid out with a coarse pavement; the other part of the N. side being unpaved, and merely covered with sand; as is likewise the whole open yard. On the south side, where the builder of the mosque has lavished all this ornament, the floor is paved with fine marble across the whole colonnade; and in those parts nearest to the tomb of Mohammed, this pavement is in mosaic, of excellent workmanship, forming one of the best specimens of that kind to be seen in the East. Large and high windows, with glass panes, (of which I know not any other instance in the Hedjaz,) admit the light through the southern wall; some of them are of fine painted glass. On the other sides, smaller windows are dispersed along the walls, but not with glass panes."

Sir Richard Burton visited the Mosque in 1273/1856 and added further details in his description.(25) At the time of his visit certain reconstructions by the Ottoman Sultan, ᶜAbd al-Majīd I, were underway.

"We began our circumambulation at the Bab el Salam, – the Gate of Salvation – in the southern portion of the western long wall of the mosque. It is a fine archway handsomely incrusted with marble and glazed tiles; the number of gilt inscriptions on its sides give it, especially at night-time, an appearance of considerable splendor. The portcullis-like doors are of wood, strengthened with brass plates, and nails of the same metal... About the centre of the western wall is the Bab el Rahmah – the Gate of Mercy. It admits the dead bodies of the Faithful when carried to be prayed over in the mosque; there is nothing remarkable in its appearance; in common with the other gates it has huge folding doors, iron-bound, an external flight of steps, and a few modern inscriptions. The Bab Mejidi or Gate of the Sultan Abd el Mejid stands in the centre of the northern wall; like its portico, it is unfinished, but its present appearance promises that it will eclipse all except the Bab el Salam. The Bab el Nisa is in the eastern wall opposite the Bab el Rahmah, with which it is connected by the 'Farsh el Hajar,' a broad band of stone, two or three steps below the level of the portico, and slightly raised above the Sahn or the hypaethral portion of the Mosque. And lastly, in the southern portion of the same eastern wall is the Bab Jibrail, the Gate of the Archangel Gabriel. All these entrances are arrived at by short external flights of steps leading from the streets, as the base of the temple [sic. the Mosque], *unlike that of Meccah, is a little higher than the foundations of the buildings around it."*

Burton goes on to describe the five minarets: that known as the Shikayliya at the north-west corner; the *mināra* at the Bāb al-Salām, that stands beside the gate of the same name; the Bāb al-Raḥma *mināra* near the centre of the western wall; and the Sulaymāniyya *mināra* of Sultan Sulaymān at the north-east corner. The minaret at the south-east corner, built by Qayt Bay, Burton calls the "Munar Raisiyah". The minarets were irregular in Burton's eyes in the sense that they were of no uniform style. The interior of the building he describes in the following terms:

"Equally irregular are the Riwaks, or porches, surrounding the hypaethral court. Along the northern wall there will be, when finished, a fine colonnade of granite, paved with marble. The eastern Riwak has three rows of pillars, the western four, and the southern, under which stands the tomb, of course has its columns ranged deeper than all the others."(26)

Another Englishman, Eldon Rutter, was in the Hejaz in 1344/1926, when the late King ᶜAbd al-ᶜAzīz had only recently taken al-Madina al-Monawarah from the Hāshemites. Rutter saw the Mosque of the Prophet (ṣ) as it appears in plates 11, 12, 13 and 16.(27) From his account comes this description of the southern *riwāq* and the Noble Tomb:

"Half-way across the Mosque we came to a marble pulpit on our left-hand, and a few paces further stood an isolated mihrâb. The latter was encased in slabs of white, black, red and green marble, arranged in elaborate patterns. It is known as Mihrâb en-Nabi – the Prophet's prayer-niche.

"Turning to our left, we passed between the pulpit and the mihrâb, and entered a forest of massive stone columns. To our right, that is, to eastward, a beautiful screen of green-painted iron and brasswork, extending from floor to roof of the Mosque, was visible through the row of columns. From its upper extremity, great curtains of dark-green silk hung in festoons, being caught up with brass chains or hooks. Unseen behind that screen lay the Prophet's tomb."

After the incorporation of the Hejaz into the Saudi state, the Al Saᶜūd rulers of Arabia became responsible for the Holy Mosques, and the first repairs, undertaken by order of the late King ᶜAbd al-ᶜAzīz were carried out in 1347/1928-9, when the *rahaba* was widened. In 1350/1931-2 repairs were made to some of the columns. The most extensive rebuilding of the Mosque has come with the prosperity of the Kingdom in more recent times. The late King ᶜAbd al-ᶜAzīz announced in a letter of 5 Ramaḍān 1368/30 June 1949 the plan to extend the Prophet's (ṣ) Mosque. The work was commenced on 5 Shawwāl 1370/10 July 1951 and, after their purchase, neighbouring houses were demolished to permit the Mosque to be extended; the foundation stone of the new constructions was laid on 5 Rabīᶜa I 1372/23 November 1952. As a result of this new building by the Saudi government, the Mosque of the Prophet (ṣ) reached an area of 22,955 square metres.(28) Subsequently, the late King Fayṣal b. ᶜAbd al-ᶜAzīz added an open rectangular area to the west of the Mosque to accommodate the great numbers attending the Mosque during the *hajj*. The new addition, *al-sāḥa*, was planned in 1393/1973 and budgeted for an expenditure of 50 million Saudi riyals.(29) At the time of writing, the government of H.M. King Fahad b. ᶜAbd al-ᶜAzīz Al Saᶜūd has announced new construction to facilitate prayers at the Mosque of the Prophet (ṣ)(30)

Other mosques of al-Madina al-Monawarah

There are several important mosques in al-Madina al-Monawarah which have been described by other authorities, including the Jumaʿ mosque[1], the Qiblatayn mosque[2], the 'Ajāba mosque[3], the five mosques of al-Fatḥ, and a number of others in the vicinity of the city.[4]

Jidda

Jidda, on the Red Sea coast of Saudi Arabia, became the port of Makkah al-Mukarramah in 26/646 in the Caliphate of ʿUthmān b. ʿAffān, replacing the earlier harbour of al-Shuʿayba. To this day, Jidda remains a major point of entry for pilgrims to Makkah al-Mukarramah as well as one of the principal commercial ports of the peninsula. The prosperity that has accrued to Jidda from the traffic passing through it has given rise to a tradition of fine architecture, both religious and domestic.

The mosques of Jidda are referred to by Ibn Jubayr who associated two of them with the second Caliph[1]:

"The city has a blessed mosque attributed to ʿUmar ibn al-Khattab – may God hold him in His favour – and another with two pillars of ebony wood, also attributed to him – may God hold him in His favour – although some attribute it to Harun al-Rashid – may God have mercy on him."

The first of these is taken to be the Shāfiʿī mosque[2] described below, and the second the mosque of ʿUthmān b. ʿAffān or the Ebony (Ābanūs) Mosque.[3] Ibn Baṭṭūṭa also referred to a mosque called the Ebony Mosque when he visited Jidda in 730/1330.[4] An earlier visitor, the pilgrim Nāṣir-i Khusraw, made a reference to the mosques of Jidda in the following terms:[5]

"La qiblèh de la grande mosquée est tournée dans la direction de l'est. On ne voit en dehors de la ville aucun bâtiment, à l'exception d'une mosquée qui porte le nom de Mesdjid er Ressoul (mosquée du Prophète)."

The commerce conveyed through Jidda was of great importance to Egypt and as a result the Hejaz was brought under the control of the Mamlūk Sultans of Cairo. In 828/1425, the Sultan Barsbay established a customs post at Jidda to exploit to the full revenue from goods arriving in the city. Jidda was thus a port of major importance to the Mamlūks, and thereafter, from 923/1517, to the Ottomans in their resistance to Portuguese encroachments in the Red Sea. During the Ottoman period, the Hejaz and Jidda with it came under the sometimes rather tenuous domination of Istanbul. A consequence of Ottoman power in the area was the introduction into the Hejaz of Ottoman architectural styles, especially with regard to minarets, and the impact of this is clear in the mosques of Jidda.

During the Ottoman period, effective local power in Jidda tended to remain with the Sharīfs of Makkah al-Mukarramah until the Al Saʿūd forces beseiged the city in 1217/1803 and eventually took it from the incumbent Sharīf, Ghālib b. ʿAwn. The Saudis retained control of Jidda until 1226/1811, when the Governor of Egypt, Muḥammad ʿAlī Pasha, took the city, ostensibly on behalf of the enfeebled Ottoman Sultanate. When Muḥammad ʿAlī's power declined under European pressure after 1256/1840, the Ottomans reinstituted direct rule in most of the Hejaz, and the region as a whole, including Jidda, remained under their government until the rebellion of Sharīf Ḥusayn b. ʿAlī in 1334/1916. In 1344/1925, Jidda passed under the rule of His Late Majesty King ʿAbd al-ʿAzīz Al Saʿūd.

al-Miʿmār mosque, Jidda

The Miʿmār mosque in the Maḥallat al-Maẓlūm area of Jidda is one of the best-preserved of the older mosques of the city. Although no full documentation or ground-plan has been published, it nevertheless has been mentioned in a number of studies of Jidda and its architecture. ʿAbd al-Quddūs al-Anṣāry attributes the foundation of the mosque to the patronage of Muṣṭafa Maʿmār Pasha and points out that there was also a Miʿmar Pasha, *wālī* of Jidda, in 1284/1867-8.[1] However, this date has been questioned by Angelo Pesce, who points out that a "Mahammar" mosque had been recorded in 1250/1834 by Maurice Tamisier in his list of the five most prominent mosques in Jidda in his day.[2]

The al-Miʿmār mosque is heavily covered with plaster which obscures much of the underlying fabric, apparently coral-aggregate blocks reinforced with wooden beams laid horizontally. This combination of materials is used in traditional building in Jidda as well as on the Red Sea coast as a whole. The Miʿmār mosque consists of a high rectangular prayer-hall on the east (*qibla*) side with a level roof, preceded on the west side by a *ṣaḥn* which is, in fact, a raised platform resting above

al-Miʿmār mosque, Jidda. East (qibla) *wall and south wall (left).*

shops and other structures built into its side walls. There is a door in the centre of the west face of the platform, on the ground level. The *ṣaḥn* that this platform creates is partly roofed over with wood resting on piers and also with corrugated metal sheeting on wooden frames to provide shade for those praying in the *ṣaḥn* of the mosque. The prayer-hall of the mosque has a series of blind arches and recesses articulating its west face, and in these are set the entrances from the *ṣaḥn* to the prayer-hall. In the sides of the prayer-hall are further openings arranged with a somewhat haphazard symmetry. Thus, in the south wall above a rectangular door on this side of the prayer-hall, there are a pair of arched windows with a small circular window set between the crowns of the window arches. A similar system occurs in the design of a window immediately to the east, set back in a rectangular recess and within which a rectangular window with a wooden grille is inserted to ventilate the interior as well as to provide illumination.

The two entrances in the south wall are reached by a

al-Miʿmār mosque, Jidda. Minaret and prayer-hall facade from the west.

pair of staircases which are set on either side of the projecting minaret base, itself set at a point somewhat west of centre along the south side of the prayer-hall. The minaret is one of the few remaining in traditional style and materials in Jidda. It has a rectangular base which reaches some two-thirds up the height of the south wall of the mosque: thereafter, the shaft is reduced in width by two successive transitional zones until it is tranformed into an octagon just about the summit of the south wall of the prayer-hall. The minaret thereafter has an octagonal form as far as the lower of the two *shurrāfas*, after which the shaft becomes circular. The two *shurrāfas* are both of similar design, although the lower is without the supports that form the underlying structure of the upper balcony. Both are formed of simple plain panels, with raised frames. The minaret is terminated by a slightly faceted, conical roof.

The east (*qibla*) wall has two rectangular windows surmounted by narrower arched windows, set at either end of the wall. Two small rectangular windows are also set higher in the *qibla* wall above the *miḥrāb*. All of these windows in the *qibla* wall are closed by wooden shutters. The central part of the *qibla* wall is built forward from the line of the wall on either side, apparently as a result of restoration. Since the mosque was photographed, a modern building has been added to its south-east corner against the *qibla* wall. There is also a walled extension of some age against the north end of this wall, which limited examination. This extension has a single doorway from the north.

The north wall of the mosque is not a regular, continuous surface. It is sufficiently interrupted to suggest that alterations to the building have been made in the past. At present there are the following openings from the east corner: an arched window, a rectangular doorway, another rectangular window, and finally, a door to the *ṣaḥn*, with moulding around it.

Strika reports that the inside of the mosque has stylised floral decoration, which suggests to him a Persian influence, and that the *miḥrāb*, seen from the interior, is apparently not ornate:(3)

"Il miḥrāb *non presenta nulla di particolare; il* minbar *invece è aggettante, ma la scaletta è parellela al muro della* qiblah, *viene cioè evitato il pulpito sporgente che potrebbe alterare la gerarchia dei valori tra* miḥrāb *e* minbar".

14 Rajab 1403/27 April 1983

al-Ḥanīfī (or Abū Ḥanīfa) mosque, Jidda

*al-Ḥanīfī mosque, Jidda. East (*qibla*) wall and south wall (left).*

al-Ḥanīfī mosque, Jidda. South entrance.

This mosque is situated in the area of Maḥallat al-Shām and, along with the Miᶜmār mosque nearby, it is one of the most distinguished remaining ancient mosques in Jidda.(1) ᶜAbd al-Quddūs al-Anṣāry records that inside the Ḥanīfī mosque there is an inscription giving the foundation date as 1240/1823-4 and that it has an inscription with lines of verse in Turkish.

The Ḥanīfī mosque is coated with plaster which conceals the underlying building material. Although freestanding on the east (*qibla*) side, and along the eastern ends of its side walls, the mosque is pressed close by adjacent buildings at the western end generally. Nevertheless, access is possible from the direction of the *sūq* on the west side. The mosque consists of a rectangular prayer-hall with a flat roof to the east, preceded on the west side by a shallow *ṣaḥn*. On the west side of the mosque is a salient set to the south of the centrally placed doorway on this side, and within the salient is the minaret. The position of the minaret is interesting, for it is placed to the right of the entrance to the mosque, on axis with the *miḥrāb*; this is a position which has antecedents in early Islamic times in mosques in Damascus and Cordoba. Although unusual in its position among the minarets of Jidda, nevertheless the Ḥanīfī minaret thus belongs to an Islamic tradition with ancient antecedents.

The base of the minaret is square with an octagonal shaft above, whose width reduces at the two successive *shurfas*. These *shurfas* are more elegant than those of the Miᶜmār mosque in that they both have *muqarnaṣ* ornament beneath forming the support of each *shurfa*. Although the minaret was covered with white plaster in 1397/1977, when I first photographed it, this plaster has now been stripped off.

The prayer-hall of the mosque is entered from the *ṣaḥn* or by doors in the north and south sides towards the *qibla* wall. The level-roofed prayer-hall itself is a deep building illuminated by light from the *ṣaḥn* and by numerous windows in the north, south and east (*qibla*) walls. The upper windows of the mosque on these three sides are all positioned at the same height, endowing the exterior of the mosque with a striking symmetry which is especially noticeable in the case of the windows of the *qibla* wall. The design of the windows varies somewhat, depending on whether they are in the *qibla* wall or the lateral walls, but essentially each one consists of pairs of narrow arched openings set into the wall, with a round window between the crowns of each pair. In the lateral walls of the mosque, pairs of windows surmount high rectangular windows. The latter are framed by blind trefoil arches, slightly pointed and in raised relief, set within recessed panels.

Against the south wall of the prayer-hall, rectangular buttresses of varying sizes reinforce the building. The doorway to the prayer-hall on this side is set at the eastern end of the wall between buttresses and deserves attention. The ornate frame above the door recalls Mamlūk mosque entrances in Cairo. A low relief frame outlines the panel and within this is a blind trefoil arch, again in low relief. This trefoil arch forms the extrado of yet another blind trefoil arch with simple *muqarnaṣ* mouldings that serves as a tympanum to the rectangular doorway beneath it. In the centre of the upper lobe of the tympanum is a raised circular boss. The wooden door is rectangular with ornate carving, in which carved discs are set in a square in the upper part of each of the two door-leaves. Above the doorway is a wooden panel with an inscription and a narrower rectangular window set immediately under the tympanum. The emphasis on the doorway that is achieved by the surrounding decoration is a tradition in the Islamic world that can be identified in mosque architecture as early as the 3rd/9th century.

The *qibla* wall of the Ḥanīfī mosque has four small rectangular windows along its length, all at the same height. Each rectangular window is surmounted by a pointed blind arch containing pairs of windows with round-headed arches and a circular window at the crown between them. These four groups of openings are arranged in two pairs on either side of the *miḥrāb* which is set in the centre of the wall. Directly above the *miḥrāb* is a blind arch, accentuated by the fact that the windows set in it are distinct from the other small windows in the rest of the *qibla* wall. Whereas the other small windows have round-headed arches, over the *miḥrāb* are a pair of narrow windows with pointed arches: the blind arched panel over the *miḥrāb* is further accentuated by the fact that it is trefoil in shape. The *miḥrāb* beneath these openings is indicated on the exterior surface of the *qibla* wall by a three-sided projection whose summit terminates in a tapering pyramidic form, reaching a point just below the windows over the *miḥrāb*.

14 Rajab 1403/27 April 1983

al-Shāfiᶜī mosque, Jidda

The Shāfiᶜī mosque in the Maḥallat al-Maẓlūm area of Jidda seems to be the oldest in the city. According to ᶜAbd al-Quddūs al-Anṣāry(1) it is known as al-Jāmiᶜ al-ᶜAtīq and is believed to have been founded in the time of the second Caliph, ᶜUmar b. al-Khaṭṭāb. However, al-Anṣāry casts doubt on the accuracy of this inasmuch as Jidda was not a town in ᶜUmar's time. Instead, he suggests that the Shāfiᶜī mosque should be dated to the reign of Malik al-Muẓaffar, Sulaymān b. Saᶜd al-Dīn Shāhanshāh II, a Rasūlid ruler of Yemen, and to 649/1251, the year of Sulaymān's death.(2) A Malik al-Muẓaffar also undertook restoration of the Masjid al-Ḥarām in Makkah al-Mukarramah.(3) A further connection with Yemen is recorded by al-Anṣāry, who refers to an Indian merchant, al-Khwājā Muḥammad ᶜAlī who, in 940/1533-4, came to Jidda bringing wood and columns from Yemen and demolished the old mosque, to rebuild it far better than it had previously been. However, he did nothing to the minaret, which goes back to the time of Malik al-Muẓaffar; this is the minaret in carved stone that exists today. An inscription in the mosque still remains, recording the work of Khwājā Muḥammad ᶜAlī. The Indian merchant also presented a fine *minbar* to the mosque. Another inscription in the mosque records the name of Sharīf Ḥusayn b. ᶜAjlān, an *amīr* of Makkah al-Mukarramah between 798 and 829/1395-6 and 1426. However, in his study of Jidda mosques, Vicenzo Strika treats the Shāfiᶜī mosque as essentially an Ottoman reconstruction.(4)

al-Shāfiᶜī mosque, Jidda. South porch and minaret.

The Shāfiᶜī mosque is a difficult building to examine from the exterior for there are shops built against the south side and only the large entrance on this side is visible, flanked by the shops. It forms a porch with a pointed arch and is plastered white, like the rest of the exterior of the mosque. By contrast, the east (*qibla*) wall of the mosque is exposed. The *miḥrāb* projection in the centre is a diminutive structure with three facets and pyramidic roofing: it reaches no higher than half-way up the *qibla* wall and has a blocked window above it. Articulating the *qibla* wall on either side of the *miḥrāb* is a series of very shallow, slightly banked buttresses, two on either side of the *miḥrāb*. At the south end of the *qibla* wall there is a doorway, the sole entrance on this side of the building. This doorway is accentuated by a rectangular frame in low relief around the round-arched entrance, the whole set in a rectangular salient that projects from the wall, like the principal doorways in the other sides of the mosque. The decoration around the doorway in the east wall is obscured by thick plaster, but it includes an entrelac band running around the arch and horizontally above it; above this is a *muqarnaṣ* register terminating the frame over the door. There were originally windows in the *qibla* wall, set between the shallow buttresses, but none of them are in use as they have been blocked by rough panels. All these windows are set at the same height. The presence of windows in the *qibla* wall of the Shāfiᶜī mosque recalls the arrangement of the windows in the al-Ḥanīfī mosque in Jidda and, to a lesser extent, the presence of windows in the *qibla* wall of the Miᶜmār mosque. Windows in the long *qibla* wall are found in other mosques in the Hejaz, in the Ashrāf mosque and the Budaywī mosque in al-Wajh, and in the ᶜAlī mosque in Khaybar. With respect to its symmetry, the Shāfiᶜī mosque's *qibla* wall recalls particularly the Hanīfī mosque in Jidda.

The north side of the Shāfiᶜī mosque is free of abutting structures for much of its length and indeed, at its eastern end, it is isolated by a low wall around a courtyard on this side. By contrast with the other sides, there are two entrances in the north wall of the mosque. From the east end, the north wall of the mosque is organised as follows: two windows of identical design give on to the prayer-hall, each consisting of a tall, narrow rectangular opening, closed by a grille. Immediately above is a blind pointed arch, stilted with its extrado ornamented by an entrelac motif. At its crown, this motif interlaces with the same motif which also forms a part of the frame of the blind arch. West of these two windows is a doorway giving directly on to the prayer-hall. The door is rectangular with the same dimensions as the nearby windows. However, rather than a blind pointed arch, the doorway is surmounted by a blind, pointed trefoil arch, forming a tympanum. The extrado again has an entrelac band, intersecting at its crown with the raised entrelac frame of the rectangular panel over the door. Finally, there is a second, very large projecting door giving on to the *ṣaḥn*: it is in effect a porch, vaulted by a pointed arch which is decorated with an entrelac frame. It appears to be situated opposite the similar southern entrance to the mosque.

Inside the enclosure wall, the mosque consists of an open *ṣaḥn* to the west, with arcades around it forming *riwāqs*. The flat-roofed prayer-hall on the east side has arcades of the same type, with pointed arches running parallel to the *qibla* wall. Such parallel arches follow an extremely ancient tradition in the Islamic world(5) which persists into more recent times both in Arabia and in neighbouring countries.

The summit of the facade of the prayer-hall on the *qibla* side of the court is surmounted by crenellations. The facade proper is also preceded by high columns bearing a flat roof that forms a porch in the *ṣaḥn*. Inside the prayer-hall, the elaborate *miḥrāb*(6) has to its immediate south (i.e. right) a staircase spiralling within the thickness of the *qibla* wall, giving access to a fixed *minbar*. Fixed *minbars* of somewhat different design are also found elsewhere in the Hejaz at Khaybar, al-ᶜUlā and in other parts of Saudi Arabia, including Nejd.

The minaret is situated in the south-west corner of the courtyard, to the left of the entrance. This position corresponds with that of the minaret of the very much later Budaywī mosque in al-Wajh. To some degree, the presence of the minaret on the south side of Shāfiᶜī mosque and to the left of the entrance recalls the Miᶜmār mosque in Jidda, although in that case the minaret is built against the wall of the prayer-hall, rather than the *ṣaḥn*.

The base of the minaret of the Shāfiᶜī mosque is concealed within the south *riwāq*, but from the point at which it emerges above the height of the enclosure wall it is an octagonal structure that reduces in girth with each of its two successive *shurfas*. Each of the *shurfas* is supported beneath by masonry whose surfaces are articulated by ranks of diminutive *muqarnas*. Around both the upper and the lower *shurfas* are wooden balustrades painted green, accessible from the interior staircase through arched doorways. In alternating facets of the octagonal shaft are pairs of narrow windows with round windows between the crown of each. The minaret terminates in an elaborate form surmounted by a gadrooned canopy and a finial. The uppermost part of this minaret is entirely different to the other minarets in Jidda, which follow the conventional Ottoman "pencil" form. Vicenzo Strika terms the minaret pinnacle "indianeggiante". Assuming that the mosque is older than the rest of the mosque and indeed goes back to about 649/1251, a Yemeni Rasūlid element or the influence of Ayyūbid Egypt or Syria might be expected. Of the important mosques of Jidda, this particularly deserves further study.

14 Rajab 1403/27 April 1983.

al-Bāshā mosque, Jidda

This mosque is situated near the sea on the edge of the old part of Jidda, the Maḥallat al-Shām.(1) The mosque has been rebuilt in recent years and is now an entirely modern structure. The photographs of the building in its former condition were taken in Jumāda I 1397/April 1977. The earlier mosque has been dated by ᶜAbd al-Quddūs al-Anṣāry to 1137/1724-5(2) and attributed to Bakr Bāshā, a *wālī* of Jidda. The name Sultan Ḥassan is given by Pesce(3) as an alternative, but another discussion of the mosques of Jidda by Strika(4) does not make the same connection. A *jāmiᶜ* Sultan Ḥassan was mentioned as the first of a list of noteworthy Jidda mosques by Tamisier following his visit there in 1248/1832.(5) According to other scholars the Bāshā mosque was the most important in Jidda.(6)

Before its reconstruction, the Bāshā mosque consisted of a *ṣaḥn* on a raised platform which was approached by a double flight of steps on the west side, leading to a prominent triumphal arch-like entrance, ornate with plaster mouldings and surmounted by

al-Bāshā mosque, Jidda, in 1403/1983.

crenellations. On the south side of the *ṣaḥn* was an octagonal freestanding minaret with a single *shurrāfa*. This *shurrāfa* had ornate *muqarnaṣ* moulding beneath while the panels of the balcony were pierced by geometric openwork. Above the *shurrāfa* the shaft continued as an octagon and passed without transition into the slender conical roof, surmounted by a finial. Although this *shurrāfa* was more complex than others in the Hejaz, nevertheless the minaret lacked the elegance of the Ḥanīfī mosque's minaret or the complexity of the minaret of the Miᶜmār mosque, both nearby in Jidda. The minaret of the Bāshā mosque had a distinct tilt.

To the east of the *ṣaḥn* platform, the simple rectangular prayer-hall of the Bāshā mosque recalled other mosques in Jidda, especially the Ḥanīfī mosque. The height of the prayer-hall is concealed somewhat in the illustration below, but both this feature and the rectangular buttresses of the lateral walls of the Bāshā mosque resembled the design of the Ḥanīfī. The overall covering of light-coloured plaster on the outer walls of the Bāshā mosque was a standard feature found in the older mosques of Jidda, as well as elsewhere in western Saudi Arabia.

The windows of the prayer-hall of the Bāshā mosque

al-Bāshā mosque, Jidda, before reconstruction (1397/1977).

were rectangular, with an upper register of round-arched windows immediately above each, and were closed by barred screens. This system of windows in two registers is one which, in varying forms, is to be found at several places around the Arabian coasts. A similar system is found as far east as Oman and Bahrayn.[2] The Bāshā mosque conformed in general to the Jidda mosque-building tradition, a point illustrated not only by the specific forms of its various elements but also by its overall design; thus the minaret was built in a position to the right of the main entrance which corresponds to the position of the minarets of the Miᶜmār and Shāfiᶜī mosques in Jidda.

In his account of the mosque, Pesce records that the *miḥrāb* was coloured green and had inscriptions. Unfortunately he does not illustrate it. According to Strika, there was once a *madrasa* associated with mosque.[8]

14 Rajab 1403/27 April 1983

al-Ṭā'if

Al-Ṭā'if stands in the highlands of the Hejaz above Makkah al-Mukarramah and, like the rest of the mountainous country of Saudi Arabia, it enjoys a far more clement climate than the foothills and the coastal plain to the west or the plateau that extends away to Nejd in the east. There is frequent rain and, as a result of its cool summer climate, the town has been a resort during the hot weather since ancient times; it continues in this role today. In pre-Islamic times, al-Ṭā'if was an important town in western Arabia, and the Prophet Muḥammad (ṣ) showed particular concern to bring it within the fold of Islam. ᶜAbd Allāh b. ᶜAbbās, a cousin of the Prophet (ṣ) and ancestor of the ᶜAbbāsid Caliphs, died at al-Ṭā'if and the mosque named after him is the principal mosque of al-Ṭā'if today. Although the town is now largely rebuilt in modern style, in 1395/1975 there were still numerous examples of al-Ṭā'if's traditional houses built in stone in a manner related to that found in other major Hejaz cities. Nevertheless, even at that time,most of the mosques had been rebuilt in a modern style.

Several mosques in al-Ṭā'if and its environs are associated with the Prophet Muḥammad (ṣ) and his expedition there, including the mosque of ᶜAbd Allah b. ᶜAbbās, the Masjid al-Kūᶜ (or *mawqaf* al-Rasūl), and the Masjid al-Khabza.[1] The mosque of ᶜAbd Allah b. ᶜAbbās was rebuilt in recent times by the Saudi government when it had long since lost its ancient form. The mosque site is the oldest in al-Ṭā'if, and has been mentioned by several travellers, including Nāṣir-i Khusraw in 442/1051, who referred to the great size of the mosque and noted that it had been reconstructed by the ᶜAbbāsid Caliphs.[2] The mosque was seen by J. L. Burckhardt in 1229/1814, but he says little of it, and noted only two other small mosques, the best of which was the mosque of the Hunūd (Indians).[3] Subsequently, the mosque of ᶜAbd Allah b. ᶜAbbās was described by Maurice Tamisier[4] in 1250/1834, while accompanying Muḥammad ᶜAlī Pasha's forces on their expedition to ᶜAsīr. It was built near one of the gates of al-Ṭā'if, against the town wall, and measured 100 paces by 60. The outer walls had openings with iron grilles, with five in the east wall, and seven and six respectively in the side walls. The three doors were not very large or distinguished. The principal external feature was a minaret which formed an octagon as far as the balcony, above which the shaft of the minaret was round, terminating in a cone. It would appear to have been of the Ottoman style familiar in the Hejaz in the *ḥaramayn*, Jidda and al-Wajh. The interior was distinguished by the size of its columns, and in general, the mosque struck Tamisier as being the most impressive he had seen in Arabia.[5]

Apart from these more famous historical mosques, there was also one in the town in 1395/1975 whose prayer-hall was recent, but whose minaret was clearly older and in Ottoman style (see illustration below). The minaret was at the south-east corner of the mosque enclosure and was a freestanding structure. It was coated with white plaster like those in Jidda and the

Minaret, al-Ṭā'if.

minaret had a single balcony. In the lower, octagonal part of the shaft there was a blind lobed arch in each of the eight facets; the arches were set just beneath the balcony. Above them, each facet of the octagon splayed outwards to support the balcony and each of the facets under the balcony was articulated with ranks of *muqarnaṣ* mouldings. Their clarity was somewhat lost through the thickness of the plaster that coated them. The balustrade of the balcony was plain. Above, the shaft of the minaret was narrower and cylindrical, with an arched entrance to the balcony. The roof was conical and the entire minaret was closely related to Ottoman models, like those in other parts of western Arabia.

al-Wajh

Al-Wajh is a natural harbour on the coast of the Red Sea, lying to the north of Yanbu^{c}. Although the town is small, the safety of the approach through the coral reefs off-shore made al-Wajh an attractive landfall in the past. The old part of al-Wajh, close to the harbour, gives an excellent idea of the character of a traditional Red Sea town. Today, the modern town beyond the group of traditional buildings reflects the developing character of the area and its infrastructure.

Unfortunately, little has been recorded of al-Wajh by travellers. Sir Richard Burton visited it on his way to the Holy Cities in 1272/1856 but described nothing of consequence of the place.[(1)] D.G. Hogarth[(2)] mentioned al-Wajh but did not describe the mosques, although not long after, Ameen Rihani[(3)] recorded the presence of two mosques in the town, apparently those described here.

During the 13th/19th century the Hejaz passed out of the control of the first Saudi state and was occupied by the Egyptian governor, Muḥammad ^{c}Alī Pasha. Al-Wajh remained under the Egyptians until 1304/1887 in contrast to the rest of the area, which was returned to the Ottomans in 1256/1840. The Egyptians held al-Wajh to secure the passage of their pilgrims into Arabia, but finally relinquished their authority to the Ottoman government. The Turks were not expelled until 1335/1917 when the British navy bombarded the town. The Hāshimites briefly held sway until al-Wajh and the rest of the Hejaz were incorporated into the territories of the late King ^{c}Abd al-^{c}Azīz.

The combination of Egyptian and Ottoman administrations in al-Wajh and the influx of pilgrims through the town have had a marked influence on the architecture. This is noticeable in the minarets of two large old mosques of al-Wajh which reflect the Ottoman style of the Holy Cities, of Cairo, and of Istanbul itself. The domestic architecture of al-Wajh as a whole displays the general character of what has been termed the "Red Sea style".

Inland from al-Wajh is the Qaṣr Zurayb, a mediaeval Islamic *khān*, it appears, built to serve the route to al-Madina al-Monawarah. There, against the interior of a curtain wall, stands an incomplete minaret built of stone like the rest of the building, and reflecting, as does the entire Qaṣr the architectural traditions of Egypt and Bilād al-Shām in the Ayyūbid and Mamlūk periods.

Qaṣr Zurayb, near al-Wajh.

al-Ashrāf mosque, al-Wajh

al-Ashrāf mosque, al-Wajh, from the north-west.

Beside the port of al-Wajh, on the south side of the town, is a large and distinguished mosque, known as *masjid* al-Ashrāf.(1) Just to the south of the mosque is the harbour-front and on this side there are no abutting structures. The mosque is also freestanding to the north and west for in these directions the ground rises steeply to the highest part of the town. On the east side the mosque is partly hidden by adjacent buildings.

The exterior and the interior of the mosque are covered with white plaster, concealing much of the fabric, which appears to be coral aggregate with regular horizontal wooden beams to stabilise the structure. As coral is readily available this is the standard building system of al-Wajh. The mosque has a rectangular prayer-hall on its southern (*qibla*) side, which is longer on its east-west axis and comparatively shallow from north to south. There is a lower building against the prayer-hall on its north side concealing much of the lateral wall from that direction. The prayer-hall is a flat-roofed structure with its principal entrance in the east side, at the north-east corner. The rectangular doorway has a wooden lintel carrying a dating inscription in relief, the letters picked out in white paint against a brown ground. The words are set in four cartouches, separated by floral discs, and the date given is 10 Muḥarram 1306/17 September 1888. Above the entrance are two round-headed blind arches: within each of these is a pair of smaller round-headed blind arches, resting on diminutive attached columns. A very similar motif is found over the main entrance to the Budaywī mosque in al-Wajh. The tradition of accentuating a mosque doorway with blind arches is one of long standing in the Islamic world.

al-Ashrāf mosque, al-Wajh. East entrance.

al-Ashrāf mosque, al-Wajh. Interior from the east door.

The interior of the prayer-hall of the Ashrāf mosque is noteworthy for the impressive height of the columns that support the level wooden roof. These colonnades are arranged in two rows bearing two rows of joists running parallel to the *qibla* wall. The circular composite columns have square "capitals" surmounted by somewhat larger rectangular piers above. The columns are reinforced by wooden bracing beams that stabilise the structure. The tradition of building mosques with colonnades parallel to the *qibla* wall goes back to the early period of Islam and the system can be seen in the Umayyad *jāmiᶜ* of Damascus of *c.* 86-96/705-15, as well as in the Umayyad phase of the Aqṣā mosque in Jerusalem and the mosque of ᶜAmr b. al-ᶜĀs in al-Fusṭāṭ, and in a number of other early mosques in the Near East. The system of bracing the columns with wooden beams is commonly found from early Islamic times onwards, and occurs in mosques in Egypt and North Africa. However, the height of the columns of the Ashrāf mosque is remarkable. The ventilation of the interior is assisted by the height of the ceiling and the numerous windows in the walls. The humidity and heat of the Red Sea coast made the provision of ventilating devices a major necessity in the days before air-conditioning.

To meet this need further, the Ashrāf mosque has ten tall rectangular windows set high in the north wall of the prayer-hall. In the west wall, again up high, are another eight windows, akin to those in the north wall. The southern (*qibla*) wall is somewhat different: in the centre of the wall is the *miḥrāb*, a curved recess on the interior surrounded by a rectangular frame, painted green. The arch of the *miḥrāb* itself is pointed. On the exterior, the *miḥrāb* is marked as a shallow curved projection, reaching just over half the full height of the *qibla* wall. To the east of this *miḥrāb* there are four tall rectangular windows with grilles below, and somewhat narrower windows closed by grilles immediately above; at the extreme east end of the *qibla* wall is a further doorway into the prayer-hall with yet another small window above it. To the west of the *miḥrāb* there are only two large windows in the lower register, with six windows above. Again, these have grilles. In the summit of the *qibla* wall, gulleys are cut to allow the rainwater to run off the mosque roof.

The flat-roofed structure built against the north wall of the prayer-hall is considerably lower in height than the prayer-hall itself. It has a single doorway on the east side and three to the north. There are no entrances on the west side. As to windows, there are two in the east wall – one of which is over the entrance – twelve in the north wall of irregular dimensions, and three in the east wall. However, all these windows are very small in contrast with those of the prayer-hall. There is no *ṣaḥn* to the mosque, and no indication that there ever was a courtyard of any kind.

The minaret is constructed against the eastern end of the north wall of the prayer-hall and is of particular interest. Its base is hidden by the low building on the north side of the prayer-hall, but above this it emerges as an octagonal structure horizontally subdivided at regular intervals by wooden stretchers, stabilising and reinforcing it. At the height of the wooden *shurfa*, the body of the minaret is transformed from an octagon into a circular form before finally contracting to a pencil point in the fashion of Ottoman minarets. One is hesitant to ascribe an immediate antecedent for this minaret, for in the Ottoman period the type was widespread. However, it is clearly related not only to the minaret of the Budaywī mosque in al-Wajh and to a number of other minarets of the Hejaz but to similar minarets in Cairo of the Ottoman period. The ultimate origin, of course, is the minaret style that emanated from Istanbul from the 9th/15th century onwards.

15 Shaᶜbān 1404/16 May 1984

al-Budaywī al-Shaḥāta mosque, al-Wajh

al-Budaywī mosque, al-Wajh. North-west corner and minaret.

The Budaywī al-Shaḥāta mosque[1] stands on the summit of the high ground on which the old part of al-Wajh is built. The mosque is situated east of the main street through the old town, only a short distance from the Ashrāf mosque. It is freestanding on all sides, with neighbouring buildings approaching it only on the east side.

Like the nearby Ashrāf mosque, the mosque is coated in plaster and the underlying building material is the same, coral aggregate. The Budaywī mosque is a rectangular complex with a *ṣaḥn* on the north side, whose enclosing wall is only a little less in height than the very long prayer-hall on the south side. There is a single door to the *ṣaḥn* in the north enclosure wall, opposite the *miḥrāb* in the centre of the south (*qibla*) wall of the mosque. There is a second door to the *ṣaḥn* from the west, approached from the street by a flight of three steps. Both these doorways are simple unadorned rectangular openings with plain wooden doors. In the north-east corner of the *ṣaḥn* is a level-roofed structure which forms a salient beyond the line of the east wall of the mosque: I take this to be for ablutions. Other structures in the *ṣaḥn* include a flat-roofed pavilion against the north facade of the prayer-hall. This rests on rectangular piers and appears to be later than other parts of the mosque. It lacks a coherent relationship to either the *ṣaḥn* or the prayer-hall, supporting the contention that it is later.

The major structure in the *ṣaḥn* is the minaret in the north-west corner, standing immediately north of the main entrance to the mosque on the west side of the enclosure. The minaret is built against the inner surface of the west wall of the *ṣaḥn*: it does not project beyond the line of the wall into the street that runs along this side of the mosque. The base of this minaret is square with the entrance in the south side. At the point just above the summit of the *ṣaḥn* wall, the minaret has a zone of transition from a square to an octagon. It continues in this form as far as the wooden *shurfa*. Above this point, the stubby minaret becomes circular and tapers somewhat until it transforms into a pencil-point summit. Like the Ashrāf mosque, the minaret clearly owes its origin to Ottoman antecedents.

al-Budaywī mosque, al-Wajh. Minaret at the north-west corner.

To the south of the minaret is the principal entrance to the mosque, a rectangular block whose design echoes the main door of the Ashrāf mosque and, in a distant manner, the entrances of mosques and *madrasas* of Mamlūk and Ottoman Cairo. Inasmuch as the doorway projects a little from the line of the west wall, it has the appearance of a separate unit, terminated at the summit on either side by a slightly splayed moulding. Within this projecting doorway block, the entrance proper is set back from the plane of the facade, terminated above with a blind trilobe arch. A slender colonette is built into either edge of the doorway salient. Immediately over the trabeate doorway is a blind arcade resting on three attached colonettes. Each of the arches decorating and accentuating the main entrance is half-round: the two arches in the centre immediately over the doorway are somewhat broader in span than the arches on either side. Finally, resting on the extrados of each arch are three small, pointed arches. I know of no similar design in Arabia or the immediate area. However, the use of blind arcades over doorways is a feature of Islamic architecture from the Umayyad period onwards.

The prayer-hall on the south side of the *ṣaḥn* is a deep flat-roofed structure with eight tall narrow rectangular windows on the west side; above each is a diminutive square window. As this side of the mosque gives on to the broad main street, it was probably always a principal source of light for the interior of the mosque. By contrast, there is a largely blank wall on the east side with four small rectangular windows set high up and closed by wooden screens pierced with geometric openings.

al-Budaywī mosque, al-Wajh. West door.

*al-Budaywī mosque, al-Wajh. South (*qibla*) wall.*

al-Budaywī mosque, al-Wajh. Miḥrāb.

At the south end of the prayer-hall, the *qibla* wall is very regular in its external form. On the west side of the central *miḥrāb* projections is a pair of rectangular windows, quite tall and closed by wooden shutters. Above each is a very small rectangular window also with a wooden frame. To the east of the *miḥrāb* is a doorway with yet another small window above it, creating symmetry with the rest of the wall; and, finally, a large rectangular window with a wooden shutter and a smaller opening above, which corresponds to the system on the west side of the *miḥrāb*.

The *miḥrāb* itself is in the form of a broad rectangular projection which reaches only a little short of the height of the *qibla* wall. A doorway opens in the west face of this projection and is preceded by three steps. Standing proud from the south face of this projection is yet another very shallow projection. On the exterior surface of the *miḥrāb* and the *qibla* wall the construction technique is clearly visible where the plaster coating has fallen away. Beneath the plaster, coral is laid in blocks and the wall is levelled and stabilised every metre or so by wooded slats running horizontally along the *qibla* wall. The lower part of the exterior wall surface is coated with grey plaster, rather than the white that covers all other surfaces on the exterior. As for the interior, which I saw but briefly, the system consists of lofty square columns carrying a flat wooden roof.

The mosque is some 95 (*hijrī*) years old, taking the original building back to about 1309/1891, before the days of a well known former *imām*, ᶜAlī ᶜIsā. In the past, the *qibla* wall lay only just to the south of the principal entrance in the west wall. The entire southern part of the prayer-hall is an extension, added by the *awqāf* administration of al-Wajh. I could not establish when this major addition took place.

15 Shaᶜbān 1404/16 May 1984

Tabūk

Tabūk lies in the north-west of the Kingdom, on the main road from Jordan to al-Madina al-Monawarah. The surrounding country presents a strikingly impressive landscape of mountains and sand, while Tabūk itself stands on a broad open plain. Its importance to the ancient trade route from Arabia to Bilād al-Shām has always derived from the presence of water in this desert area and its significance in ancient times is indicated by its role in the pre-Islamic period as an outpost of the Byzantines or of their Arab allies. In the Islamic period, it became a halt on the *hajj* route from the north and, in later Ottoman times, the Hejaz railway ran through the town. Today, Tabūk is a modern and growing place of major importance in the area.

The mosque of the Prophet Muḥammad (Ṣ), Tabūk

The mosque of the Prophet Muḥammad (ṣ) in Tabūk stands on the place where the Prophet (ṣ) prayed during his expedition to the town in Rajab 9/November-December 630. The Prophet (ṣ) made his expedition northwards from al-Madina al-Monawarah after the reverse suffered by the Muslim forces at the hands of the Byzantines and their allies at Mu'ta in Jumāda I 8/ September 629. In the course of this major expedition, the Prophet (ṣ) reached Tabūk where he received the submission of various Christian and Jewish communities from Adhruḥ, Maqnā and ᶜAqaba (Aila); a simultaneous expedition was sent eastwards under the great Muslim general, Khālid b. al-Walīd, to bring about the submission of the ruler of Dūmat al-Jandal, Ukaydir. Apart from the mosque at Tabūk, other mosques were established as a result of the Prophet's (ṣ) march, including one outside Tabūk(1) and another at Wādī'l-Qurā'.

The present mosque at Tabūk was built by His Late Majesty King Fayṣal b. ᶜAbd al-ᶜAzīz Al Saᶜūd in 1394/1974 and is constructed in a style which reflects Islamic building in the Kingdom a decade or so ago. The mosque of the Prophet (ṣ) erected by King Fayṣal is larger than the mosque that preceded it on the site, and of which several photographs still exist. However, the previous mosque was by no means ancient. On 24 March and again between 8 and 11 May 1907 (25-28 Rabīᶜ I, 1325), two Franciscan fathers, A. Jaussen and F. Savignac(2), visited Tabūk in the course of their archaeological researches in north-west Arabia and they record that the *amīr al-ḥajj*, ᶜAbd al-Raḥmān Pasha, had funded the construction of a mosque which was not complete at the time. This mosque, they state, marked the place where the Prophet (ṣ) had prayed at Tabūk. This same mosque was seen by H. St. J. Philby in 1370/1951(3) when he recorded an inscription on a plaque over the doorway to the mosque in the name of the Ottoman Sultan, ᶜAbd al-Ḥamīd II b. ᶜAbd al-Majīd, and of Khādhim Pasha, which gave the date of completion as 1325 AH (14 February 1907–3 February 1908).

The position of the mosque of the Prophet (ṣ) within Tabūk is interesting. It is in the western part of the town on higher ground, close to the *qalaᶜ*. The *qalaᶜ* as it presently stands is dated 1064/1653-4, when it was restored on the orders of the Ottoman Sultan Muḥammad IV, as recorded by an inscription in ceramic tiles.(4) Some of the masonry in the *qalaᶜ* is apparently re-used, confirming the Ottoman inscription. The antiquity of the predecessor of the *qalaᶜ* is implied but far from clear, although there is textual evidence of an outpost for the Byzantines in Tabūk before Islam. It seems quite likely that the present *qalaᶜ* marks the site of some earlier administrative building of Tabūk and, once he had taken the town, the Prophet (ṣ) established his own place of prayer in its general vicinity.

7 Dhū'l-Ḥijja 1402/24 September 1982

Mosque of the Prophet (s), Tabūk. North facade(?), c1327/ 1909.

Mosque of the Prophet (s), Tabūk.

Jāmi^c, al-^cUlā

Al-^cUlā is a town of the Islamic period situated on the old Syrian *hajj* route and it was also a major station on the disused Hejaz railway. Settlement in this area goes back to extremely ancient times: just to the north of al-^cUlā is Dedān, the centre of the Lihyanites, while north again is the Nabataean site of Madā'in Ṣāliḥ. The district was known as Wādī'l-Qurā' in the early Islamic period, when it was the object of a number of Muslim expeditions, reflecting its importance as an oasis area. The Prophet Muḥammad (ṣ) prayed in Wādī'l-Qurā', passing the area on his famous expedition to Tabūk. The agriculture which has always given the district its importance is based on wells and the skilful husbanding of irrigation through a system of *qanāt*.[1]

The *jāmi^c* is situated within the closely built town, flanked by narrow streets on all sides except the south where neighbouring buildings abut it and conceal the exterior surface of the *qibla* wall.[2] The *jāmi^c* is built of cut stone like the rest of al-^cUlā, much of which has been taken, in all likelihood, from earlier buildings. The prevalence of Lihyanite and other ancient inscriptions on re-used stones in the houses of al-^cUlā supports this contention. Some areas of white plaster still attached to the exterior walls of the *jāmi^c* show that it was formerly coated entirely with plaster.

The *jāmi^c* lacks a courtyard, consisting only of a flat-roofed prayer-hall, a chamber of considerable size. There is an entrance on the north side opposite which is the *miḥrāb*, set in the centre of the south *(qibla)* wall. The *miḥrāb* of the mosque appears to have a fixed *minbar* niche to the west, a system seen at Khaybar, Jidda, Dūmat al-Jandal, Sudūs, and other mosques in the south-west of Saudi Arabia.

In the north-west corner of the *jāmi^c* there is a rather roughly built minaret that is inspired by Ottoman-style models. It is built within the prayer-hall in order not to project into the neighbouring streets. The shaft is circular with two *shurfas*. The lower part of the minaret is concealed within the mosque, however, and I could not establish its shape. Of the two *shurfas*, the lower is a roughly polygonal structure supported on wooden struts projecting at right angles from the minaret shaft. Above this point, the minaret continues circular but with a reduced diameter as far as the height of the second *shurfa*. At the summit is a still narrower cylindrical shaft terminated by a conical roof. The architect was undoubtably familiar with the Ottoman-style minarets that are seen in western Arabia in Makkah al-Mukarramah, al-Madina al-Monawarah, Jidda and elsewhere. However, the flat-roofed prayer-hall is quite without relation to Ottoman models although it recalls the prayer-halls of mosques in Jidda to some extent.

1397/1977

Jāmi^c, *al-^cUlā. Minaret.*

Khaybar

Khaybar has a well recorded history in the early Islamic period and was the object of a major expedition by the Prophet Muḥammad (s) in 7/628. Today, the modern town has been constructed some distance from the principal ancient site, whose houses and palm groves are dominated by the Ḥiṣn or Qalaᶜ Marḥab, the fortress taken from the Jews by the Muslims in the Prophet's (ṣ) lifetime. There are two principal historical mosques in the old town, one attributed to the time of the Prophet (ṣ) or to the Caliph ᶜAlī b. Abī Ṭālib. The foundation of this may be ancient but the present structure is of more recent date. The second mosque of historical interest in Khaybar is the mosque in the Ḥiṣn Marḥab. Although possibly of ancient foundation, it is hard not to believe that its present state reflects renewal of a fairly extensive nature in modern times: Philby refers to the fact that during the 1930s (1350s AH) a governor appointed to Khaybar by the late King ᶜAbd al-ᶜAzīz Al Saᶜūd had restored the citadel as the local seat of government.[1] It seems unlikely that the mosque in the Ḥiṣn and the mosque going back to the time of the Prophet (ṣ) at its foot do not display the results of these restorations in their present state.

Mosque of the early Islamic period, Khaybar

The mosque in Khaybar attributed either to the time of the Prophet (ṣ) or to the fourth Caliph, ᶜAlī b. Abī Ṭālib[1], stands at the southern foot of the Ḥiṣn Marḥab. Its construction includes the basalt that abounds in the country around the town. However, the upper parts include mud-brick and the roofing beams are of palm trunks, readily available in the great groves of Khaybar. The masonry is secured by mud-mortar and the entire mosque is coated externally and internally with a thick white plaster.

Early mosque, Khaybar. Minaret from the north.

Early mosque, Khaybar, from the north-west.

The mosque is a large rectangular structure whose principal features include a fairly narrow *ṣaḥn* on the north side, a prayer-hall on the south side and a minaret in the north-west corner, to the right of the main entrance to the mosque. The wall that surrounds the *ṣaḥn* is in fact nearly the same height as the wall around the prayer-hall. For parts of its length, the enclosure wall of the mosque lacks a covering of plaster on the exterior surface.

The entrance to the north wall of the mosque, immediately to the east of the minaret, is the only access to the building, apart from a small doorway at the western end of the *qibla* wall on the south side of the mosque. The north entrance is interesting inasmuch as it is stressed by the slight rise of its frame above the level of the rest of the enclosure: the door itself is of plain wood with cross bars.

Within the *ṣaḥn* there is no pavement. There is an unusual feature running along the north side of the *ṣaḥn*, a low *dikka* or *maṣṭaba*, an element which I am not familiar with in this particular position in other mosques in the region. At the north-west corner of the *ṣaḥn* the minaret is a rectangular structure with its longer side on an east-west axis. The staircase to the summit of the minaret runs up the east side of the tower, with several stages, and it gives access finally to the flat roof of the tower, which is surrounded by a low parapet. The minaret itself is lit internally by small inverted V-shaped apertures. Although there are various types of exterior staircase to minarets in Arabian mosques, and though the rectangular minaret is a very common type, nevertheless, I am not aware of any other minaret within Saudi Arabia that is akin to this curious but pleasing structure. At the westernmost end of the *ṣaḥn*, between the prayer-hall and the minaret, are remains of roofing.

The prayer-hall on the south side of the *ṣaḥn* is a simple structure, displaying the same elegance of form as the minaret. It consists of four rows of rectangular piers all running parallel to the *qibla* wall on the south side. On the roof of the mosque, there are rows of raised ridges which run above the wooden beams that bridge the space between the piers. These ridges are plastered white. Within the prayer-hall and projecting from the rectangular piers are short ledges formed of flat stones at about head height, which served as rests for copies of the Holy Qur'ān, safe from the dust rising near the floor of the prayer-hall.

As already mentioned, the second door to the mosque is in the *qibla* wall. Apart from this, and some simple rectangular windows to provide ventilation more than light, the principal feature of the *qibla* wall is the *miḥrāb*. This is of a type that appears in various forms in several parts of Arabia and must be regarded as indigenous and perhaps of considerable antiquity. The *miḥrāb* is a recess which has a rather curious opening that narrows before ending in a slightly pointed arch. To the west of this, and set above floor level, is a narrower niche with a round-headed arch, occupied by three steps. As elsewhere in Arabia, this second element constitutes a fixed *minbar*. Both this and the *miḥrāb* proper are contained within a deeply curved niche which forms a projection on the exterior of the *qibla* wall, culminating in a slightly domed roofing. It is opened by a rectangular window in its west side which provides illumination for the interior of the entire *minbar* and *miḥrāb* niche.

6 Dhū'l-Ḥijja 1402/23 September 1982

Early mosque, Khaybar. Interior of the qibla *wall, looking east.*

Early mosque, Khaybar. Miḥrāb *and* minbar *niche in the* qibla *wall.*

Mosque of the ḥiṣn, Khaybar

Within the walls of the *ḥiṣn* (or *qalaᶜ*) of Marḥab at Khaybar is a small mosque built against the south wall, on the interior of the *ḥiṣn*.[1] Although its form is dictated in many respects by the limitations imposed by its confined position within the fortress, it nevertheless includes features found in the early mosque to the south of the hill which was attributed to the time of the Prophet (ṣ) or to the Caliph ᶜAlī b. Abī Ṭālib.

Like the previous mosque, the *ḥiṣn* mosque is built of stone, fixed with mud-mortar and then given a coating of white plaster. To the north there is an open area, but much of the roofing has now fallen, and it is clear that is was once partly covered. Preceding the southern (*qibla*) wall (actually the south wall of the *ḥiṣn*), there are now two rows of rectangular piers running parallel to the *qibla* wall. There was once a third row of piers, it seems, although as mentioned already, the roof has vanished. The system of construction is identical to that of the mosque at the southern foot of the hill, with rectangular piers built in the same way, carrying a roof of palm trunks. The mosque is unpaved.

Mosque of the ḥiṣn, *Khaybar.* Qibla *wall (right) and prayer-hall.*

The *qibla* wall is without any features other than the *miḥrāb*, whose sides have partly fallen. The *miḥrāb* is a curved recess with a pointed arch but, most interestingly, it has a fixed *minbar* on the west side, within the *miḥrāb*, formed of three steps. Although the form differs from that in the more impressive lower mosque discussed already, the similarity with the previous mosque's *minbar* is obvious.

6 Dhū'l-Ḥijja 1402/23 September 1982

al-Thamad

Southern mosque, al-Thamad.

Al-Thamad is a small town south of Khaybar on the road from al-Madina al-Monawarah. The town has two mosques of some interest, both of recent origin. The southern mosque is covered with whitewash and its construction material is obscured, although this is probably concrete. It lacks a *ṣaḥn* and consists only of a level-roofed prayer-hall with a very large *miḥrāb* forming a rectangular projection somewhat lower at its summit than the *qibla* wall itself. The minaret of the mosque, on the north side, is a curious construction in two storeys, the lower part of which is a rectangular tower with a staircase giving access to the summit of the minaret. The tower provides a platform on which rests a tetrahedron with a terminating ornamental finial crowning it. At various points on the top of the wall of the mosque, including the area above the *miḥrāb* on the *qibla* side, are open triangular crenellations.

A second mosque in al-Thamad, further north in the village, is also apparently of recent date. It is a rectangular enclosure with a flat-roofed prayer-hall to the south and an open *ṣaḥn* to the north. The prayer-hall is without any particular distinguishing features, apart from a *miḥrāb* in the centre of the *qibla* wall which forms a curved projection reaching no higher than half the height of the *qibla* wall. Immediately to the west is a shallower rectangular projection adjoining the *miḥrāb* which, from its position, may relate to the *minbar*. There are no windows in the *qibla* wall, in contrast to al-Thamad's southern mosque, but, instead, windows are set in the side of the prayer-hall. The most striking feature of this northern mosque is the minaret, near the north-west corner of the open *ṣaḥn*. It is a rectangular tower, ascended from the *ṣaḥn* by a staircase against the south wall, and serving as a base for a conical finial at the summit. Although of no great age, the design is of interest and of a type confined, it seems, to this western area of Saudi Arabia.

6 Dhū'l-Ḥijja 1402/23 September 1982

Northern mosque, al-Thamad.

The Tihāma

al-Qunfudha

Situated on the Red Sea coast, al-Qunfudha seems to be a town of ancient origin. Travellers' estimates of its size in former times vary, but today it is quite large and of some importance on the coast road from Jidda to Jīzān and Yemen. The town has been almost completely rebuilt and modernised in recent years, as a result of the current prosperity of the Kingdom.

Al-Qunfudha's traditional role has been that of an entrepôt for the coastal plain and mountains of the hinterland, while shipping along the coast would put in at the anchorage. Various goods were handled by the port, including myrrh, hides, honey[1] and grain from the interior. When Carsten Niebuhr passed through al-Qunfudha in 1176/1762 loads of coffee from Yemen were taxed there by officials appointed by the Sharīf of Makkah al-Mukarramah.[2]

View of al-Qunfundha in 1247-8/1832, by Rupert Kirk, with mosque in the central area

Niebuhr comments on the size of al-Qunfudha, but he says nothing of the mosques of the town. By fortunate chance, a watercolour scene of the town was painted by Rupert Kirk in 1247-8/1832[3], in the course of a Red Sea voyage during which he painted several other scenes of Saudi Arabian territory, including Jīzān and Farasān. In the far distance in Kirk's watercolour of al-Qunfudha is a distinctive mosque with a square minaret surmounted by a dome. The entire mosque is white-washed. The building appears to have been one of those seen by Eldon Rutter in 1343/1925[4], by Philby in 1355/1937[5], and by Dr Theodore Prochazka jr. in 1395/1975[6]. Prochazka photographed two mosques, one of which appears to be that illustrated by Kirk, thus giving it a date earlier than 1247-8/1832. Since Prochazka's visit to al-Qunfudha the old mosques have been replaced by modern ones, as I discovered when I went to al-Qunfudha on 8 Shaᶜbān 1404/19 May 1984.

The mosques of al-Qunfudha have attracted the attention of travellers in the past[7], especially Rutter, who commented on their remarkable nature. He pointed out the peculiarity of the minarets of al-Qunfudha which were unlike others he had seen, describing them as "square and squat, some fifty feet in height, and the top is surmounted by a little round tower".[8]

In comparison with the building tradition of the Tihāma and the highlands of the interior the architecture of these mosques of al-Qunfudha was most unusual. The building material was coral aggregate blocks reinforced with wooden beams laid horizontally. This is the building material of the better traditional buildings of al-Qunfudha as a whole, as well as the rest of the Red Sea coast. Each of the mosques photographed by Prochazka appears to have consisted of a rectangular structure with a walled *ṣaḥn* to the south and a level-roofed prayer-hall to the north. The most striking feature was the minaret, a very large square tower, in each case far more bulky and larger than any other minaret I have seen in the Tihāma, the Hejaz or, for that matter, anywhere else in Saudi Arabia. On the flat roofs of the minarets were small rectangular pavilions, surmounted by high, slender-domed finials. The minarets seem to represent either a purely local al-Qunfudha tradition or, alternatively, an Islamic style emanating not from Arabia but from beyond. There is some reason for relating the style of the vanished minarets of al-Qunfudha with those of North Africa, both in their square form and the presence of a canopy on the top. If this is correct, it must be assumed that this style reached al-Qunfudha as a result of the town's role as a Red Sea port, and yet never penetrated inland.[9]

Tihāmat ᶜAsīr

The coastal plain of Tihāmat ᶜAsīr is generally level towards the Red Sea, rising to the east to the foothills of the ᶜAsīr highlands. To the north the coastal plain is narrowed by lava fields around al-Qaḥma. The plain is traversed by a number of large *wādīs* which flow from the mountains in the east towards the sea. The area is extremely hot in summer with a heavy humidity that increases towards the coast; in winter the climate is more moderate. The principal town is Jīzān (*classical*: Jāzān) which is a port on rising ground in the far south; the port is modern and only a few fortifications from earlier times remain, with the rest of Jīzān reconstructed more recently.

The hinterland of Jīzān is a rich agricultural area, among whose principal towns are Ṣabyā and Abū ᶜArīsh. Of these, the latter has a distinguished history in the area, going back to the 7th/13th century.[1] It seems to have undergone an efflorescence with much building in the 12th/18th century and, when visited by Combes and Tamisier[2] in 1250/1834, it was a fortified town of some consequence in the commerce of the area, with brick-built *wakālas* for merchants to store their goods. There were several mosques, one of which had a minaret. In later times Abū ᶜArīsh gave way to the nearby town of Ṣabyā, the capital of the Idrīsī. In the early years of the 14th/20th century a two-storey palace and a fine mosque were mentioned among the principal features of Ṣabyā.[3] Of a different architectural character is the town of Muḥāyil in the north, among the foothills on the road from the highlands to the coast. There is extensive agriculture in the vicinity and in Ottoman times several forts were built in the neighbourhood.

ᶜAlāwiyya mosque, Ṣabyā

The ᶜAlāwiyya mosque in Ṣabyā is of particular importance because it is the only mosque in the town in this style as far as I could determine. The mosque is said to be two hundred years old, but there is no inscription on the exterior to substantiate this. The building material of the mosque is hidden by plaster which conceals most of the surfaces. Other substantial buildings in Ṣabyā are constructed of baked brick and basalt. I was told that the covering plaster that is used at Ṣabyā and elsewhere in the area comes from Jīzān. Philby also speaks of the production of *nūra* and *juṣṣ* plaster from gypsum as a major industry of Jīzān at the time of his visit in 1355/1936 and, although mostly produced for the local use of Jīzān itself, he also refers to the export of this plaster to Ṣabyā and Abū ᶜArīsh.[1]

ᶜAlāwiyya mosque, Ṣabyā. South facade and ṣaḥn.

The ᶜAlāwiyya mosque is similar to those of Abū ᶜArīsh in general terms, although it has certain distinctive features. It has the usual rectangular *ṣaḥn* which is rather deep in relation to its width and in this respect contrasts with other mosques in the area. The *ṣaḥn* has a single entrance towards the eastern end of the south wall with a high rectangular frame. The floor of the *ṣaḥn* is lower than the surrounding ground-surface, which in itself argues for the mosque being of some antiquity, as the ground has risen beyond the level of the mosque floor since its construction.

Immediately to the right (east) of the entrance is a fixed staircase ascending towards the south wall of the *ṣaḥn*. This is the only place in the mosque where provision is made for the call to prayer, for there is no minaret as such. Similar staircases occupy the same position in mosques in Abū ᶜArīsh. Eldon Rutter also mentions a construction in a mosque in al-Birk, to the north, which was apparently akin to the staircase in the ᶜAlāwiyya mosque.(2) In 1343/1925 Rutter saw a mosque in al-Birk where the *mu'adhdhin* "mounted to the top of four or five stone steps in one corner of the building, and chanted the adân – the call to prayer". The simple mosque Rutter describes was not in itself comparable to the ᶜAlāwiyya, but the staircase indicates that the system at Ṣabyā was also found further north along the Red Sea coast. In Abū ᶜArīsh, the similar staircase in the ᶜAbbās mosque is in the same position as that in the ᶜAlāwiyya mosque in Ṣabyā.

An interesting feature of the south wall of the *ṣaḥn* of the ᶜAlāwiyya mosque is a curved *miḥrāb* niche west of the entrance, in such a position that it impinges on the *ṣaḥn*. It was apparently intended for those who prayed outside the limits of the small mosque on a low platform to the south, when the numbers were too great within the enclosure. I have personally seen no similar niche in other Arabian mosques. To the south of the *ṣaḥn* on this platform is a series of modern water tanks for ablutions.

The prayer-hall on the north side of the *ṣaḥn* is rectangular, roofed by six domes which are arranged in two rows of three, running parallel to the *qibla* wall. The profiles of the domes are rather coarsely finished and all are whitened with plaster, like the south facade of the mosque and the wall around the *ṣaḥn*. The facade of the mosque on the north side of the *ṣaḥn* has an interesting system of articulation. To left and right are two entrances to the prayer-hall from the *ṣaḥn*, both with pointed arches and rising somewhat higher than a curved *miḥrāb* with a pointed arch that lies mid-way between the two doors. In the west side of each doorway is a short

ʿAlāwiyya mosque, Ṣabyā. South facade of the prayer-hall.

stretch of wall partly blocking the entrance, preceded by a projecting ledge built in the west corner.

Inside the mosque, the principal *miḥrāb* is on axis with the *miḥrāb* in the south wall of the prayer-hall, and forms an extremely bulky projection in the centre of the *qibla* wall on its exterior surface. This large *miḥrāb* salient reaches the summit of the *qibla* wall and, in its present condition, its dark external colouring contrasts with the white plaster that covers all the other surfaces of the mosque.

12 Rajab 1403/25 April 1983

*ʿAlāwiyya mosque, Ṣabyā. North (*qibla*) wall.*

Old mosque, Ṣabyā

Old mosque, Ṣabyā. Remains of north (qibla) *wall and arcade of the prayer-hall.*

On the north edge of Ṣabyā, in the area of ruins that marks the site of the old residence of the Idrīsī rulers of the Tihāma, are the remains of a mosque of unusual design and of considerable size. A seeming reference to this mosque was made by Cornwallis, suggesting that it was a building of some note in its heyday[1], while Philby[2] spoke of the principal mosque of Ṣabyā as "a masonry building plastered with stucco inside and out". However, I am not entirely convinced that Philby's mosque is that under discussion here. As the Idrīsī state flourished in the Tihāma in the latter part of the 13th/19th century and the early 14th/20th century, it is presumably to this period to which the mosque should be attributed.

The ruined mosque is built of courses of well cut black basalt alternating with baked brick, the materials used for a number of other important buildings in Ṣabyā. The surfaces of the mosque's walls are rendered smooth with fine thick ochre plaster, but they lack the extremely elegant carved decoration that covers other buildings in Ṣabyā.

Although the former extent of the mosque is not entirely clear, much of its original design can be established. Running parallel to the northern *qibla* wall is a single incomplete arcade consisting now of five octagonal piers bearing round-headed arches; the arcade was once longer. The roofing is lost, but may be assumed to have been level originally; in this, it contrasts with other mosque roofs in this region where vaulting with several domes is the tradition.

On the northern *qibla* side, the almost entirely ruined wall nevertheless preserves the *miḥrāb*, a curving projection on the exterior and internally vaulted by a round-headed arch, with a half-dome devoid of ornament. The *miḥrāb* is set back in a high and shallow rectangular recess.

12 Rajab 1403/25 April 1983

Old mosque, Ṣabyā. Miḥrāb.

ᶜAbbās mosque, Abū ᶜArīsh

ᶜAbbās mosque, Abū ᶜArīsh, from the south-east.

The ᶜAbbās mosque in Abū ᶜArīsh is one of the finer mosques in the Tihāma although not the largest in the town. The mosque is coated with thick white plaster which hides the fabric entirely. In the Old Mosque in Abū ᶜArīsh, and in buildings in nearby Ṣabyā, the building material for the better architecture is baked brick and basalt and it may be that the ᶜAbbās mosque is of the same materials. In its design, the mosque adheres to the essential features of the style prevailing in Abū ᶜArīsh itself, Ṣabyā, Jīzān (in former times), and Farasān.

The ᶜAbbās mosque has an open rectangular *ṣaḥn* on the south side and a long shallow prayer-hall on the north, roofed by three domes and with a minaret at the east end approached by a staircase from the *ṣaḥn*. The entrance to the mosque is through a simple rectangular doorway in the east end of the walled *ṣaḥn*. The frame of this entrance is somewhat higher than the rest of the enclosure wall, a common feature of mosques in Saudi Arabia. The paved courtyard is divided into two separate areas by a low parapet parallel to the *qibla* wall. Water for ablutions is stored outside the entrance to the enclosure. In the south-east corner of the *ṣaḥn*, built against the east wall, is a short flight of steps leading to a low platform which I was told is used to give the prayer-call. Platforms in the *ṣaḥn* in this particular position are common in this area as well as in the highlands of ᶜAsīr. However, in this particular case the device would appear to be redundant, given the presence of the large staircase minaret at the east end of the prayer-hall, directly opposite the small platform in the *ṣaḥn*.

ᶜAbbās mosque, Abū ᶜArīsh. Minaret.

ᶜAbbās mosque, Abū ᶜArīsh. South facade of the prayer-hall.

The minaret is approached by a staircase that rises to it from the north-east corner of the courtyard. This staircase is an elaborate and bulky structure with a stepped balustrade forming a bannister of triangular section. Beneath the staircase in the east face is an arched opening. At the summit of this aesthetically pleasing structure is the square minaret with a narrow pointed arch in each of the four faces. The summit of the canopy-like tower is covered by a shallow dome. The minaret recalls that of the Ashrāf mosque in Abū ᶜ Arīsh (before it lost its staircase) and it may also preserve the form of the original staircase of the Old Mosque in the town.

The facade of the domed prayer-hall of the ᶜAbbās mosque is extremely simple: on the *ṣaḥn* side are three entrances, each vaulted by a pointed arch and all regularly spaced. The domes of the prayer-hall are all of the same size and profile, with an octagonal ornamental balustrade built around the base of each, and terminated at each corner of the octagon by an ornamental finial. A variation on this decoration is extended to the *miḥrāb*, which is a five-sided projection in the centre of the *qibla* wall exterior; this *miḥrāb* is surmounted by a small parapet formed of panels. The panels have openings and at the junction between each panel is a finial. Otherwise, the *qibla* wall is without feature on the exterior.

13 Rajab 1403/26 April 1983

*ᶜAbbās mosque, Abū ᶜArīsh. North (*qibla*) wall.*

Wāfi^c mosque, Abū ^cArīsh

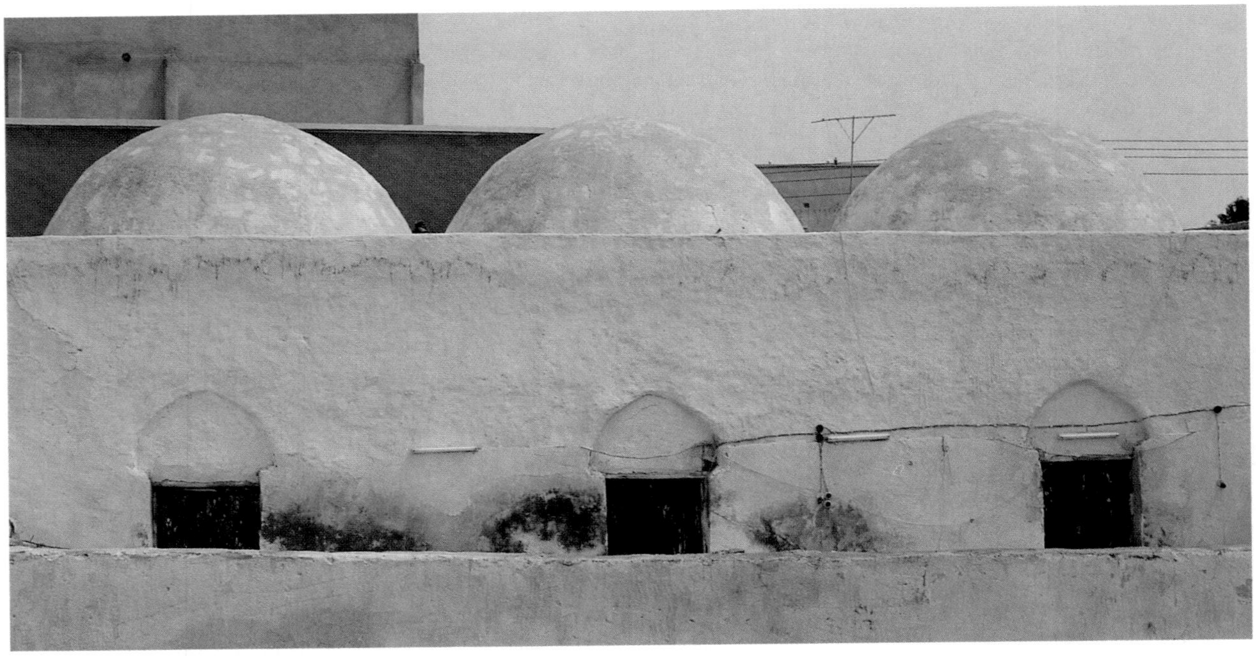

*Wāfi*ᶜ *mosque, Abū* ᶜ*Arīsh.* Ṣaḥn *and south wall of the prayer hall.*

The Wāfiᶜ mosque is a small mosque in Abū ᶜArīsh which encompasses the principal features of larger mosques in the area. The mosque is apparently of no great age, but its date could not be ascertained. The walls are too much covered with whitewash to determine the building material, although the wall of the *ṣaḥn* on the south side is reconstructed in concrete blocks. The mosque is very similar to the larger al-ᶜAbbās mosque in the same town in its overall plan. The *ṣaḥn*, surrounded by a low wall, has a rectangular doorway on the east side of the enclosure, with a frame which rises higher than the *ṣaḥn* wall, once again in a way similar to that in the ᶜAbbās mosque. The prayer-hall of the Wāfiᶜ mosque has three entrances on the south side from the *ṣaḥn* , opposite the *qibla* wall and distributed with precise symmetry. Above each rectangular entrance is a somewhat roughly shaped tympanum. The three domes of the prayer hall are all of the same diameter and height, a characteristic of several mosques on the Tihāma plain and on Farasān.

*Wāfi*ᶜ *mosque, Abū* ᶜ*Arīsh. South facade of the prayer-hall and* ṣaḥn *wall.*

Masjid, Abū ᶜArīsh

Masjid, *Abū ᶜArīsh, from the south.*

The largest mosque in traditional style in Abū ᶜArīsh is referred to variously as the *masjid* ᶜUthmān Rifaᶜī, *masjid* Abū ᶜArīsh(1), or, according to Philby(2), the mosque of the Ashrāf. He says that it stood close to an Ashrāf fortress called "Daujani", but this has vanished. The local historian Muḥammad Aḥmad al-ᶜAqīlī agrees with Philby in attributing it to the Ashrāf but is more precise than Philby inasmuch as he gives the prominent figure of the area, Ḥamūd Abū Mismār (early 13th/19th century) as the builder. Both writers have published photographs of the mosque, which is useful, as it has been restored heavily in recent times.

The mosque is a very large rectangular building, wider from east to west than it is deep, and indeed, it is the largest mosque in traditional style that I have seen in the Tihāma.(3) It has an L-shaped *ṣaḥn* running along the south and the west sides of the prayer-hall, surrounded by an enclosure wall which is recent, or at least, restored.(4) The entrance to the *ṣaḥn* is from the south side of the enclosure. The prayer-hall is roofed by eighteen domes arranged in a six by three formation, all of an equal diameter and uniform height. They exceed in number the domes of any other mosques in Abū ᶜArīsh itself, in Ṣabyā or in Farasān. The prayer-hall has six more

Masjid, *Abū ᶜArīsh. North* (qibla) *wall.*

or less pointed arches on the south side and three on the west side. The extremely thick arches are supported by square capitals which, in turn, are borne by heavy rounded columns of great size. They are coloured reddish-brown in contrast to the ochre-white plaster that covers the rest of the mosque exterior. Modern screens now close the arches, a part of the recent restoration, but Philby's published illustration shows that in 1355/1936 the arches on the *ṣaḥn* were open, with only a small ledge to separate the prayer-hall from the *ṣaḥn*.[5] The north (*qibla*) wall of the mosque is now closed along its entire length, although formerly there were pairs of openings on each side of the centrally placed *miḥrāb*. These are now blocked. The *miḥrāb* is a six-sided projection on the exterior with a faceted, pitched roof. Throughout this area, the local mosque-building tradition shows a preference for *miḥrābs* of some size, but this carefully constructed form is unusual, reflecting the generally high quality of design in this mosque.

The minaret stands at the extreme south-east corner of the prayer-hall, a slender rectangular structure with arched openings in the sides, surmounted by a small shallow dome. At the time of Philby's visit and al-ᶜAqīlī's photograph, there was a staircase to this minaret from the *ṣaḥn*, but the staircase has since vanished.

13 Rajab 1403/26 April 1983

Old mosque, Abū ᶜArīsh

A mosque described as the Old Mosque (*al-masjid al-qadīm*) stands in Abū ᶜArīsh and is one of the very few old buildings in an otherwise rapidly modernising town. Although altered in recent times, the original form of the Old Mosque is fairly clear. It is constructed of alternating courses of baked brick and basalt, a combination of materials used in other major buildings in the area. The enclosure wall of the *ṣaḥn* has vanished and the building now consists of a rectangular prayer-hall, the longer side on the east-west axis like other mosques in Abū ᶜArīsh, Ṣabyā and Farasān. The mosque was once larger; it is now reduced to a prayer-hall, with only a single arcade parallel to the *qibla* wall, roofed by two domes. Although there were formerly three, the western dome has vanished. Of the two remaining, the central dome above the *miḥrāb* is larger. Both have octagonal zones of transition between the square bay beneath and the base of the dome.

Old mosque, Abū ᶜArīsh, from the south.

The facade of the mosque on the south side now consists of a broad central arch nearly corresponding in its span to the diameter of the central dome in front of the *miḥrāb*. A smaller arch flanks it on either side. The present facade is not in its original form, for the remains of the springing of arches on the facade indicate that there were once arcades taking off to the south; these have now collapsed. Whether the vanished arcade was vaulted by a further three domes is unclear. On the exterior of the north (*qibla*) wall, the *miḥrāb* is in the form of a broad flat rectangular projection, with a single window in the centre. At the west end of the mosque is a staircase leading to the roof, but, unlike similar structures in the area, there is no minaret at the top of the staircase, although it may have disappeared.

The mosque is obviously of some age and is regarded as such in Abū ᶜArīsh, as its name shows; no date was suggested for it during my visit. However, Philby refers to the fact that there had been a mosque of the Zaydīs in Abū ᶜArīsh which had lost one of its domes during fighting in or about 1286/1869.[1] If this is indeed the mosque to which Philby refers, then it would appear to date to the 13th/18th century.

13 Rajab 1403/26 April 1983

Muḥāyil

Mosque Muḥāyil.

Muḥāyil is a small town in the low hills at the foot of the southern Hejaz mountains on the road from Abhā to the coastal plain. It marks a junction on the road from the ^{c}Asīr highlands northwards to Jidda and Makkah al-Mukarramah, and the route southwards to Jīzān and Yemen. Muḥāyil has many modern buildings now and has changed since I first visited it in 1393/1973 but a traditional-style mosque is still intact and typifies the mosques of other smaller places in the Tihāmat ^{c}Asīr foothills.

The mosque consists of a simple prayer-hall, built of stone like all the other traditional buildings in this neighbourhood. It is covered with a pale ochre plaster in conformity with the tradition often encountered in this region for coating the exteriors of mosques with a light plaster. At the four corners of the prayer-hall are stepped corner crenellations, another feature of mosques in the south-western highlands and foothills generally.

The very large *miḥrāb*, flanked by two square windows and set centrally in the *qibla* wall, tapers somewhat as it rises: at a point coinciding with the summit of the *qibla* wall, the *miḥrāb* is crowned by a curved cap of narrower radius than the *miḥrāb* proper beneath. It is this *miḥrāb* style on the exterior of the *qibla* wall which is so prevalent and so striking in this locality and which imparts to these small mosques an appearance of heavy solidity.[1]

11 Rajab 1403/24 April 1983

Farasān

The islands of Farasān in the Red Sea lie off-shore from Jīzān at a distance of some 60-75 kilometres. The principal island, Farasān al-Kabīr, is a low-lying coral atoll like the other islands of the group. The main settlement is on Farasān al-Kabīr and was described to me as Umm Farasān. The town lies inland some distance from the harbour at which the ferry docks from Jīzān. Although the town is expanding and has numerous modern houses, there are still several fine houses in traditional style, built of coral aggregate and of great elegance. There are several distinctive mosques akin to those of the Tihāmat ^{c}Asīr coastal plain.

Jāmi^{c}, Umm Farasān

The *jāmi^{c}* of Umm Farasān is a large building on the north side of the town.[1] Like other traditional mosques and houses in Umm Farasān, the *jāmi^{c}* is built of coral aggregate. It is dated precisely to 27 Rabī^{c}a I 1307/21 November 1889 by a slightly blurred inscription carved in plaster over the west entrance to the mosque. It is therefore the oldest surviving mosque of Umm Farasān and striking among Arabian mosques for the very fact that it is dated.

The *jāmi^{c}* is freestanding, although the space to the south is no more than a narrow passage between the *jāmi^{c}* and neighbouring structures. Built against the exterior of the *jāmi^{c}* at the northernmost extremity of the west wall are the ablutions facilities with a well nearby. These ablutions are immediately left of the entrance to the enclosure on the west side of the building. This entrance is one of only two into the mosque: the second entrance is on the east side. Of the two the west entrance is more impressive: it gives directly on to the *ṣaḥn* and is preceded by four steps rising from the surrounding street. Flanking these steps is the south wall of the ablutions area. The arch of the

Jāmi^{c}, *Umm Farasān. East wall of the* ṣaḥn.

entrance is pointed and set within a rectangular frame which rises higher than the line of the *ṣaḥn* wall. In the spandrels of the exterior surface shallow ornament is carved in the plaster, while over the crown of the arch is a deeply carved palmette that is similar in its essential elements to a floral motif that appears some forty years later in the Nejdī mosque in Umm Farasān. On either side of the crown of the arch are rectangular panels bearing the date and an inscription, and below them on each side are discs and stars against a background of brick-like rectangles, incised in the plaster. The west doorway, like the entire exterior of the *jāmi^{c}*, is whitewashed, but around the doorway are traces of a pale-blue colouring that once covered more of the plasterwork.

The entrance on the east side of the *jāmi^{c}* also gives access directly to the *ṣaḥn* and is approached by four rising steps, but the plaster decoration of the arch is far simpler, culminating at the summit in a palmette.

Unfortunately, it was difficult to establish the interior

Jāmi^{c}, *Umm Farasān. West door.*

Jāmi^{c}, *Umm Farasān. East door.*

Jāmi^{c}, *Umm Farasān, from the north-west.*

plan because of the high walls of the *ṣaḥn*. It clearly consists of a deep rectangular enclosure with a courtyard to the south and a prayer-hall to the north, vaulted by eight domes. The open *ṣaḥn* is occupied by a number of structures: among them is a rectangular building with a vaulted roof along most of the south side. The building's longer axis runs east-west and at the four corners it has very large and prominent stepped finials. In the walls are roughly triangular groupings of diamond-shaped openings providing the building with ventilation.

On the north side of the *ṣaḥn* and built against the south facade of the prayer-hall is a flat-roofed structure resting on rectangular piers. This structure is not as wide as the sanctuary facade, but it rises somewhat higher than the roof of the prayer-hall. Finally, in the north-east corner of the *ṣaḥn* against the prayer-hall facade, is a small domed structure that appears to be a diminutive minaret. As a result of these buildings in the *ṣaḥn*, only a very limited amount of its overall area is open. Similar structures providing shade in the *ṣaḥns* of mosques, built with varying degrees of permanence, are found in mosques elsewhere in the Red Sea area, in the Budaywī mosque in al-Wajh, and in the Mi^{c}mār mosque in Jidda.

There is no access to the prayer-hall except through the *ṣaḥn*. The hall is a rectangular building roofed by eight domes in a four by two formation, with the longer axis lying east-west. No dome is accentuated more than any other. The domes are terminated by *hilāls* (crescents). Eight domes is an unusual number among Tihāma mosques, where three domes or multiples of three appear to be more common.

There are only two windows in the lateral walls of the prayer-hall and four in the north (*qibla*) wall, set in pairs on either side of the central *miḥrāb*. The two windows in the east wall of the mosque have open-work plaster screens with geometric motifs.

The *miḥrāb* is a very large rectangular projection on the exterior of the *qibla* wall, terminated by a roof that curves down and away from the wall. This system of *miḥrāb* design is similar to that in the nearby Nejdi mosque and to that in a small, recent mosque also in Umm Farasān.

14 Rabī^{c}a II 1404/17 January 1984

jāmi^{c}, *Umm Farasān. Window in the enclosure wall.*

al-Nejdī mosque, Umm Farasān

al-Nejdī mosque, Umm Farasān, from the south.

In the western part of the old area of Umm Farasān there is a large and distinguished mosque built by Ibrāhīm al-Nejdī al-Tamīmī in 1347/1927-8, just to the north-west of the house of the founder.(1) The founder was a merchant engaged in the pearling trade, dealing with Red Sea ports but also further afield as far as India. The decline of this commerce set in with the collapse of the natural pearling industry, as a result of the introduction of cultured pearls.

As with all other traditional buildings on Farasān, the building material of the Nejdī mosque is coral aggregate,(2) in roughly shaped, extremely hard blocks. The mosque is coated on the outer wall surfaces with an overall beige plaster and with a thicker white plaster for decoration. The craftsmen who built the mosque were from Yemen and Jidda. The mosque remains in its original state and has undergone no apparent restoration.

The Nejdī mosque has a very large rectangular *ṣaḥn* to the south and a domed prayer-hall to the north. Enclosing the *ṣaḥn* to the east, south and west is a low wall whose principal entrance is in the east side. This eastern entrance is preceded by a single step and the doorway has a rectangular frame rising high above the *ṣaḥn* wall. The doorway is surmounted at the summit by a moulded cornice; set back from the plane of the entrance frame is an ornate blind, lobed arch, culminating in an ogee at the crown, within which is a stylised palm motif. The doorway proper beneath this is a round-headed arch with a moulding, giving access to the *ṣaḥn*.(3) Immediately to the right (i.e. north) of this entrance is an ablution facility and a well against the exterior of the mosque.

The other entrances to the *ṣaḥn* are less striking. One is a simple opening situated off-centre in the south wall of the *ṣaḥn*, while a third entrance is set in the west side of the *ṣaḥn* wall. This last entrance is set within a rectangular frame but is far lower and less ornate than the entrance opposite, in the east wall of the courtyard.

al-Nejdī mosque, Umm Farasān. Tympanum over the east door.

Much of the *ṣaḥn* is empty and the floor well paved with plaster. In the south-east corner are two structures which are no longer intact. In the corner is a room which was built to accommodate the *mu'adhdhin*, while next to it is the base of a minaret, most of which has long since fallen. The remains of the minaret are some two metres high, including a rectangular base and an entrance in the west face with an arch terminating in a slight ogee. Above this, the minaret still survives sufficiently to show that its shaft was octagonal. On the evidence available, it may have been a minaret of a design comparable to the Ottoman-style minarets further north in Jidda, al-Wajh and the Holy Cities.

al-Nejdī mosque, Umm Farasān. Ṣaḥn *with minaret base and the* mu'adhdhin*'s room.*

The prayer-hall on the north side of the *ṣaḥn* is accessible only through this courtyard. Uniquely among Arabian mosques with which I am acquainted, the prayer-hall is preceded by a shallow "pavilion" which is an integral part of the original structure. Its level roof is very slightly pitched. This pavilion has a single entrance in its eastern side, but there are larger entrances directly into the prayer-hall from the *ṣaḥn* on either side of the pavilion. The entire facade of the prayer-hall and the pavilion is treated as a unified and coherent whole, based on the symmetry of its organisation and its plaster decoration.

al-Nejdī mosque, Umm Farasān. South facade of the prayer hall.

al-Nejdī mosque, Umm Farasān. South-west corner of the prayer-hall.

The lateral entrances to the prayer-hall which flank the pavilion are identical to each other and a description of the western entrance will serve for both. The rectangular doorway proper is closed by a simple wooden door, which contrasts with the complex wall surfaces flanking it. On each side of the doorway is a narrow rectangular plaster panel, the field of which consists of circles with diamond-like motifs whose concave sides fill each circle. At the summit of the panel is a rectangular band of highly stylised floral motifs which echo an Islamic decorative tradition whose antecedents lie in ᶜAbbāsid Samārran-style plaster of the 3rd/9th century. Above the entrance and its lateral ornamental panels is a tympanum with a round arch. It is outlined by a stylised scroll motif in plaster, culminating at the crown in a palmette which recalls to some extent the palm motif over the east entrance to the *ṣaḥn*. The tympanum is subdivided internally into three by vertical bands decorated with stylised motifs betraying echoes of fleurs-de-lys. The three panels formed by this subdivision are pierced by small square windows framed by floral motifs, drill-holes and grooves.

al-Nejdī mosque, Umm Farasān. Plaster decoration on the south facade of the prayer-hall.

al-Nejdī mosque, Umm Farasān. South-east corner of the prayer-hall.

The ornateness of the plaster screens above the two lateral doorways of the prayer-hall is matched by the treatment of the outer wall surfaces of the pavilion that projects from the facade into the *ṣaḥn*. The lateral walls of the pavilion are articulated by shallow rectangular recesses that frame a variety of blind arches and arched openings. The east side of the pavilion consists of three arches, each flanked by a pier surmounted by a simple rectangular continuation above. Of these arches, that to the south is open and serves as an entrance to the pavilion from the *ṣaḥn*, preceded by a flight of steps. To the north, the next two arches are closed in their lower reaches by pierced plaster screens, one with a large diamond pattern filled by floral scroll motifs. The other panel has a "tree of life" motif culminating in a palm-like form that recalls the motif over the east door to the *ṣaḥn* of the Nejdī mosque. A similar motif is set over each of the three arches at the point at which the ornament around the extrados culminates in a finial. In the upper part of the wall, the two lateral arches are ornamented by panels with highly complex blind arches with lobes and ogees above them, whereas a hanging "drape" in plaster relief decorates the panel above the central arch.

The treatment of the west side of the pavilion is the same as that at the east end, except there is no door on the east side; instead there are three open arches closed below by pierced plaster balustrades. The decoration of these is by no means as complex as those so far described at the east end of the pavilion, for the carved decoration in the western panels is incomplete. This indicates that here, at least, the plaster decoration was carved *in situ*.

The south facade of the pavilion is treated essentially in the same manner as the eastern and western sides. Six rectangular piers and a single column support the roof, with six intervening rectangular plaster panels set back slightly from the plane of the piers; in the upper part of each panel is an arch. The outermost panels at either extremity of the facade are broader than the rest and the arches which they contain are of a wider radius than the others. These outer arches are also distinguished by the fact that they are round-headed whereas the other four narrower arches are all pointed. All six arches are blocked below by open-work plaster balustrades arranged symmetrically so that the three panels on the left match the three corresponding panels on the right.

al-Nejdī mosque, Umm Farasān. Miḥrāb *in the north (*qibla*) wall.*

The motifs carved in these panels are basically of the same repertoire as those in the sides of the pavilion. A number of the designs in these six panels are incomplete, like certain parts of the decoration on the west end of the pavilion. The south facade of the pavilion, like the side walls, has various types of ornate blind arch in the upper panels above the six open arches. The two central blind arches are lobed and culminate in an ogee, while flanking these on either side is a trilobed blind arch. Finally, at the outermost points on either side of the south facade is yet another broad blind arch with an ogee.

The most complex part of the Nejdī mosque is this plaster decoration on the walls of the pavilion and the south wall of the prayer-hall. Its complexity is matched in Umm Farasān by the fine plaster in the nearby house of the mosque's founder, Ibrāhīm al-Nejdī al-Tamīmī, and in another house in the town, that of Aḥmad al-Munawwar al-Rifāʿī, built in 1341/1922-3. However, fine plaster-carving traditions can be identified elsewhere in the architecture of south-western Saudi Arabia at Ṣabyā and (in the past) at Jīzān. Further south, there is very finely carved plasterwork on buildings at Zabīd in North Yemen as well as elsewhere in the Yemeni Tihāma.

The prayer-hall of the Nejdī mosque, against which this projecting pavilion is built, is a rectangle, broader from east to west than from north (*qibla*) to south. As already explained, the only access from the *ṣaḥn* is through two doors in its south wall or by a door in the east wall of the pavilion. Apart from the ornate south wall of the prayer-hall and the pavilion, the exterior is very plain. There are three round-headed windows set low in the west side of the prayer-hall and three more in the *qibla* wall, one to the west of the *miḥrāb* and two more to the east. In the east wall there are only two windows, while the ablutions block on this side forms a salient against the wall of the mosque, adjacent to the east door to the *ṣaḥn*. The arched windows in the east, north and west sides of the prayer-hall are nearly all the same in their general design, and are closed by wooden shutters. However, the central window on the west side of the prayer-hall is different. It is filled by a plaster screen which is partially pierced, although the ornament was never completed.

The *miḥrāb* is a prominent projection on the exterior surface of the north (*qibla*) wall in the form of a broad rectangle covered by a curving roof. In the lateral walls of the *miḥrāb* are groups of three windows in each side, consisting of two small round-arched windows and a rectangular space between them. There are also three openings in the north face of the *miḥrāb*.

The north-east and the north-west corners of the

al-Nejdī mosque, Umm Farasān. Interior of the prayer-hall from the qibla *wall window.*

mosque on the exterior have very substantial corner buttresses intended to counter the thrust of the domes of the roof. For the same reason, the walls of the prayer-hall are massively thick to withstand the weight. The roof consists of twelve domes in a four by three formation, in which four domes run along the east-west axis. Each dome terminates at the summit in a finial. There are also other finials in plaster on the *qibla* wall and the west wall of the prayer-hall. There are three on the *qibla* wall, one at each corner and one over the *miḥrāb*. These continue along the west wall, where again there is one finial at each corner and one at the centre. There were presumably intended to be finials on the south and east walls of the prayer-hall. All the finials on the walls of the mosque are pierced by open-work geometric patterns and are unusually ornate.

Internally, the prayer-hall is dominated by the support system for the twelve domes in its roof, which rests on arcades springing from attached piers in the lateral walls and in the *qibla* wall. From these rise slightly pointed arches which spring at their intermediate points from substantial octagonal piers. The arcades thus formed support the twelve domes, one over each of the bays into which the interior is subdivided. Each of the heavy dome-supporting piers is surmounted by a simple capital.

In the interior of the mosque there is decorative plaster around the extrados of the windows, while there is also an ornate plaster screen inside the prayer-hall, dividing it from the pavilion in the *ṣaḥn*.

14 Rabīᶜa II 1404/17 January 1984

al-Nejdī mosque, Umm Farasān. South side of the prayer-hall from the qibla *wall window.*

Mosque, Umm Farasān

Mosque, Umm Farasān. South facade of the prayer-hall.

In the central part of Umm Farasān is a mosque of no great age. Its interest lies in the evidence it presents of a small-scale version of the tradition that also gave rise to the much more grandiose al-Nejdī mosque, or the earlier *jāmi*ᶜ of Umm Farasān.

This small mosque is set on the north side of a very deep rectangular courtyard with an entrance in the west side and another at the eastern extremity of the north (*qibla*) wall. A very recent unfinished structure is built against the interior of the south wall of the *ṣaḥn* and another modern structure, likewise unfinished in concrete, straddles the east wall of the *ṣaḥn*. Otherwise the unpaved *ṣaḥn* is empty. The mosque is entirely whitewashed except on the surface of the *qibla* wall where the exposed cement and coral is visible from the exterior.

The prayer-hall is built against the north (*qibla*) wall of the *ṣaḥn* but the width of the prayer-hall is considerably less than the length of the *ṣaḥn* wall on this side. The prayer-hall itself is rectangular and far shallower from north to south than laterally. It has a single entrance in the centre of the south wall, opposite the *miḥrāb* in the north wall. The arched doorway has a diminutive rectangular window immediately above it. The roof consists of three domes running along the east-west axis, all of equal diameter and height. The *miḥrāb* is a rectangular projection in the centre of the north wall, reaching over half-way up the height of the *qibla* wall. The summit of the *miḥrāb* is terminated by a sloping roof.

The mosque is related in type to the *jāmi*ᶜ of Umm Farasān and the al-Nejdī mosque nearby, but parallels can also be drawn with mosques further afield, in Ṣabyā, Abū ᶜArīsh, and in former times, in Jīzān. There are also mosques related to this basic type further south in Yemen.(1) It seems to be a fundamental mosque form of the south-west coast of Arabia and areas in contact with it.(2)

14 Rabīᶜa II 1404/17 January 1984

The Tihāma mountains

Towards the Yemen frontier, in the extreme south-west of Saudi Arabia, the land is mountainous. The rugged Tihāma area is cut through by steep-sided *wādīs* running from the mountains further east. There are some settlements in the valleys but most are built on the mountain sides that tower above. Of these mountains of the Tihāma, that of Banī Mālik and Jabal Fayfā' are among the most spectacular in terms of their landscape and both are remarkable for their traditional architecture and mosques.

Jabal Banī Mālik lies north-west of Jabal Fayfā' and is somewhat lower. The two mountains share similar characteristics, with numerous small communities perched on rocky outcrops on high ground with stone-built architecture of a markedly defensive nature. Every available space and fold in the mountainsides is given over to farming, with terraces running like sheer staircases from the peaks to the valleys beneath. Although the mountains are cool, especially the higher Jabal Fayfā', lack of water has been a problem until recent times and there are plaster-lined water tanks everywhere to catch what they can of the rainfall run-off. Water tanks are usually found beside or within the mosques, to store water for ablutions. According to the people of the villages, the difficulty of the terrain encouraged the building of numerous mosques so that each small community had its own place of prayer, in order to avoid the difficulty of travelling distances to pray.

Mosque, al-Muqanda, Banī Mālik

Mosque, al-Muqanda. East wall of the prayer-hall and the ṣaḥn.

The village of al-Maqanda lies almost at the summit of Jabal Banī Mālik. Beyond a group of houses, at the north-west end of the village, a small stone-built mosque is set on a slope. Because of this, the mosque is built up on a raised platform on its northern (*qibla*) side, while it is set back into the slope on the south side. The limitations imposed by the site are presumably responsible for the rather unusual arrangement whereby the *ṣaḥn* lies east of the prayer-hall, rather than to the south where it might be expected. The sole access to the mosque is through this *ṣaḥn*, by means of a simple rectangular doorway in the north wall. The *ṣaḥn* is some 10-12 metres from east to west and its only features are a series of platforms on the south side, the covers of water cisterns cut into the ground. These platforms and the *ṣaḥn* floor are all covered by a hard yellowish plaster.

Mosque, al-Muqanda. Prayer-hall roof from the south-east.

The enclosure wall of the *ṣaḥn* and the prayer-hall are built in the same roughly shaped dry-laid masonry found everywhere in the Banī Mālik mountains; the crenellations on top of the wall around the *ṣaḥn*, however, are coated with a hard white plaster which is also found on the uppermost part of the walls and on the merlons on the rim of the prayer-hall roof. The *miḥrāb* in the north wall of the prayer-hall is plastered on the exterior surface as well. The rest of the exterior of the *qibla* wall surface and the other exterior wall surfaces of the mosque are left unplastered, while the inner walls of the *ṣaḥn* and the surfaces of the prayer-hall facing the *ṣaḥn* are plaster-covered. Whitewashing or plastering the *miḥrāb* of the *qibla* wall is found in other mosques in this area, while the plastering of at least some of the prayer-hall wall surfaces and crenellations also conforms to the same local tradition.

The prayer-hall on the west side of the enclosure is

Mosque, al-Muqanda. View from the north-west with the qibla *wall.*

rectangular with each of its corners surmounted by a stepped finial; over the centre of the wall on each side is an intermediate merlon. Of these merlons, those on the south and the north sides coincide respectively with the position of the doorway to the prayer-hall and with that of the *miḥrāb*. This doorway is the sole point of access and is a simple rectangle like the main door to the complex as a whole. The door of the prayer-hall is situated directly opposite the *miḥrāb,* a slightly banked and very large rectangular salient in the centre of the *qibla* wall. The *qibla* wall continues eastwards beyond the prayer-hall to become the north wall of the *ṣaḥn*. The overall effect of this is that the *miḥrāb* is far off-centre in terms of the entire mosque, although central in relation to the prayer-hall. The *miḥrāb* reaches a height somewhat less than that of the *qibla* wall, while the outermost corners of the *miḥrāb* roof are terminated by a finial on either side.

On the opposite side of the *ṣaḥn* to the prayer-hall there is a flat-roofed *riwāq*, separated from it by a narrow unroofed space. At the west end it is delimited by the enclosure wall, and at the east end by a lintel bridging the space between prayer-hall and *riwāq*. There are several examples of such *riwāqs* built close to the prayer-halls of other mosques in Banī Mālik and the nearby Jabal Fayfā'. As with other mosques in Banī Mālik, there is no minaret.

12 Rabīᶜa II 1404/15 January 1984

Mosque, al-Qahaba, Banī Mālik

Mosque, al-Qahaba. View from the west, showing ablutions and ṣaḥn *wall.*

Al-Qahaba is one of the small mountain communities in the Banī Mālik highlands.[1] The village runs along the summit of high ground, and, perched on the south side, close to the terraced mountain slope, is the mosque of the community. As a result of its position and the confined space available, the mosque is built up on a platform on the south side while the north (*qibla*) side rests on the hill. On the north side and at some distance to the east, there are houses, but nowhere are they contiguous with the mosque.

Nothing could better illustrate the attempts to cope with the limitations and exigencies set by the terrain of the Tihāma mountains than the narrow staircases and platforms which allow people to approach the mosque of al-Qahaba from the level of the village and from the cultivated terraces of the hillside. The mosque is approached from the east from the hillside terrace which gives access to the mosque platform. The terrain drops sharply to a lower terrace on the south side, where there is another path leading to the mosque and a steep flight of steps ascending to the south-east corner of the platform. Another staircase runs up the south face of the platform from the west.

The building material of the mosque is almost certainly stone, coated with thick whitewashed plaster that has recently been renewed. Philby reported that this was done in Banī Mālik every year before Ramaḍān in accordance with local custom. However, I was informed in al-Qahaba that the work was done whenever necessary and that when it became necessary, someone would undertake the responsibility.

The mosque of al-Qahaba is a small structure, the orientation of the *qibla* and the topography placing it somewhat askew in relation to its irregular platform on the south and east sides. The sole entrance to the mosque is in the eastern extremity of the south wall, leading into the *ṣaḥn*. Projecting at a right angle from the south wall (in fact an extension of the east wall of the *ṣaḥn*) is a short stretch of wall, flanking the approach to the entrance from the right. At the base of this wall is a *maṣṭaba* or stone bench.

The simple doorway into the mosque enclosure gives access to a shallow rectangular *ṣaḥn*, along the north side of which is the small prayer-hall. Distinctive features of the *ṣaḥn* are extremely large finials on the summit of the walls, which are of a size unusual even in this region where these devices are often striking. The flat-roofed prayer-hall is a simple structure, with its corners stressed by finials far smaller than those surmounting the walls of the *ṣaḥn*. There is also a triangular cresting over the centre of the south wall of the prayer-hall on axis with the *miḥrāb*. On the exterior of the north wall of the mosque the *miḥrāb* forms a simple but very prominent rectangular projection which does not reach much more than half-way up the height of the *qibla* wall. Like the rest of the exterior of the mosque, the *miḥrāb* is plastered white.

Finally, just west of the mosque are the ablutions facilities, constructed on the platform on which the mosque stands. The ablutions are enclosed by thick white-plastered walls, providing privacy. The design of these is reminiscent of the *maṭāhir* in the villages in ᶜAsīr around Abhā.

12 Rabīᶜa II 1404/15 January 1984

Mosque, Nīd al-Ḥaqū, Banī Mālik

Mosque, Nīd al-Ḥaqū. South facade of the prayer-hall.

The hamlet of Nīd al-Ḥaqū is perched on the summit of the Banī Mālik mountain overlooking the terraces.[1] These descend, undulating with the folds of the slopes, to the valleys beneath. At the west end of the settlement is a small mosque set on a terrace below the summit. The mosque, which is heavily plastered, is built of stone, and is situated on a plastered platform or esplanade. This platform is approached through a doorway on the eastern side, an arrangement dictated by the constricted space available on the terraced slopes. On the west and north (*qibla*) side, the platform falls away sharply as a result of the terracing. In effect, this platform is a *ṣaḥn* without the conventional enclosure wall, while the prayer-hall is freestanding on the north side. On the south side of the platform, in the south-west corner, is a channel for the ablution system from which water is drained away down-hill.

The simple rectangular prayer-hall, covered by a level roof, has a single entrance in the centre of the south wall, opposite the *miḥrāb*. Above this door there is a small projecting, ledge-like frame of stone, like those which also appear above the windows in the south and west walls of the prayer-hall. These ledges serve to prevent the flow of water over the doorway and the windows during rainfall, which is not infrequent in these mountains. A further precaution against rain is a gully cut in the summit of the south wall, just west of the doorway, to drain rainwater from the flat roof. This rainfall seems to collect in a cistern in the platform where it is stored for ablutions.

The only ornament on the mosque exterior consists of simple stepped finials at all four corners of the roof. An open triangular motif, of two flat stones leaning against each other at a steep angle, is set on the centre of the wall at the intermediate points on the east, west and south sides. The *miḥrāb* is a large rectangular projection which stops short of the summit of the *qibla* wall in accord with what seems to be the general tradition of the district. At each of the two outer corners of the flat *miḥrāb* roof are small finials. The *miḥrāb* exterior is covered with whitewash, as distinct from the pale ochre plaster on the rest of the mosque exterior. Although this treatment differs from the all-over whitening that is found elsewhere in the district, the concept of pale plaster for the mosque as a whole conforms to the custom in general terms, while pure white plaster in this case is reserved for the most significant architectural feature of the mosque, the *miḥrāb*. There are examples of accentuation of the *miḥrāb* by plastering in other areas of south-west Saudi Arabia, in the Tihāma, in ᶜAsīr and in Najrān.

12 Rabīᶜa II 1404/15 January 1984

Jāmiᶜ, al-Wushr, Fayfā'

Jāmiᶜ, *al-Wushr. East wall.*

Al-Wushr is a scattered village on the ridge of Jabal Fayfā' and the *jāmi*[c] stands to the west of the road that traverses the mountain top. Compared with other mosques in this area it is quite large and I was told that it is over 150 years old. My informant, who was about 55-60 years of age, said that the mosque was already old in his father's day.

Although it is stone-built, like all other mosques in the Tihāma highlands, the building material is concealed by the thick ochre plaster that covers the walls. However, around the uppermost parts of the walls of the prayer-hall is a band of white plaster that also covers the finials on the roof. The overall design recalls the prayer-hall and *rīwāq* of the mosque of al-Muqanda on Banī Mālik. The *jāmi*[c] is a rectangular building, deeper on its north-south axis than it is wide. At the south end is a flat-roofed area, described as a *muẓalla,* occupying the entire southern third of the structure. This is entered from a door in the centre of the south side, opposite the *miḥrāb*. Another doorway, approached by a rising flight of steps, gives access to the *muẓalla* from the east. These are the only points of entry to the mosque.

At the north end of the structure is the level-roofed prayer-hall, reaching about the same height as the roof of the *muẓalla*. The prayer-hall is separated from the *muẓalla* by an unroofed area, in effect an extremely shallow *ṣaḥn*, again akin to the Muqanda mosque in Banī Mālik. At the east end of this narrow *ṣaḥn* is a tank for storing water, built as a great salient on the outside of the mosque.

Access from the *ṣaḥn* to the prayer-hall is through a single doorway in the south side. This doorway is on axis both with the south door to the *muẓalla* and with the *miḥrāb*. The prayer-hall, a simple rectangular building like all the others of Fayfā' and Banī Mālik, is illuminated by its single door in the south side and also by two pairs of small rectangular windows in each of the east and west walls of the mosque. As with other mosques in the Tihāma mountains, stepped finials ornament the four corners of the building, while at the intermediate point on each side, there is a stepped crenellation at the summit of the wall: thus, one crenellation stands over the doorway to the prayer-hall and on line with it is another over the *miḥrāb*. The *miḥrāb*, like others in the district, is a great square salient surmounted on the two outer corners by simple but large and prominent finials covered with white plaster. The level, plastered roof of the *miḥrāb* reaches somewhat less than the full height of the roof of the mosque.

13 Rabī[c]a II 1404/16 January 1984

Jāmi[c], *al-Wushr. Roofing over the south* riwāq *and the prayer- hall.*

Jāmi[c]*, al-Marmār, Fayfā'*

Like the other mosques of the Fayfā' and Banī Mālik mountains the small *jāmi*[c] of the village of al-Marmār on Fayfā' is perched on a terrace on the side of the slope at the edge of the scattered settlement. I was told that the mosque is 150 years old or more.

The mosque is stone-built and heavily plastered, covered with a fresh coat of whitewash at the time of my visit. The *jāmi*[c] is a simple rectangle with a *ṣaḥn* on the south side and a flat-roofed prayer-hall on the north. The *ṣaḥn* is not as long from east to west as the prayer-hall, its west wall ceasing somewhat short of the west end of the prayer-hall; in the space thus created a water catchment tank is situated whose cover rises quite high above the ground. The walls of the *ṣaḥn* on the west and south sides are lower than at the east end, where the rectangular entrance to the entire structure is set. In other parts of Arabia emphasis on doorways to mosques is common, and this entrance belongs to this tradition. Against the exterior of the south wall of the enclosure there is a low stepped *maṣṭaba*, akin to that by the doorway to the mosque of al-Qahaba in Banī Mālik, and to the *maṣṭabas* of houses in the region.

The prayer-hall is entered from the *ṣaḥn* by a doorway which is set in the centre of its south wall, directly opposite the *miḥrāb* in the north wall. Lighting inside the mosque is limited, with only four small rectangular windows, a pair in the west wall and another pair in the east. In this respect, the *jāmi*ᶜ of al-Marmār corresponds to the other small mosques of Fayfā' and Banī Mālik, where the lighting of the interiors is similarly sparse.

Jāmiᶜ, *al-Marmār, from the south-west.*

Jāmiᶜ, *al-Marmār. Roof of the prayer-hall from the north with the* qibla *wall in the foreground.*

The *miḥrāb* of the *jāmiᶜ* forms a curved projection on the exterior surface of the *qibla* wall, reaching to only about half the height of the *qibla* wall. It is noteworthy inasmuch as most of the *miḥrābs* I have seen in this area are rectangular. Apart from the *miḥrāb* the only other external features of the mosque are simple corner finials and intermediate merlons along the sides: this arrangement means that a merlon stands above the door to the prayer-hall from the *ṣaḥn* and another is set above the *miḥrāb*, on top of the *qibla* wall.

On the east side of the mosque enclosure there is a platform through which the door to the *ṣaḥn* is approached. In this platform are water storage tanks whose covers rise somewhat above the level of the platform floor. A continuation of the platform to the west has further storage tanks. The source of water for these cisterns is rainfall.

13 Rabīᶜa II 1404/16 January 1984

The southern Hejaz and ᶜAsīr

The mosques of the mountains of the southern Hejaz and ᶜAsīr are only very briefly mentioned by earlier travellers to the district. This may well be the result of the inaccessibility of the highlands of south-western Saudi Arabia in the past and the insecurity that prevailed before the region was incorporated into the Saudi state. Maurice Tamisier refers to the type of simple mosque described below in Bilād Zahrān, which he noted in the ᶜAsir highlands in 1250/1834 and which he said was for the use of shepherds.(1)

Little information beyond that recorded by Tamisier or the earlier second-hand reports of Burckhardt in 1229/1814 regarding the southern mountains(2) was added over the next century(3), until H. St. J. Philby made an exploratory expedition in the mountains of the south-west in 1355/1936-7.(4) However, Philby tended only to mention mosques in passing, along with the copious topographical information and accounts of his personal dealings. Occasionally he records some useful architectural details, all the more valuable when the mosque he describes has been rebuilt in modern times. This is the case in his account of the *jāmiᶜ* of Manādhir, the largest village of those that constituted Abhā before it grew into a single town. Today, Abhā is an almost entirely modern town and nothing remains of the structure of the old *jāmiᶜ* that Philby mentioned. The Manādhir *jāmiᶜ* was not large enough to accommodate all the men of Abhā and, as a result, some people prayed in mosques in the other villages of Abhā. He reckoned the congregation of the *jāmiᶜ* at 500 with fifteen rows of worshippers each with some thirty to thirty-five men. He described the procession of the governor, his entourage and troops entering the mosque from the government palace and passing through the market-place and the streets of the village. Of the arrangement of the mosque Philby says:(5)

"In the [mosque] the Mihrab, *oriented practically due north, occupied the middle of the back wall, with another niche on its right (as we faced it) with a few steps leading to a seat which serves as a pulpit for the reading of the sermon. On the entry of the* Imam *by a door in the back wall, the Muadhdhin intoned the summons to prayer in the traditional Najdi manner with almost conversational and encouraging suavity."*

The description tells little of the overall mosque design, but it suggests strongly that the building had a fixed *minbar* of the type that we find elsewhere in the Hejaz and Nejd. There is no evidence one way or the other that the Turks influenced the building, despite their presence in the town until the end of World War I.

Subsequently, other travels were described in the south-western highlands, but only scant material relevant to the mosques of the area was published.(6) An interesting drawing of a mosque in al-Bāḥa has been published(7) which shows the entrance and the minaret, a circular structure surmounted by a turret-like *shurrāfa* and terminated by a cone-shaped structure with a finial. The doorway to the minaret is high up, approached by a staircase inside the enclosure. On the enclosure wall is a conical form on a square base, apparently a decoration serving the same role as the rather different merlons further south in the highlands.

Mosque in fields, Bilād Zahrān

This mosque was located in open ground among fields in the mountainous region of Bilād Zahrān in the southern Hejaz; it lay near the old track through the highlands that preceded the modern highway from al-Ṭā'if to Abhā. The mosque is a particularly fine example of a type that is found throughout the Near East in desert and rural areas. It consisted of no more than the outline of a mosque enclosure and *miḥrāb* niche laid out as a line of stones, correctly oriented towards Makkah al-Mukarramah. However, it departed from the normal examples of the type inasmuch as the curved *miḥrāb* niche was formed by an elaborate low-walled structure, with piled stones forming two "columns" at the points at which the *miḥrāb* commenced. The whole was built against a great natural rock embedded in the ground. The *miḥrāb* was further distinguished by the whitening of some of the stones with plaster and the use of white stones. Similar mosques appear in many parts of the country and also beyond the borders of Saudi Arabia, in Jordan, Oman and elsewhere.

Jumāda II 1393/July 1973

Mosque in the countryside, Bilād Zahrān. The miḥrāb *and* qibla

*Jāmi*ᶜ*, al-Suqā', *ᶜ*Asīr*

Al-Suqā' is a sizeable village in the country west of Abhā, situated in a valley surrounded by hillside terraces under cultivation. The *jāmi*ᶜ of al-Suqā' is the most striking building in the village, with its white plastered walls standing out sharply from surroundings of tower houses and vividly green slopes.

The basic traditional building material of the region and of this mosque is stone, which can best be seen where the thick covering of plaster has fallen away, revealing the roughly cut masonry beneath. Although the plaster obscures the underlying structure, there are sufficient consistent elements in the construction to indicate that the entire mosque is of the same date, 1259/1843-4, which is inscribed on the wooden door to the mosque on its south side.

The plan of this *jāmi*ᶜ is a rectangle with the prayer-hall on the north side, an open *ṣaḥn* to the south and, bordering this on the south side, a flat roofed *riwāq*. In the south-east corner of the *jāmi*ᶜ is a low rectangular minaret. The mosque is without lateral *riwāqs* and the

Jāmiᶜ, *al-Suqā', from the north, with the* qibla *wall in the foreground.*

Jāmi^c, *al-Suqā'. West side with the prayer-hall (left) and south* riwāq.

west side of the enclosure is occupied by the ablution facilities. The *jāmi^c* is entered through a doorway in the south side, between the ablutions and the south *riwāq*, and gives access to the *ṣaḥn*.

Jāmi^c, *al-Suqā'. Ablutions facilities.*

The ablutions facilities to the left of the entrance include a group of *maṭāhir* formed by low walls in L-shaped units. Built against the interior surface of the west enclosure wall, these walls form individual booths to provide privacy for people performing their ablutions. In front of these *maṭāhir* are a series of very low platforms in which plastered water runnels and basins known as *marūsa* are excavated for ablutions. The entire floor and ablution system is waterproofed by *quḍāḍ*, a hard cement-like plaster used throughout the district. Like the ablutions facilities of mosques elsewhere in the region, those in the *jāmi*ᶜ of al-Suqā' are not roofed in any way.

Apart from the ablutions, the courtyard is empty, excepting a staircase at the east end which gives access to the roof of the south *riwāq* and to the minaret. The south *riwāq* roof is partly supported by four massive circular piers, covered with plaster. As well as these unusual and unnecessarily substantial piers, the roof is also supported by wooden columns. A doorway adjacent to the staircase leading to the roof of this *riwāq* is framed by a raised zig-zag moulding in plaster, and nearby is a panel of scroll motifs in plaster. Other plaster decoration on the south *riwāq* serves the purpose of unifying the entire facade, so that a row of inverted V-shaped motifs runs horizontally across it above the lintels on the massive piers.

Jāmiᶜ, *al-Suqā'. South* riwāq.

The square minaret has slightly banked walls and reaches a greater height on its northern side, rising by steps along its east and west sides to culminate in two corner crenellations, stepped like others on the prayer-hall roof. The minaret is entered through a doorway in its north side, to which access is gained by the staircase from the *ṣaḥn* already mentioned. There may be another point of entry from within the south *riwāq*.

Jāmi^c, *al-Suqā'*. Miḥrāb.

The prayer-hall on the north side of the *ṣaḥn* is entered by a single rectangular doorway. This is set in the centre of the south wall opposite the *miḥrāb* and is preceded by a porch which is a late addition. On either side, quite low down in the south wall of the prayer-hall, are two rectangular windows. Like the entrance, these windows are framed by relief decoration in plaster. The wall surfaces between are ornamented with decorative plaster panels in relief, including five-pointed stars, inscriptions and V-shaped motifs around the windows in double registers, as opposed to the single register around the entrance. A band of V-shaped motifs in relief runs across the facade of the prayer-hall corresponding to the same decoration on the face of the south *riwāq*, once again unifying the overall wall surface into a visually coherent whole. This band is interrupted on either side of the entrance by two vertical channels designed to drain away rainwater from the prayer-hall roof. These channels are given formal coherence within the prayer-hall facade by their symmetry and by the decorative rectangular frames that enclose each of them at the summit. The motif seems to echo South Arabian decoration from very ancient times.

The summits of the prayer-hall walls are particularly striking. At each corner, crenellations with four steps terminate the building, while a similar merlon stands over the entrance, on axis with the *miḥrāb*. This system is common, but the striking feature of the *jāmi*^c of al-Suqā' is the size of the crenellations and merlons which have an almost sculptural quality. The motif of crenellation is taken up in the large square *miḥrāb* projection. It is terminated with steps on each side surmounted by a column ornamented with V-motifs in shallow relief, akin to those on the prayer-hall and *riwāq* facades. The *miḥrāb* is also the most ornate feature on the exterior of the mosque, although there is also a certain amount of plaster decoration with floral scrolls on the exterior of the east wall.[1]

10 Rajab 1403/23 April 1983

Jāmi^c, *al-Suqā'. South facade of the prayer-hall.*

Jamal, ^cAsīr

Jamal is a small settlement to the east of Ṭabab, with numerous old houses and towers and surrounded by agricultural land. There are two mosques of some antiquity. The smaller of these two mosques, on the north-eastern edge of Jamal, is in ruins. It is built on a low rocky outcrop overlooking the road from Ṭabab and al-Sūqā'. The roof and the west wall have vanished but the rest of the walls remain in good condition, extremely well built in dry-laid masonry, and apparently never plastered. The mosque consists of a prayer-hall only, with no *ṣaḥn*, probably because of the limited size of the available space, as well as the nature of the mosque.

Small mosque, Jamal.

Small mosque, Jamal.

There is only one doorway in the centre of the south wall, opposite the *miḥrāb* in the centre of the *qibla* wall. This doorway is bridged by a particularly long wooden beam. The *miḥrāb* is in the form of a deeply curved recess which is vaulted by a pair of long stones forming a steep keel-arch. On the exterior surface, the *miḥrāb* forms a curving projection that narrows into a canopy.

The second of these two older mosques in Jamal is within the main complex of houses of the settlement and is built on rising ground: as a consequence it is approached by steps. This mosque I was told is 500 years old, but dating must be treated with caution and may mean only that the mosque is older than any living generation.

Old mosque, Jamal, from the south-east.

Old mosque, Jamal. Miḥrāb *and door in south facade of the prayer-hall.*

This mosque is stone-built and the walls and *ṣaḥn* floor are whitened with plaster. The entrance is at the western extremity of the south enclosure wall, the rectangular doorway stressed by its projection above the line of the wall. There is also a slight prominence on the summit of this wall which is on axis with the *miḥrāb* and serves to indicate its direction from outside the mosque. Within the enclosure is a wide, shallow *ṣaḥn* and a rectangular level-roofed prayer-hall on the north side. In the centre of the north wall of the *ṣaḥn* is a narrow rectangular entrance, closed by a wooden double door, painted green. Projecting, flat stone slabs above the door serve to break the flow of rainfall over the entrance. To the west of this entrance to the prayer-hall is a *miḥrāb* in the centre, taking the form of a tall, slightly narrowing, recess. It is framed by a moulding and, in contrast to the rest of the prayer-hall wall, the recess is painted blue. There is an inscription to the left of this *miḥrāb* and a second between the *miḥrāb* and the doorway to the prayer-hall, but unfortunately they could not be examined.

10 Rajab 1403/23 April 1983

Mosque, Sharama, ᶜAsīr

Sharama is a small settlement lying between Ṭabab and Jamal, to the north-west of Abhā. There are a number of houses of the traditional highland type and one very unusual mosque. I could elicit no firm date, except that it was old. The mosque is stone-built and stands on the edge of a complex of houses that approach close on all sides, except the north (*qibla*) wall which is entirely free of adjoining structures.

This mosque has a courtyard on the south side and a flat-roofed prayer-hall on the north. On the east side, built as one with the complex as a whole, is an ablutions facility which can be approached from outside the mosque from the north or from the direction of the *ṣaḥn*. Apart from this access to the mosque via the ablutions, the principal entrance to the mosque of Sharama is from the south into the *ṣaḥn*, placed opposite the *miḥrāb*. The *ṣaḥn* is open and in its south-east corner, overlooking the *ṣaḥn*, the roof of the ablutions and the prayer-hall, is a staircase leading to a platform. This platform recalls the staircase-platforms in the corresponding position in mosques in the Tihāma at Ṣabyā, Abū ᶜArīsh and elsewhere in the area.

Mosque, Sharama. South facade of the prayer-hall and the ṣaḥn.

The prayer-hall has a single entrance in the south wall, on axis with both the ***miḥrāb*** and the entrance on the south side of the ***ṣaḥn***. To the west of the door to the prayer-hall is a flight of stone steps climbing the face of the wall, giving access to the prayer-hall roof. The steps are simple stone slabs projecting from the wall like corbels, each some seventy centimetres higher than its successor. This simple but effective staircase to the roof is a device found in other parts of the region, where I have also seen the walls of field terraces on the mountainsides fitted with such steps.

On the prayer-hall roof there is a particularly unusual tower structure which stands just to the right (or east) of the ***miḥrāb*** below, inside the prayer-hall. This tower has a rectangular base projecting well beyond the line of the ***qibla*** wall and also beyond the broad rectangular ***miḥrāb*** salient. The tower is banked slightly and the upper part is articulated on each of the faces, except that to the south, by shallow blind-arched recesses. By contrast, on the south face, giving on to the roof of the prayer-hall, there is a deep recess vaulted by a round-headed arch which cuts into the thickness of the

Mosque, Sharama. South face of the minaret.

*Mosque, Sharama. North (*qibla*) wall and minaret.*

tower. The recess has the character of a *miḥrāb* on the mosque roof, although the tower was described to me by the people of Sharama as a minaret. Also on the south face of the tower are two roughly constructed merlons at each corner, adding emphasis to the *qibla* direction. On its summit, the tower is terminated by a tall and narrow cylindrical finial, capped by a domical form. As the entire tower is solid it can only be ascended externally and to achieve this it has a flight of corbelled steps inserted into its west face.

The outer surfaces of the mosque as a whole are left unplastered, with the sole exception of the minaret, which is coated with yellowish *quḍāḍ* plaster over the upper two thirds. Within the *ṣaḥn*, the walls are all covered with white plaster. This treatment also includes the facade of the prayer-hall (towards the *qibla* in the north). The application of white plaster is a tradition found in varying forms in many parts of south-western and western Arabia. The roof of the prayer-hall is plastered as well, sealing it against the rainfall that is heavy and frequent in these mountains. To drain this, water runways are set in the mosque walls, where they are visible on the south face of the prayer-hall.

10 Rajab 1403/23 April 1983

Jāmi^c, Ṭabab, ^{c}Asīr

Jāmi^c, *Ṭabab. Foundation inscription.*

Ṭabab is a sizeable village north-west of Abhā and to the west of the road to al-Ṭā'if. The mosque is on the east side of the town, situated between the modern asphalt road as it enters the village, and a large *wādī*. Unusually among the mosques of the area, the *jāmi*ᶜ of Ṭabab has a very detailed modern inscription panel in marble recording its foundation. It was founded in the reign of Imām Saᶜūd b. ᶜAbd al-ᶜAzīz b. Muḥammad b. Saᶜūd in the year 1221/1806-7 and was restored in the reign of His Late Majesty King Fayṣal b. ᶜAbd al-ᶜAzīz in 1392/1972-3. It is particularly interesting that we should have a mosque remaining in this area from the time of the first Saudi state, whose authority was extended to this area in 1215/1801.

The *jāmi*ᶜ of Ṭabab is currently being restored and there is a new minaret in concrete in the south-east corner. Other restorations are underway apart from the minaret but much of the original mosque remains, including the prayer-hall, built of fine dry-laid masonry in which larger stones are stabilised with smaller packed stones and wedges. The stones that form the projecting rectangular *miḥrāb* on the exterior of the *qibla* wall are particularly large. In this area as a whole, stone laying without mortar is a highly developed craft and the *jāmi*ᶜ of Ṭabab is a fine example of this.

The entrance to the *jāmi*ᶜ enclosure is on the west side, giving directly on to the narrow *ṣaḥn* that occupies the south half of the mosque. At the time of my visit, much

Jāmiᶜ, *Ṭabab, from the north-west.*

of the facade of the prayer-hall on the *ṣaḥn* was exposed, and the interior was visible. The prayer-hall is a long building on its east-west axis and shallower, comparatively, on its north-south axis. The flat roof rests on three arcades running parallel to the north (*qibla*) wall with arches which are approximately pointed, but are irregular in profile – some actually flatten off at the crown. The underlying structure of these arcades is stone, but all are covered with thick white plaster. The *miḥrāb* in the centre of the *qibla* wall is a rectangular recess, arched on the interior and forming a square projection on the exterior surface, where it reaches to the summit of the wall. The greater part of the interior of the mosque is coated with white plaster, contrasting with the exterior surfaces where plaster is confined to the frames around the windows and a band around the summit of the walls. The vertical channels to drain away rainwater from the roof are also plastered, although this is a purely functional device. The number of drain-channels testify to the heavy rainfall in this part of Saudi Arabia. The only

Jāmi^c, *Ṭabab. Interior of the prayer-hall and* miḥrāb *in the north* (qibla) *wall.*

decoration on the mosque is the stepped crenellations on the corners and at the intermediate points along the walls. These are made of concrete and are modern, but they may replace earlier crenellations. It is an interesting example of the persistence of traditional forms despite the introduction of new building materials.

10 Rajab 1403/23 April 1983

al-Aṣfal mosque, Masqī, ᶜAsīr

al-Aṣfal mosque, Masqī, from the north-east, showing the north (qibla) *wall.*

Masqī is a village of some size which lies to the south-east of Abhā in the highlands. The mosque known as Masjid al-Aṣfal is situated on the western side of the low hill on which much of the old part of Masqī lies. The mosque is freestanding, lying between the last houses of the village and the fields that come close to it. It is a large building which is particularly well constructed, like the architecture of Masqī generally; in its design it is very close to the al-Shahīr mosque in the same town, and both are presumably of similar date.

The Aṣfal mosque consists of a rectangular enclosure, entirely constructed of stone. The walls on the exterior are left unplastered with the exception of a band of the local white *quḍāḍ* around the summit of the walls, which also covers the finials and merlons. Otherwise, the well laid masonry is left plain. The plaster on the wall summits is probably as much to protect the masonry from the consequences of frequent and heavy rainfall as for decoration. The entrance is situated on the west side of the mosque enclosure from a street running around the edge of the village at this point. It is a simple rectangular doorway, apparently restored. The interior of the enclosure has extensive ablutions facilities in the southern and eastern areas, shielded from the *ṣaḥn* by low walls. On the north side of the *ṣaḥn* are two buildings that constitute the prayer-halls against the north (*qibla*) wall. The varying dimensions of these two buildings and the arrangement of the ablutions area gives the *ṣaḥn* an appearance of irregularity which is encountered in the al-Shahīr mosque and in other mosques in this area of the mountains.

al-Aṣfal mosque, Masqī. South-west side of the ṣaḥn.

The ablutions facilities consist of extremely complex and well designed *maṭāhir* separated from the rest of the *ṣaḥn* by walls and entered from a point directly opposite the street; thus, people may perform their ablutions first before turning from the *maṭāhir* right into the *ṣaḥn* and the prayer-hall. The *maṭāhir* constitute a series of booths defined by L-shaped walls with individual areas divided by stone screens. The *maṭāhir*, the associated water-channels, and the pavement of the *ṣaḥn* are all covered with the hard thick *quḍāḍ* plaster that is used everywhere in ᶜAsīr for water-proofing. In this ablutions area there is a shower room near the entrance which is plastered and has minute finials at the four corners; the whole structure is also covered with *quḍāḍ*. I was informed that the water for ablutions in these channels feeding the *maṭāhir* or the shower is poured by the *mu'adhdhin* or whoever else is available to assist people's ablutions. Although the mosque lacks a minaret, in the south-east corner of the courtyard, beyond the ablutions area, there is a small staircase running up against the east wall of the mosque and forming a solid block from whose platform-summit the prayer-call is given. The position of the staircase allows the *mu'adhdhin* to perform ablutions and then ascend to give the *adhān*.

al-Asfal mosque, Masqī. Ablutions facilities.

al-Asfal mosque, Masqī. Ablutions facilities.

al-Asfal mosque, Masqī. South facade of the prayer-hall.

The two prayer-halls on the north side of the enclosure are separate and independent structures. That to the east, the larger of the two, is rectangular with banked walls and advances into the *ṣaḥn* further than the smaller western building. The eastern hall has a level roof and a single entrance in the centre of the south wall. The entrance is rectangular, closed by a modern door painted green and framed by a broad white band above and to the sides, with a green dado beneath on either side. Above the entrance is a shallow porch of a type seen elsewhere in the area to protect the doorway from the flow of rainwater. To the left of the doorway is an inscription incised in the plaster but I had no opportunity to transcribe it. Directly above the entrance is a merlon and there is another merlon on the opposite side of the prayer-hall, above the *miḥrāb*. The stepped crenellation over the *miḥrāb* has one more step in it than any other merlon or finial on the building. The stepped corner finials of this larger prayer-hall are remarkable for their size.

My brief examination of the deeper eastern prayer-hall from the threshold showed that its level roof is made of substantial wooden beams which rest on green-painted wooden columns and carry the roof-bearing beams(1) running at right angles to the *qibla* wall. The upper wall surface of the prayer-hall is plastered white, while a dado below is painted the same green as the wooden columns. The *miḥrāb* in the centre of the *qibla* wall is a curved recess terminated with a horizontal covering some way short of the summit of the wall. The floor is covered by carpets and there are cases for keeping the Holy Qur'ān by the *qibla* wall. There are also open wooden boxes attached to the columns at the summit, just beneath the roof: these are used to store the Holy Qur'ān away from the dust of the floor. This solves the question of how best to keep the Holy Qur'ān safely in an appropriate place. The arrangement may be compared to the use of stone shelves inserted in columns that are found in mosques in Nejd.

The second, smaller hall to the west of the first is much shallower; unfortunately it was impossible to examine its interior as it was locked. The design of this prayer-hall is akin to that to the east, with a single entrance opposite the *miḥrāb*. The same type of impressive finial merlon surmounts the entrance, while especially large corner finials stand at the four corners of the building. Over the *miḥrāb* is another finial which is not stepped but built to terminate the rectangular *miḥrāb* projection.

11 Rajab 1403/24 April 1983

*al-Asfal mosque, Masqī. Prayer-hall, looking towards the north (*qibla*) wall from the entrance.*

Shahīr mosque, Masqī

The Shahīr mosque is built against a group of houses on the south-west side of Masqī, and is only free of adjoining structures on the west side: as a result it was not possible to examine the mosque from the exterior, nor could the external shape of the *miḥrāb* be satisfactorily ascertained. In its construction, the Shahīr mosque is very similar to the Aṣfal mosque in the same village, using the well laid, unmortared masonry of the region. The prayer-hall, the interior of the courtyard, including the ablutions area and the pavement, are all waterproofed with hard *quḍāḍ* plaster.

The mosque consists of a walled courtyard on the south side with a level-roofed prayer-hall on the north side. It is entered either by a doorway in the southern extremity of the west wall or through a second doorway in the south wall, although this is presently blocked. The courtyard includes within its area the *maṭāhir* which are arranged against the south wall. This position corresponds to that of the ablutions facilities in the Aṣfal mosque in Masqī, and also to those of the *jāmiᶜ* of Suqā'. In the Shahīr mosque, the ablutions facilities include water channels and receptacles for water (*marūsa*) raised above the plastered floor. Between the ablutions and the prayer-hall on the north side, the courtyard is empty.

Shahīr mosque, Masqī. South-west corner of the courtyard.

The prayer-hall has a single rectangular doorway in the centre, closed by a green painted door with carving. The doorway is accentuated by a band of white plaster around it and flanked by plaster panels in shallow relief. The panel to the west is in the form of a pointed blind arch, terminated by a finial and shaped like a *miḥrāb*. The panel to the east is inscribed and bears the date of the mosque's construction, 1225/1810. Above the entrance is a "porch" of projecting stones to break the rainwater flowing from above the door. There is also a single course of slightly projecting stones running horizontally across the width of the south wall of the prayer-hall. As with many other mosques in the mountains, a water channel has been cut in the summit of this wall to allow rainwater to run off the roof. The water collected by this channel is stored in a tank under the courtyard, near the door of the prayer-hall.

Shahīr mosque, Masqī. Decorative panel in south wall of the prayer-hall.

Shahīr mosque, Masqī. South facade.

At the west end of the prayer-hall facade is a short staircase with four steps, approached by a low step in the *ṣaḥn*. The staircase is not intended to reach the summit of the mosque roof. Instead, I was told that it serves as a platform from which to call the prayer.

Inside the prayer-hall are finely finished wooden columns with capitals supporting the joists of the roof, which run at right-angles to the *qibla* wall and which themselves support lathes. The capitals of the columns take a simple T-shape. The single *miḥrāb* in the centre of the *qibla* wall is a deep rectangular recess, opposite the entrance, and is bridged by a pointed arch. The interior walls of the prayer-hall have a green dado painted below with the upper wall surfaces painted purple. The same colours are used on the columns attached to the walls and for the *miḥrāb* recess. The floor of the mosque is carpeted. Given the points of similarity between the Shahīr mosque and the Aṣfal mosque of Masqī, it is quite reasonable to take them to be of similar date.

11 Rajab 1403/24 April 1983

Jāmiᶜ, Aḥad Rufayda, ᶜAsīr

Jāmiᶜ, *Aḥad Rufayda.* Ṣaḥn *and south wall of the prayer-hall.*

Aḥad Rufayda lies east of Abhā and Khamīs Mushayṭ. It is a large town with many examples remaining of traditional architecture in the old quarter, as well as an increasing number of modern buildings. The *jāmiᶜ* lies on the western side of a large public square, where the Sunday (*yawm al-aḥad*) market, from which the town takes its name, was in progress at the time of my visit.

The *jāmiᶜ* is an exceptionally large mosque because of the extent of the *ṣaḥn*, a vast, walled, unpaved courtyard on the south side. It is far greater in area than the mosques which I saw elsewhere in the region. The prayer-hall runs the full width of the enclosure on the north (*qibla*) side. The east side is obscured on the exterior by shops and other buildings built against it. One of the two entrances to the *ṣaḥn* is on this side, approached from between the adjoining buildings. The south side is free of buildings and the second entrance to the *ṣaḥn* is situated here in the centre of the wall, on axis with the main entrance to the prayer-hall and to the *miḥrāb* in the centre of the *qibla* wall. The west side of the *ṣaḥn* is also unencumbered by other buildings. The only structure in the great *ṣaḥn* is a minaret at the south-east corner, a square tower which is stumpy and low, coloured with an ochre plaster. This distinguishes it from the enclosure walls of the *ṣaḥn* and the prayer-hall, all of which are coated with white plaster. The minaret is

Jāmiᶜ, *Aḥad Rufayda. East side of the minaret.*

approached by a staircase running along the inner surface of the east wall of the *ṣaḥn* up to an opening in the north face. There also are openings in the east and west faces of the tower, in its upper part. A wooden canopy at the top of the minaret is clearly a later addition. The minaret is unusual among those that I have seen in ᶜAsīr, and it is interesting that the local feature of a staircase to call the prayer from the *ṣaḥn* should be kept, even when a conventional minaret has been added to the building.

On the north side, the prayer-hall takes the form of a long low structure with a flat roof. It has three rectangular entrances in the south side, distributed symmetrically, of which the principal door is that opposite the *miḥrāb*. A single rectangular window is set between each door, and a pair of windows are set at either extremity of the wall. In the west lateral wall are three windows, but there are none in the east side wall, which is concealed by shops. In the north (*qibla*) wall there are three windows west of the *miḥrāb* and two to the east.

The *miḥrāb* forms one of two salients on the exterior of the *qibla* wall. It makes a curved projection rising about two-thirds the height of the wall. To the east is a second, larger salient in the form of a rectangle, the same height as the *miḥrāb*. In its east face, this rectangular projection has a door for the *imām* to enter the mosque. I did not see the interior to discover if the *minbar* was also placed within this rectangular projection, where it might be expected.

11 Rajab 1403/24 April 1983

Jāmiᶜ, Aḥad Rufayda. Door in the miḥrāb, north (qibla) *wall.*

Wādī Najrān

Wādī Najrān lies in the extreme south-west of Saudi Arabia and has been settled since ancient times, as its archaeological ruins show. It is a valley of great fertility; the *wādī* rises in the mountains to the west and, when in flood, carries its waters out to the Empty Quarter desert in the east. The numerous settlements of Najrān are scattered along the banks and tributary channels of the *wādī*. The main town in the past was Abā Saᶜūd, but a new city, Madīna Fayṣal, has now been built to the east. The rest of the settlements are small villages, set between the *wādī* channel and the bare mountains that rise steeply behind the valley on either side. The village settlements of Najrān consist of distinctive houses of impressive design grouped together amidst their palm groves and gardens: each of these settlements has at least one small mosque. Although various aspects of Najrān and its antiquities have been described in the past,[1] very little has been said of its traditional mosques, which are among the finest in Saudi Arabia.

Mosque, Dahdha al-Ṣuqūr, Najrān

This small mosque is used by the inhabitants of the nearby houses, and lies on the south side of the main asphalt road through Dahdha al-Ṣuqūr, amidst gardens and trees. Like other mosques of this type in Najrān, it is a diminutive building, built of mud and coated with mud-plaster on the exterior and the interior. The enclosure forms a rectangle within which the *ṣaḥn* lies to the south and the small prayer-hall the north, the direction of the *qibla* in Najrān. The only entrance to the mosque is that in the east side, which leads to the *ṣaḥn* rather than to the prayer-hall. The door is a simple rectangle.

The *ṣaḥn* is of a particularly interesting type, like all those that I saw in Najrān. Its walls are surmounted on the east, south and west sides by triangular crenellations, each of which is capped by a small finial and pierced by a triangular opening. All the crenellations on the *ṣaḥn* walls are treated in the same way, although some of them have been damaged; the form of these ornamental motifs is typical of Najrān.

The small *ṣaḥn* is empty except for a staircase to the

South mosque, Dahdha al-Ṣuqūr, from the south-west.

roof of the prayer-hall, built at a right angle to it against the inner face of the west wall of the enclosure. The staircase is constructed, like all of those in this group of Najrān mosques, with a split palm trunk laid flat side up and at an angle to the roof, forming a ramp. On the foundation thus provided, a flight of shallow mud-brick steps is constructed. At the base of the steps is a rectangular mud platform, with three steps on its east side leading up from the unpaved *ṣaḥn* floor. At the summit of the staircase is a very narrow access to the roof of the mosque through the top of the prayer-hall wall. The staircase is used by the *mu'adhdhin* to give the call to prayer.

The prayer-hall is a rectangular building which is a little deeper than the *ṣaḥn* and has a level roof. There is only one entrance to it from the *ṣaḥn*, set in the centre of the south wall, opposite the *miḥrāb*; as with the entrance to the *ṣaḥn* in the east side, there is only a simple wooden door. There are two windows in each of the side walls of the prayer-hall, and, apart from the doorway, these are the only natural sources of illumination inside the mosque.

The *miḥrāb* was examined only from the exterior and is similar to others in Najrān: it is a very large and prominent salient, forming a curved projection on the exterior of the *qibla* wall and rising the full height of the wall. It terminates in a slightly irregular manner as a result of erosion.

The prayer-hall roof is decorated with merlons of a quite different type to those on the wall around the *ṣaḥn*: the former are all solid in contrast with the pierced ornaments of the *ṣaḥn* enclosure wall. At the four corners of the prayer-hall roof are crenellations, while between them, on all four sides of the roof, are pairs of intermediate merlons. The two merlons on the *qibla* side are very carefully positioned to flank the summit of the *miḥrāb*.

2 Shaʿbān 1404/3 May 1984

South mosque, Dahdha al-Ṣuqūr. View of ṣaḥn *to the west.*

South mosque, Dahdha al-Ṣuqūr. North (qibla) wall.

North mosque, Dahdha al-Ṣuqūr, Najrān

North mosque, Dahdha al-Ṣuqūr, from the south-west.

This mosque in Dahdha al-Ṣuqūr, to the north of the main asphalt road, is the most beautiful that I visited in Najrān. It is built of mud-brick and coated with mud-plaster like all the rest of the traditional Najrān mosques discussed here, but the windows, the merlons and entire *ṣaḥn* are emphasised by a coating of white plaster.

North mosque, Dahdha al-Ṣuqūr, from the south-east.

The mosque consists of a prayer-hall with the usual level roof on the north side of an open rectangular *ṣaḥn*, which is surrounded by a low wall. The *ṣaḥn* is entered through a doorway at the southern end of the east wall, the sole point of access to the building. The frame of the rectangular doorway rises a little above the summit of the *ṣaḥn* wall, a system found in many parts of Saudi Arabia although here the doorway is not as accentuated as examples elsewhere.

On top of the *ṣaḥn* wall there are ornamental crenellations of a complexity of design that distinguishes them from others that I have seen in Najrān. At the south-west and south-east corners of the *ṣaḥn* there are simple stepped finials, but at the intermediate points on the east, west and south walls are elaborate triple merlons with three triangular peaks and a single triangular opening piercing each. The merlon in the centre of the south wall is on axis with the *miḥrāb* in the centre of the *qibla* wall.

On the west side of the *ṣaḥn* is a staircase apparently using the system of construction usual in Najrān, with mud steps resting on palm trunks; the whole is coated in white plaster. The staircase rises in two stages, the upper stage ascending the south face of the prayer-hall to reach its point of access to the roof just west of the entrance to the prayer-hall beneath.

The prayer-hall has a single entrance, a simple rectangular doorway, leading from the *ṣaḥn*, but not directly opposite the *miḥrāb*, which is rather unusual. There is also a small window in the same south wall of the prayer-hall. Apart from the illumination provided by these openings, the interior is also lit by pairs of windows in the east, west and north (*qibla*) wall. The windows in the (*qibla*) walls flank the *miḥrāb* on either side, and there is a small window in each lateral face of the square *miḥrāb* projection. This *miḥrāb* dominates the north wall and is set in the centre of it, rising to the summit of the *qibla* wall.

On the summit of the walls of the prayer-hall there are further crenellations similar to those on the *ṣaḥn* wall. At the four corners there are finials, while in the centre of the east, west and south walls there are single, complicated, pierced merlons with triple finials, like the intermediate ones on the *ṣaḥn* walls. On either side of these are smaller stepped crenellations. The treatment of the *qibla* wall is somewhat different, for not only are the smaller flanking crenellations dissimilar to those in corresponding positions on other walls, but the decoration above the *miḥrāb* is the most complicated in the mosque. It consists of a four-peak structure, with two openings piercing it in the form of triangles. All of these ornamental forms on the roof are partly or entirely covered with white plaster. This contributes to the impressive finish of the mosque, which not only has a white plastered courtyard but also white frames and white aurora rays around the windows, contrasting with the dun mud-plaster of the exterior surfaces of the mosque.

2 Shaᶜbān 1404/3 May 1984

North mosque, Dahdha al-Ṣuqūr. Staircase against the south wall of the prayer-hall.

North mosque, Dahdha al-Ṣuqūr. North (qibla) *wall.*

Mosque of Muḥammad Manṣūr, Dahdha al-Ṣuqūr, Najrān

The mosque of Muḥammad Manṣūr stands amidst fields and palm plantations near a tower house of the traditional Najrān type in Dahdha al-Ṣuqūr.(1) The mosque is built and plastered with mud, and consists of the usual walled *ṣaḥn* on the south side and a level-roofed prayer-hall on the north. On the east side, set at an angle with its longer side on a north-east to south-west orientation, is a mud-brick house, built to accommodate the *mu'adhdhin* of the small mosque. Between the house and the east side of the mosque is a plastered pavement, in effect a very low platform. It gives access to the entrance to the house, and also serves as a broad passage to the mosque, whose only entrance is in its east wall, leading to the *ṣaḥn*. The passage is also an open courtyard for the house.

Mosque of Muḥammad Manṣūr, Dahdha al-Ṣuqūr, from the west.

Mosque of Muḥammad Manṣūr, Dahdha al-Ṣuqūr. South facade of the prayer-hall.

Inside the unpaved *ṣaḥn* the only feature is a staircase against the west wall of the enclosure, preceded at the base by a low flight of steps from the *ṣaḥn* floor. The staircase support is of the local type with split palm trunks carrying the mud steps. On all three sides, the enclosure wall of the *ṣaḥn* is surmounted with triangular pierced crenellations, large and pleasing forms which are taken up as a motif on the top of the walls of the *mu'adhdhin's* house. This suggests that both the mosque and the house were built at the same time.

The prayer-hall on the north side of the *ṣaḥn* has only one entrance in the centre of its south side, from the *ṣaḥn*, which is set directly opposite the *miḥrāb* in the middle of the *qibla* wall. The doorway is unusual inasmuch as it has a slightly raised frame in mud-plaster, with a pediment with curving sides – an unexpectedly baroque effect.

Mosque of Muḥammad Manṣūr, Dahdha al-Ṣuqūr. Miḥrāb *in the north (*qibla*) wall, from the entrance.*

Mosque of Muḥammad Manṣūr, Dahdha al-Ṣuqūr, from the north-west.

The tops of the walls forming the prayer-hall are decorated with merlons, but of a solid stepped type, rather than the pierced forms that decorate the walls of the *ṣaḥn* below. At each corner of the prayer-hall is a right-angled merlon. On the east and west sides at intermediate points are two merlons, whereas on the longer north (*qibla*) and south walls there are three merlons to each wall.

The interior of the mosque is plastered white, in contrast with the plain dun mud of the exterior. Internally, the prayer-hall is lit by the light from the entrance, by three rectangular windows in each side wall, and by two in the *qibla* wall, one on each side of the *miḥrāb*. The *miḥrāb* is a very deeply recessed, curved niche, vaulted by a flattened arch, and forming a commensurately prominent projection to a point some half-way up the height of the *qibla* wall. Around the *miḥrāb* on the interior surface of the *qibla* wall is a raised dado which continues above the *miḥrāb* as a frame and which culminates in a triangular motif directly above its centre. The only other features inside the prayer-hall are two substantial rectangular piers which carry the roof and which lie parallel to the *qibla* wall.

2 Shaᶜbān 1404/3 May 1984

Mosque of Muḥammad Ṣāliḥ Azaᶜjūr, Dahdha al-Ṣuqūr, Najrān

Mosque of Muḥammad Ṣāliḥ Azaᶜjūr. East wall.

The mosque of Muḥammad Sāliḥ Azaᶜjūr is surrounded by farms and palm groves in the Dahdha al-Ṣuqūr district of Najrān. The mosque is built of mud-brick, and on the exterior is plastered with mud. It follows the usual plan with a prayer-hall to the north and a shallow rectangular *ṣaḥn* to the south. The walls of the *ṣaḥn* are unusual, being higher overall than is normal in Najrān mosques. They are on two levels, the higher beginning just south of the single entrance to the mosque in the east wall. These stretches of wall are in fact the same height as the walls of the prayer-hall. The entrance gives directly on to the *ṣaḥn*. This solitary door is flanked on either side by shallow ornamental buttresses, while above the entrance is an inscription in two lines, in raised relief from the mud-plaster wall surface. It reads: *"lā-ilāha ilā Allah/Muḥammad rasūl Allāh"* ("There is no deity but God/Muḥammad is the Messenger of God"). Inside the *ṣaḥn*, against the east wall, is a staircase to the prayer-hall roof which passes directly above the entrance to the mosque.

Mosque of Muḥammad Ṣāliḥ Azaʿjūr. East doorway.

Mosque of Muḥammad Ṣāliḥ Azaʿjūr, from the north-east.

All the prayer-hall walls and the *ṣaḥn* walls are surmounted by the same type of crenellations as found in other parts of Dahdha al-Ṣuqūr and Najrān as a whole (page 100): each triangular crenellation is pierced by a triangular opening and is surmounted by a finial. In the mosque of Muḥammad Ṣāliḥ Aza[c]jūr there is no differentiation between the type, size or complexity of the crenellations on the *ṣaḥn* walls and those on the prayer-hall. They have the effect of unifying the building visually, and in the case of the prayer-hall, serve to heighten it still further.

The interior of the prayer-hall is lit through the entrance from the *ṣaḥn* and through pairs of windows in the side walls and two set on either side of the *miḥrāb* in the north (*qibla*) wall; however, some of these windows are blocked up. The *miḥrāb* is a remarkable structure which I saw only from the exterior. It is a rectangular projection that reaches some half-way up the height of the *qibla* wall and has a slightly gabled roof which also slopes a little longitudinally. Around the sides of the *miḥrāb* at mid-height is a band of tall inverted V-motifs in relief in the mud plaster. Among the mosques of Najrān, the form of this *miḥrāb* is unusual and its quality of design is as fine as all else in the mosque.

3 Sha[c]bān 1404/4 May 1984

Mosque of Muḥammad Ṣāliḥ Aza[c]jūr. Miḥrāb *projection in the north (*qibla*) wall.*

Mosque, Sha[c]b Burān al-Ḥārith, Najrān

Sha[c]b Burān al-Ḥārith is a tributary of the Wādī Najrān channel, lying on the north bank, towards the western end of the settlements. The mosque belongs to a group of houses not far from the point at which the tributary empties into Wādī Najrān. It is built on a raised platform, which it shares with neighbouring houses, and is separated from the nearby houses to the south and east, while an unpaved track runs along its west side. The *qibla* wall is not accessible because it is closed off by the enclosure wall of a courtyard.

The prayer-hall lies on the north side of the mosque and to the south of it are two courtyards: that against the prayer hall being the walled *ṣaḥn* proper while the more southerly courtyard has a low wall and provides access from the south. The entrance to the *ṣaḥn* is by means of a simple rectangular doorway. To the east of this door, on the exterior of the mosque, is a flight of steps rising to slightly higher ground and to a narrow street running along the east side of the mosque. In contrast with the enclosure walls of other mosque courtyards in Najrān,

*Mosque, Shaᶜb Burān al-Ḥārith. North (*qibla*) wall.*

there are no crenellations or other decorative forms on the *ṣaḥn* walls of this mosque.

There are two points of access to the prayer-hall. The first is a rectangular doorway in the centre of the south wall of the building, accessible from the *ṣaḥn*, already discussed above. There is a second entrance to the prayer-hall directly from the street, approached by steps, as the mosque stands somewhat higher than the street. The walls of the prayer-hall are decorated on top with merlons: simple ones at each corner and triple merlons pierced by triangular openings at the mid-point on each wall. A merlon thus stands above the south door to the prayer-hall from the *ṣaḥn* and another stands over the *miḥrāb* in the centre of the north wall. All these crenellations are coated with fine white plaster, distinguishing them from the rest of the mud-built mosque. An interesting use of white plaster occurs on the exterior of the *qibla* wall, where a great rectangular panel extends down the wall from the crenellations in the centre and then continues to coat the upper surface of the *miḥrāb* projection. The *miḥrāb* is a very pronounced rectangular salient with a slightly pitched roof. In its size it is typical of Najrān, but I do not recall another example of such a use of white plaster on the *qibla* wall and the *miḥrāb* roof.

2 Shaᶜbān 1404/3 May 1984

Mosque, Shaᶜb Burān al-Ḥārith, from the south-west.

Mosque, Bilād Banī Salmān, Bilād Banī ᶜAlī, Najrān

The mosque of Bilād Banī Salmān, Bilād Banī ᶜAlī stands on the west side of open ground near a group of houses in traditional Najrān style. It is built in mud-brick with an enclosed rectangular *ṣaḥn* on the south side and a prayer-hall to the north. The mosque is unusually large because of the length of the prayer-hall on its north (*qibla*)-south axis. It is also unusual that the *ṣaḥn* is not as wide as the prayer-hall.

Mosque, Bilād Banī Salmān, Bilād Banī ᶜAlī, from the south-west.

Mosque, Bilād Banī Salmān, Bilād Banī ᶜAlī. South wall of the prayer-hall and west wall of the ṣaḥn.

The mosque has a single entrance in the east side, leading to the *ṣaḥn*. The door is simple, made of wood, and the wall above rises higher than at any other point around the *ṣaḥn*. There are three triangular apertures above the entrance. The summit of the enclosure wall is ornamented by pierced merlons of the type seen in the mosque of Muḥammad Manṣūr in Dahdha al-Ṣuqūr (page 104). Against the inner surface of the east wall of the *ṣaḥn* is a staircase of the palm-trunk type seen in other mosques in Najrān. At the base, in the south-east corner, is a short flight of steps rising from the unpaved floor of the *ṣaḥn*.

Mosque, Bilād Banī Salmān, Bilād Banī ᶜAlī. East side of the ṣaḥn.

Mosque, Bilād Banī Salmān, Bilād Banī ᶜAlī. South facade of the prayer-hall, with the south wall of the ṣaḥn *in the foreground.*

The prayer-hall overlaps the *ṣaḥn* on the west side very slightly, and still more so to the east. In its south wall, opposite the *miḥrāb*, is a single doorway giving access from the *ṣaḥn*. Over this doorway is an inscription in raised relief with the words "*ma shā' Allah*" ("What God wills") in a Kufic-like script. Beneath, incised in the wall surface in a different, coarser style is the name of the craftsman, "*al-muᶜallim Aḥmad*". To the west (left) of the entrance is a single rectangular window and there are four others in each of the west and the east sides of the prayer-hall. In the *qibla* wall there is a single window west of the *miḥrāb*, and a small window in the east face of the *miḥrāb*.

At the four corners of the prayer-hall are the usual stepped corner crenellations. On the east and west sides there are also two pairs of intermediate stepped crenellations. However, on each of the south and the north walls there is only a single merlon, one above the door from the *ṣaḥn* and one above the *miḥrāb*. The *miḥrāb* forms a rectangular projection on the exterior of the *qibla* wall, its upper surface sloping like the roof of the *miḥrāb* in the Shaᶜb Burān al-Ḥārith mosque. The exterior of the *miḥrāb* has been whitened with plaster, as has the *ṣaḥn*, while the exterior walls of the mosque are decorated with white plaster patterns against the dun-coloured mud walls.

2 Shaᶜbān 1404/3 May 1984

Mosque, Bilād Banī Salmān, Bilād Banī ᶜAlī. East wall of the prayer-hall.

Mosque, Bilād Banī Salmān, Bilād Banī ᶜAlī. North (qibla) *wall.*

Mosque of ᶜAlī Sālim Maṣlūm, al-Aswār, Najrān

Mosque of ᶜAlī Sālim Maslūm, al-Aswār, from the south-east.

*Mosque of ᶜAlī Sālim Maslūm, al-Aswār. North (*qibla*) wall.*

Mosque of ᶜAlī Sālim Maslūm, al-Aswār. North wall with miḥrāb *and palm-trunk staircase.*

The mosque of ᶜAlī Sālim Maṣlūm in al-Aswār is a mud-built structure in an open area, serving the inhabitants of a nearby group of houses. Although it lacks a formal *ṣaḥn*, nevertheless there is an area of level ground, defined by small stones against the south wall of the mosque, which seems to be an *ad hoc ṣaḥn*.

The prayer-hall is a small and simple building in the form of a rectangle with a single rectangular doorway in the centre of the south wall, opposite the *miḥrāb* in the north (*qibla*) wall. In both the eastern and western lateral walls are pairs of rectangular windows. These are the only windows to the prayer-hall, one of which is closed by an air-conditioner. Inside the building is a large rectangular pier that carries the flat roof.

The *miḥrāb* takes the form of a square projection on the exterior of the *qibla* wall, and nearly reaches the summit of the wall. In its general appearance, the *miḥrāb* is typical of those found elsewhere in Najrān but is remarkable inasmuch as a staircase to the roof rests on the *miḥrāb* itself. This staircase is in the usual Najrān style, formed of a palm-trunk foundation and mud-brick steps. Its base, at the western end of the *qibla* wall, rests on a mud-brick platform, while the upper end of the staircase leans against the summit of the west wall of the *miḥrāb*. I have seen no similar staircase to a mosque roof via the *miḥrāb*.

Around the summit of the prayer-hall walls are stepped crenellations, one at each corner, while on all four sides of the mosque there are also single merlons set mid-way along the length of each wall.

2 Shaᶜbān 1404/3 May 1984

II

Central Saudi Arabia

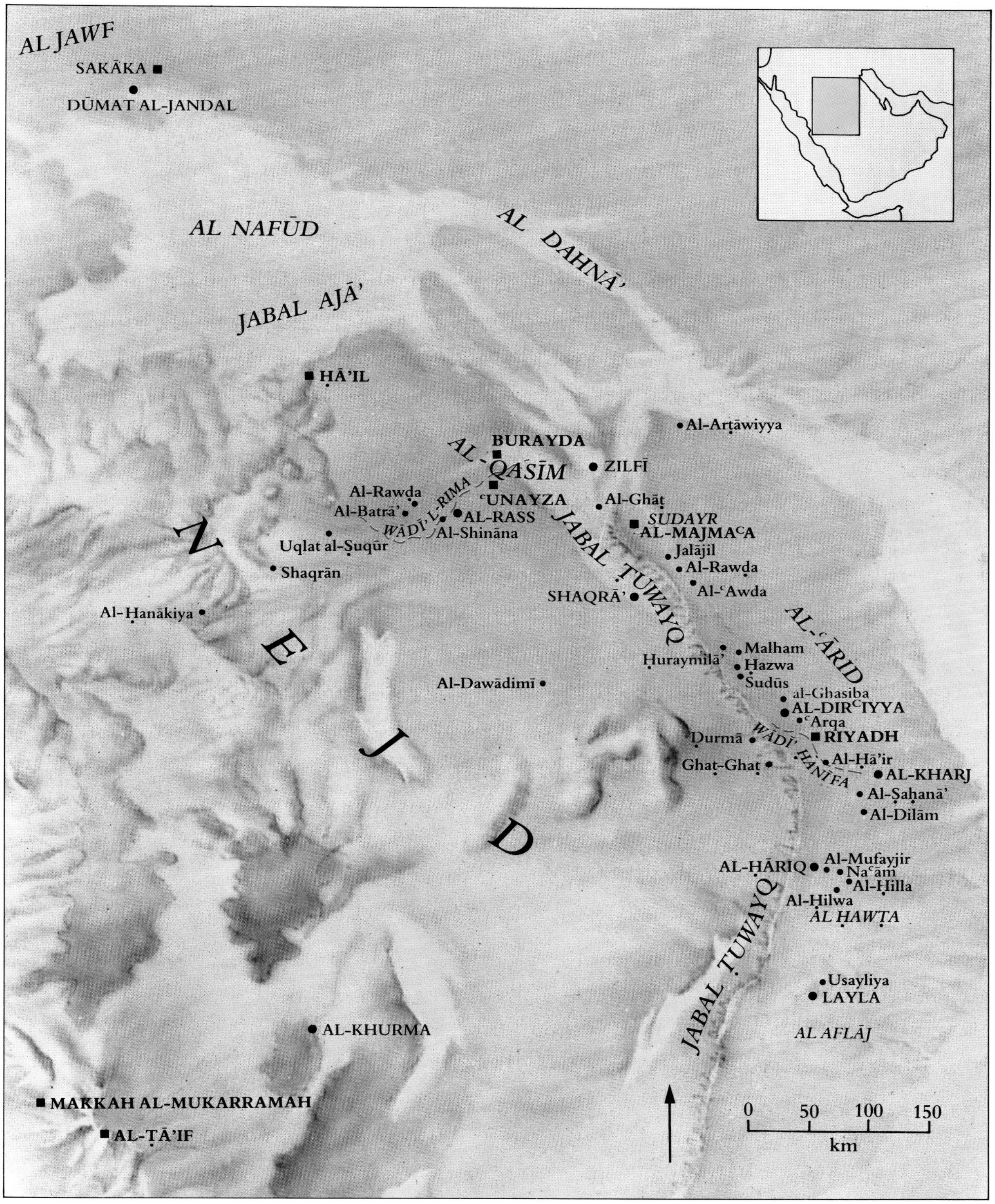

Beyond the Hejaz mountains, the vast plateau of Nejd extends eastwards towards the Arabian Gulf, with only a limited number of physical features interrupting the gravelly plains and sand bars. Of these features, the Jabal Ṭuwayq escarpment is one of the most prominent, running in a vast arc from al-Qaṣīm in the north to end in the south in the Empty Quarter. There are other escarpments in central Arabia but none of such length. Many of the settled areas of central and southern Nejd lie in the *wādīs* east of the escarpment or on the plain at its western foot. Apart from the Jabal Ṭuwayq escarpment, there are also sporadic mountain outcrops, rising abruptly from the floor of the central Arabian plain. These are more frequent towards the geographical border of Nejd and the Hejaz, but there are also large mountain formations deep within Nejd, among which the most striking are Jabal Ajā' and Jabal Salmā near Ḥā'il, the mountains of al-Ṭayy' of ancient times.

Within Nejd there are a number of clearly defined districts. In the far north, the main group of agricultural settlements are in the vicinity of al-Jawf and along the Wādī'l-Ṣirhān, a deep valley forming a natural corridor from eastern Jordan into the heart of north Arabia. The importance of the area in ancient times and in the early Islamic period is reflected in the number of its antiquities. The stone-built architecture of the al-Jawf oasis displays features which it shares with the indigenous buildings of the Ḥawrān to the north, while its mud buildings are akin to those further south in Nejd.

Separating al-Jawf and Ḥā'il is the great sand-sea of the Nafūd. Although arduous for travellers to cross in the days of camel caravans, nevertheless there was water to be had and it provided no real obstacle to communication. Ḥā'il, the main city of Jabal Shammar, was preeminent in central Arabia for a brief period. It is now an almost entirely modern city, with only a few monuments surviving from its past, but there is evidence that the traditional mosques of Ḥā'il were of a type similar in some respects to those of al-Qaṣīm and Sudayr, to the south-east.

Al-Qaṣīm is traversed by the great Wādī'l-Rimah which rises near the *ḥarra* east of al-Madina al-Monawarah and Khaybar and extends nearly to Kuwayt. The district of al-Qaṣīm has numerous towns and villages, among which Burayda, the capital of the province, ᶜUnayza and al-Rass are the most prominent. The region is important for agriculture, especially as a result of modern development, but it appears that this district also supported a large settled population in the past. Merchants from al-Qaṣīm were traditionally active throughout the Near East and even beyond, and the urban tradition and prosperity of the area is reflected in the fine mosques and houses in mud-brick which are still conserved.

In the eastern part of al-Qaṣīm are the rolling dunes of the narrow sand deserts that extend from the south up into the Nafūd. On the eastern side of the sands is Zilfī and the district of Sudayr, yet another important agricultural region of the Kingdom and settled since ancient times. These more central areas of Nejd have numerous towns and villages concentrated along the *wādīs* that cut through the plateau east of the Jabal Ṭuwayq escarpment. These traditionally settled areas of central Nejd – Sudayr, al-Maḥmal, al-ᶜĀriḍ, al-Kharj and al-Ḥawṭa, and Washm on the western side of the Ṭuwayq escarpment – share a common mud-brick architecture which is preserved to varying degrees, juxtaposed today with modern concrete buildings. Mosques in traditional styles in the region show a strong adherence to certain designs, apparently over a long period; however, within this area there is also a certain variation of design, particularly with regard to the shape of minarets. The principal city of the area is Riyadh, the capital of the Kingdom; now a vast modern city, in origin it was a small town of mud-brick surrounded by palm groves and farms like those still to be seen elsewhere in Nejd.

To the east of these settled areas of Nejd is the sand desert of al-Dahnā', the inland oasis of al-Aḥsā', and the Arabian Gulf towns of Saudi Arabia. To the south is the immense sand desert of the Empty Quarter, which forms an obstacle both to direct movement and to settlement in this direction. Communications since ancient times have skirted the north-west edge of this desert, running through the oasis area of Aflāj to Wādī'l-Dawāsir and Najrān, and to Yemen beyond.

The whole of central Arabia has the characteristic desert climate of the area, although the far north tends to be somewhat cooler, especially in winter. In summer, Nejd is extremely hot and arid, while in winter the weather is sometimes bitterly cold, particularly at night. In some years winter and spring and even early summer can be very wet. The possibility of heavy rain makes the provision of plaster-lined water drainways a matter of particular importance in building construction. Given these extremes of climate, the thick mud-brick walls of Nejdi traditional buildings are a necessary and practical means of excluding heat in summer and insulating against cold in winter. The same materials of mud-brick, and more infrequently, stone, are used for traditional houses and mosques alike, with columns made of stones cut to the shape of a drum and placed above one another to form a column shaft which is then plastered. The materials of Nejdi traditional buildings are such that quite frequent renovation and replastering must always have been necessary. However, the ready availability of mud-plaster, palm-wood and tamarisk for roofing meant that this was never a great problem.

Northern Nejd

Mosque of ᶜUmar b. al-Khaṭṭāb, Dūmat al-Jandal, al-Jawf

Mosque of ᶜUmar b. al-Khaṭṭāb and Dūmat al-Jandal, from the Qaṣr Mārid.

An old mosque in Dūmat al-Jandal, in the region of al-Jawf in northern Saudi Arabia, is attributed to the second Caliph, ᶜUmar b. al-Khaṭṭāb (13-23/634-44). The mosque may well have been founded at an early period although much of the present structure appears to be later. The mosque of ᶜUmar is at the foot of the hill on which an ancient fortress stands, the Qaṣr Mārid. Like other old buildings in Dūmat, the mosque is built of stone. It is closely confined by neighbouring buildings and only the *qibla* wall on the southern side is free of encumbrances, forming the side of a street. The mosque enclosure is entered from the *qibla* side through a door near the curious minaret which is, in effect, a free-standing structure built across the street. In 1395/1975 ancient buildings still adjoined the minaret on the western side but these and buildings to the south have since been removed, isolating the minaret in these directions.

Mosque of ᶜUmar b. al-Khaṭṭāb. Minaret in 1402/1982.

Mosque of ᶜUmar b. al-Khaṭṭāb. North facade of the prayer-hall with the ṣaḥn *in the foreground.*

The minaret is a tall, four-sided, tapering tower, culminating in a pyramidic roof, whose well laid masonry may indicate that it was built at an early date. In the base of the minaret is the passage through which the street passes. Its interior is reached by a staircase inside the mosque enclosure which gives access to an internal spiral staircase. In its upper reaches the staircase connecting the five floors of the minaret has collapsed; as a result, the minaret can no longer be ascended.

The rest of the mosque consists of an open courtyard with a level-roofed prayer-hall on the *qibla* side. Occupying the north-eastern side of the courtyard, with access from it, is a low building which serves as a prayer-place: it has a curved *miḥrāb* projection in its *qibla* wall. There is a flight of steps to the roof of this chamber. The main prayer-hall on the opposite side of the *ṣaḥn* has three rows of heavy rectangular stone piers, all running parallel to the *qibla* wall. These carry wooden lintels and the flat wooden roof rests directly on them.

The *miḥrāb* and the *minbar* in the *qibla* wall are of a type found in other mosques in Saudi Arabia. The *miḥrāb* is set in the centre of the wall as a rather roughly shaped recess, which is narrow and sharply pointed. Immediately to the west of the *miḥrāb* is a similar niche with three stone steps in the base to form a fixed *minbar*. When used by the *imām* to deliver the *khutba*, the *miḥrāb* is thus to his right. The *miḥrāb*, the *minbar* and the lower part of the *qibla* wall, are all coated with white plaster; there are remains of white plaster elsewhere in

Mosque of ᶜUmar b. al-Khaṭṭāb. Prayer-hall.

Mosque of ᶜUmar b. al-Khaṭṭāb. Minaret in 1395/1975.

the prayer-hall. On the exterior surface of the *qibla* wall, the *miḥrāb* forms a shallow protrusion. There is also a staircase from the street to the prayer-hall roof, built against the *qibla* wall.

The attribution of the mosque to the Caliph ᶜUmar b. al-Khaṭṭāb was recorded by the first European traveller known to have reached Dūmat al-Jandal, the Finn, Georg Augustus Wallin[1], who visited the town and other parts of north Arabia in 1261/1845. He stated that the mosque had been "repaired by Ibn Sa'ood in the beginning of Wahhabism". There seems no reason at present to dispute Wallin's observation as far as the prayer-hall and the *ṣaḥn* are concerned: both seem to have been rebuilt at some date, and, in view of Wallin's statement, this was presumably carried out after the Saudi expedition to Dūmat al-Jandal in 1208/1793-4[2], when the *imām* was ᶜAbd al-ᶜAzīz b. Muḥammad b. Saᶜūd. The minaret appears to be of a different period and it may go back to a date much nearer to the time of the mosque's foundation.[3] Shaykh Ḥamad al-Jāsir has suggested that the mosque may perhaps be later than the time of ᶜUmar b. al-Khaṭṭāb and that it should be attributed to the Umayyad Caliph, ᶜUmar II b. ᶜAbd al-ᶜAzīz.[4]

1395/1975
10 Dhū'l-Ḥijja 1402/27 September 1982

Mosque of ᶜUmar b. al-Khaṭṭāb. Miḥrāb *and* minbar.

Ḥā'il

Ḥā'il has undergone a great deal of modernisation and the principal antiquities that remain now are the various fortified buildings, the Qaṣr al-Aᶜyirif, Qaṣr al-Muzaᶜba and Qaṣr al-Qishla. The mosques of Ḥā'il have also been rebuilt as part of this modernising process. Thus, as a result of the deterioration of the old mud-brick *jāmiᶜ*, the building was demolished in 1400/1980 and rebuilt anew; at this time, the old *jāmiᶜ* was nearly a century old.[1] This old mosque was photographed by Gertrude Bell in 1331/1913 during her visit to Ḥā'il.[2] Her photograph shows the *sūq* of Ḥā'il and the *jāmiᶜ* of the Al Rashīd: the minaret appears to have been of the circular type that is found further south in al-Qaṣīm, with steeply tapering sides but of no great height. It was surmounted by crenellations. A colonnade with high pillars ran around the exterior of the mosque, forming the *sūq*.

Earlier travellers recorded little of the mosques of Ḥā'il. W.G. Palgrave was in the city in 1279/1862 and made a sketch plan of Ḥā'il in which he shows the "Public Mosque" in a position which corresponds to that of the present *jāmiᶜ*.[3] He spoke briefly of the "great official mosque" of Ṭalāl b. Rashīd, governor in Ḥā'il for the Saudi *imām* of Nejd, Fayṣal b. Turkī:

"When the formulas of prayer are over, about half the congregation rise and depart. Those who remain in the mosque draw together near the centre of the large and simple edifice, and seat themselves on its pebble-strewn floor, circle within circle; some lean their backs against the rough square pillars, I might better call them piers, that support the roof…"[4]

Palgrave's predecessor in Ḥā'il, Wallin, says nothing of the appearance of the mosque, and nor does Guarmani, who reached Ḥā'il two years after Palgrave. However, Guarmani makes it clear that the mosque was close to the place of the *amīr*.[5]

Mosque, Ḥarṭa al-Zubāra, Ḥā'il

At Ḥarṭa al-Zubāra, on the outskirts of Ḥā'il, an old traditional mosque still stands, constructed in mud-brick. It is a sizeable rectangular building, much of its area being the open *ṣaḥn*, and without a minaret. Low walls flank the large courtyard while at the north-east and the south-west (*qibla*) ends are covered *riwāqs* whose level roofs rest on rectangular piers with rectangular capitals. I have not seen rectangular piers further south in Nejd and they seem to be associated with the Ḥā'il area. Palgrave's description of the *jāmiᶜ* of Ḥā'il in 1279/1862 (see above) shows that it too had square piers; the mosque of al-Wāṣit, near Ḥā'il, also has rectangular piers supporting the roof.[1]

The *qibla riwāq* of the mosque of Ḥarṭa al-Zubāra

has two rows of piers supporting the roof, which rests directly on them, without intervening arches. The *riwāq* forming the prayer-hall is open on the side of the *ṣaḥn*. In the *qibla* wall are two entrances, one near the western corner and one immediately east of the *miḥrāb*. The first of these two doors is interesting for it still bears traces of stylised floral decoration of a type once found throughout Nejd. In their design and use of a wooden lock, these doors are also typical of the Nejdi tradition of door construction. However, today it is rare to find a wooden door of the old type still *in situ*, and rarer still to find painted doors. These entrances in the *qibla* wall are

Mosque, Ḥarṭa al-Zubāra. North-west wall.

framed with a paler plaster than that coating the rest of the exterior.

The single *miḥrāb* of the mosque is a massive structure projecting from the centre of the *qibla* wall. It is rectangular in ground-plan but its corners are rounded and it tapers as it rises to the summit of the wall. It is a striking architectural form and unlike the *miḥrābs* further south in Nejd.

The *ṣaḥn* is entered by doors set at the mid-way point in the side walls; these are made of wood, like those in the *qibla* wall. The north side of the *ṣaḥn* is bordered along its full length by a *riwāq* similar to that on the *qibla* side. It is not of uniform construction, however – parts have square piers supporting the roof, and other parts have round columns. The height of the flat roof also varies slightly, suggesting different periods of construction for some stretches of this *riwāq*. Part of the *riwāq* has been walled off from the *ṣaḥn*.

1 Rajab 1403/14 April 1983

*Mosque, Ḥarṭa al-Zubāra. Door in the south-west (*qibla*) wall.*

Mosque, Ḥarta al-Zubāra. Miḥrāb.

al-Qaṣīm

Al-Qaṣīm is an exceptionally fertile area of central Arabia, lying south of Ḥā'il and north of the central areas of Nejd. The great Wādī'l-Rimah, the longest *wādī* in the peninsula, flows through the area. The entire region has a history of commerce and of agriculture and in recent times the towns and the farms of al-Qaṣīm have increased greatly in size. The importance of its principal towns in the economy of Arabia in the past is reflected in the very fine mud-brick architecture, of which some traces still remain in Burayda and ᶜUnayza; this is also indicated in the fine mosques which were built in these two towns during the past century or so.

Jāmiᶜ, ᶜUnayza

The *jāmiᶜ* of ᶜUnayza is the largest among the mosques in traditional style in the town. It is a particularly impressive monument and its minaret, one of the most striking in Nejd, is the tallest in ᶜUnayza. A very much earlier mosque on the site is associated with Zuhrī' b. Jarrāh al-Thawrī who established the settlement of ᶜUnayza about 630/1232-3.(1) The present *jāmiᶜ* is later, perhaps going back about a century; the minaret is dated to 1309/1891-2.

The *jāmiᶜ* stands on the western side of the central town area of ᶜUnayza and, until recently, the neighbourhood had many fine old houses built in mud-brick. The *jāmiᶜ* is covered overall with mud-plaster which has fallen away in places, exposing underlying stonework. Although concealed under the mud-plaster surface, much of the building is presumably built of mud-brick.

The mosque is rectangular with the main entrance on the south-east side, from the direction of the town square. The great double doors which I photographed in 1395/1975 were subsequently replaced by modern ones. The original entrance seems to have been of a design unique among the mosques of Saudi Arabia. The entrance as a whole was rectangular and unusually broad, closed by double doors. Nevertheless, the individual door-leaves were of a proportion standard in Nejd; it was only the manner in which they were arranged in this entrance that made them unusual. Each door-leaf was very substantial: three heavy beams ran across the face of each, held in place by great iron nails. The panels formed between the cross-pieces were decorated with X-shapes painted on the plain background of the wood. The entire entrance was approached by steps and the doors were flanked by pilasters on square capitals. These pilasters served to support the ornamental lintels over the doors, on which a pierced cresting ran across the width of the entrance.(2) Sloping upwards above this entrance is the side of a staircase to the roof which is constructed inside the mosque. This staircase impinges somewhat on the decoration of the doorway.

The interior of the mosque is divided between a *qibla riwāq* on the western side and another *riwāq* to the east, separated by an open but relatively narrow *ṣaḥn*. The south entrance of the mosque gives directly on to the *ṣaḥn*. The pointed arcades of the *riwāqs* rest on large columns and support the level roof. Although the *ṣaḥn* is very narrow, the arrangement of the interior recalls the *jāmiᶜ* of al-Riyadh of the time of Imām Turkī b. ᶜAbd Allah, and the now rebuilt *jāmiᶜ* of Jalājil.

In the centre of the *qibla* wall, the *miḥrāb* forms a

curved projection which rises to the top of the wall without tapering in any way. In this wall are also a number of rectangular windows which serve to illuminate the interior. There are similar windows in the side wall of the mosque.

The tapering minaret at the south-east corner of the *jāmiᶜ* is exceptionally high, with a broad base to provide adequate support. Structurally, it is entirely freestanding and built so that its curved base extends beyond the line of the mosque walls,to infringe on the pavement. In the south side of the minaret is an entrance from the street, which is preceded by a short flight of steps; the entrance has a wooden door. The sharply tapering shaft of the minaret recalls those elsewhere in al-Qaṣīm and ᶜUnayza: it is subdivided into segments, so that each segment projects with a slight ridge from its predecessor below. Internally, this minaret is apparently associated with the staircase from the *ṣaḥn* which is situated over the main mosque doorway.

1395/1975
1 Ṣafar 1403/18 November 1982

Postscript
On my last visit to ᶜUnayza, the mosque was being rebuilt. The minaret remained intact.

26 Rabīᶜa II 1405/17 January 1985

Jāmiᶜ, *ᶜUnayza. South-east side and minaret in 1395/1975.*

Jāmiᶜ, *ᶜUnayza. South-east entrance and minaret base in 1395/1975.*

Jāmi^c, ^cUnayza. Entrance in south-east wall in 1395/1975.

Small mosque, ^cUnayza

A small mosque in the southern part of the palm plantations that border ^cUnayza still survives (1404/1984) intact. It is an interesting building in mud-brick and stone. The minaret and the enclosure walls are built virtually as one. The circular minaret stands in the east corner of the mosque, running without interruption or transition out of the north-east wall. At the base of the minaret, approached by a low flight of steps, is a wooden door painted with geometric motifs in the local ^cUnayza style. The minaret tapers to a crenellation of stepped merlons, picked out in plaster. By contrast with the minaret, the flat-roofed prayer-hall with its high windows is without significant decoration.

1394/1974
1 Ṣafar 1403/18 November 1982

Small mosque, ^cUnayza.

al-Mushayqaḥ mosque, Burayda

The Mushayqaḥ mosque[1] lies on the north-western side of a broad open area of ground and was founded by ᶜIsā al-ᶜAbd al-Karīm Al ᶜIsā in 1317/1899-1900. The mosque was restored in 1353/1934-5 by ᶜAbd al-ᶜAzīz b. Ḥamūd al-Mushayqaḥ[2] and is a fine example of the principal type of traditional mosque in Burayda. It is still in a good state of preservation, with only limited additions of recent date.

The mosque is constructed of roughly cut stone in the lower courses of its walls, but plastering of mud on the upper surfaces obscures the building material. A hard, water-proof plaster is used to line the water runnels cut into the walls of the mosque in order to cope with the winter and spring rains that can be surprisingly heavy. The mosque is freestanding on all sides except the north-west where it abuts a modern building. The *qibla* wall is oriented toward the south-west, the direction of Makkah al-Mukarramah.

The mosque is a large rectangular building, comprising a simple prayer-hall with a flat roof on the *qibla* side of the enclosure and a rectangular *ṣaḥn* surrounded by fairly high walls on the north-east side. There are two doorways to the mosque, both in the north-east wall of the enclosure and giving access directly to the *ṣaḥn*. The doors are set at either extremity of this wall, and are simple rectangles whose frames rise above the line of the summit of the enclosure wall. Both doorways are outlined with white plaster. The entrance on the right-hand side is used to enter the mosque and that to the left is used to leave.

The *ṣaḥn* has a sandy floor like other mosques in Burayda, while raised ridges run across the floor parallel to the *qibla* wall, in the manner seen in other mosques of Burayda and in Nejd as a whole. There are wooden posts in the *ṣaḥn* to support coverings for protection from the sun for those praying there. In the *ṣaḥn*, rising from the east corner, is a circular minaret with a broad base and a tapering shaft.[3] The minaret is entered from within the *ṣaḥn* and effectively constitutes a free-standing structure within the overall ground-plan. The minaret wall surface is articulated by two bands of slightly raised, inverted V-shapes in low relief, in a style common throughout Nejd. At the summit of the minaret is a plaster-coated decoration of stepped crenellations. The interior of the minaret is illuminated by small triangular openings.

On the north-west side of the *ṣaḥn* a staircase leads to the roof of the prayer-hall, with access through a rectangular doorway from the *ṣaḥn*. The prayer-hall is on a raised platform like the Ḥuwayza mosque (page 126), for it rests on an underground *khalwa*, an enclosed place for prayer which is common in Nejd and is found in particular in the mosques of Burayda. The upper prayer-hall built on this *khalwa* has been closed off in recent times by the insertion of screening walls. There is a new entrance and air-conditioners. The original upper prayer-hall was rather similar to that of the Ḥuwayza mosque, with a row of simple columns surmounted by plain capitals which bore the roof, without the intervention of arches. Above the colonnades is a high balustrade

al-Mushayqaḥ mosque, Burayda. Minaret in the corner of ṣaḥn.

al-Mushayqaḥ mosque, Burayda. North-east wall and minaret.

running around the roof of the prayer-hall. The *miḥrāb* in the centre of the *qibla* wall forms a tapering curved projection to the full height of the *qibla* wall.

1 Ṣafar 1403/18 November 1982

al-Mushayqaḥ mosque. North-east facade of the prayer-hall and the ṣaḥn.

al-Ḥuwayza mosque, Burayda

The Ḥuwayza mosque is one of the older mosques of Burayda, its foundation being dated to 1335/1916-17.(1) It was built by Fahad al-ᶜAlī al-Rashūdī and does not appear to have undergone much alteration since it was founded. As with other mosques in Burayda, the principal building material of the mosque is mud-brick, although plaster on the walls conceals the degree to which parts of the building might be of stone.

The mosque is of considerable size, with high walls around the *ṣaḥn*. It is entered through simple rectangular doorways on the north-west and north-east sides, the latter opposite the *qibla* wall. The south-east side of the mosque has been disturbed by the construction of a stretch of wall in concrete blocks. The open *ṣaḥn* of the Ḥuwayza mosque is a sandy rectangular space of the type that is customary in Burayda. Concrete blocks run across

al-Ḥuwayza mosque. Ṣaḥn.

the *ṣaḥn* parallel to the *qibla* wall, forming lines between those standing in prayer; there is also a curved *miḥrāb* niche, formed from concrete blocks, in the *ṣaḥn*. Wooden poles serve to support coverings for shade in the courtyard.

The most striking feature of the mosque is the design of the flat-roofed prayer-hall on the south-west side, towards the *qibla*. It is approached by two flights of steps and stands on a raised platform above the level of the *ṣaḥn*: the flights of steps are set at either end of the prayer-hall facade. The platform effect is created by the fact that beneath it is an underground prayer-hall, or *khalwa*. On the platform immediately beyond the south-eastern staircase to the principal prayer-hall, the *riwāq al-qiblī*, is a second staircase, leading to the roof of the *qibla riwāq*. The construction of this staircase is inferior to that of the rest of the mosque, and may indicate reconstruction.

al-Ḥuwayza mosque, Burayda. Prayer-hall.

The principal prayer-hall is a very imposing structure, with five rows of lofty columns supporting the flat roof. The wooden roof rests directly on the square capitals of the columns, without any intervening arches, a feature common in the mosques of Burayda and also seen at Zilfī to the south-east. The rafters of the roof are composed of groups of wooden beams and run from column to column, parallel to the *qibla* wall. In this respect the mosque accords with a general tendency in Nejdi mosques for arcades and colonnades to run parallel to the *qibla*. This tradition is found in very early Islamic times in mosque architecture. The effect of the high columns is particularly impressive with the lower part of the shafts coloured grey and the upper part covered with a pale ochre plaster which is also used for the whole prayer-hall interior.

The interior of the prayer-hall is all the more striking because of its contrast with the plain mosque facade: this is surmounted only by an undecorated balustrade, part of the parapet around the prayer-hall roof, broken by wooden spouts that cast rainwater away from the building into the courtyard.

The columns of the prayer-hall have numerous small shelves which serve as places to rest copies of the Holy Qur'ān. In the centre of the *qibla* wall is a simple *miḥrāb* niche with a curved recess, whose exterior design is concealed by a recent concrete construction against the wall.

The minaret of the Ḥuwayza mosque is a square structure set at the north-west corner of the prayer-hall, with a staircase leading to it from the *ṣaḥn* and reaching the prayer-hall roof. This minaret is built against the interior surface of the north-west wall of the *ṣaḥn* and stands over its doorway, which is set in this stretch of the enclosure wall.

The early Islamic origin of the colonnades parallel to the *qibla* wall that are found in the Ḥuwayza mosque has already been mentioned. Another early feature of the mosque, and of others in Burayda, is the level roof which rests directly on the columns of the prayer-hall.[(2)] This system of building is of great antiquity in Islam: the Mosque of the Prophet (S) at al-Madina al-Monawarah had a similar system in its original form, with a level roof resting on wooden columns. The *jāmiʿ* of Kufa in Iraq[(3)], rebuilt in 50/670 by the Umayyad governor, Ziyād, was renowned for the great height of its columns, on which the flat roof of the *qibla riwāq* rested directly. Interestingly, there were five rows of columns in this mosque on the *qibla* side, as there are in the Ḥuwayza mosque. These form five aisles, or *balāṭ*, parallel to the *qibla* wall. The same design was used in the *jāmiᶜ* of the famous Round City of Baghdad, founded in 149/766 by the ᶜAbbāsid Caliph al-Manṣūr, with a level roof once again resting directly on columns of wood.[4] This tradition of construction is one of great antiquity, and it may be that the system survives in various parts of Arabia, including Burayda; certainly the high columns of the Ḥuwayza mosque seem to echo the description of the 1st/7th-century *jāmiᶜ* of Kūfa.

1 Ṣafar 1403/18 November 1982

al-ᶜAyīrī mosque, Burayda

The ᶜAyīrī Mosque in Burayda is a further example of the traditional mud-brick mosques of Burayda. Its foundation is dated to Shawwāl 1360/October-November 1941 and is named after Aḥmad b. ᶜAlī al-ᶜAyīrī.[1] The mosque follows the usual rectangular ground-plan although it is smaller than some of the other mosques of Burayda. It stands in an area of the city which is notable for its distinguished traditional buildings, and these surround the mosque on all sides. The low walled *ṣaḥn* is on the north-east side of the enclosure and is entered via three simple entrances from the street that runs along this side of the mosque. In the east corner of the open *ṣaḥn* is a broad-based, circular minaret, whose shaft tapers emphatically to a narrow summit. The minaret intrudes slightly on to the street outside the mosque. It is entered from within the *ṣaḥn* by two doorways in the face of the tower. This minaret is the only part of the mosque to carry decoration: it is ornamented by three bands of V-mouldings in relief and surmounted at the summit by a row of plastered crenellations. I was told in Burayda that this minaret is the oldest part of the mosque.

The prayer-hall with its level roof occupies the south-western side of the mosque. It has a staircase to the roof set at the south end of the facade leading from the *ṣaḥn*. The *qibla* wall is somewhat unusual for the treatment of the *miḥrāb* which is marked on the exterior as a rectangular projection in the upper part to serve those praying on the roof of the mosque. The *qibla* wall has a number of large rectangular windows distributed on either side of the *miḥrāb*. These are framed with a hard ochre plaster.

1 Ṣafar 1403/ 18 November 1982

al-ᶜAyīrī mosque, Burayda, from the west, with the prayer-hall roof in the foreground.

al-ᶜAyīrī mosque. Minaret.

al-Māḍī mosque, Burayda

The Māḍī mosque in Burayda was pointed out to me as having one of the oldest minarets in the city, although the rest of the building, it seems, has been reconstructed. The minaret was said to go back about a century, but I could not ascertain a date for other parts of the mosque, which resembles the Ḥuwayza and the Mushayqaḥ mosques. The foundation of the mosque is attributed to Māḍī al-Māḍī.(1)

The Māḍī mosque is built of the same materials as other mosques in Burayda – unfired brick, and stone with mud-plaster coating the surfaces. The building is a very large rectangle with an open *ṣaḥn* on the north-east side which is sand-covered like others in Burayda. There are entrances to the courtyard through each of the lateral walls. In the north corner of the *ṣaḥn* is the minaret, with a broad circular base. It is entered through a small rectangular doorway at some height from the ground via a small staircase from the *ṣaḥn* floor. The tapering shaft of the minaret is decorated with five bands of raised, inverted V-motifs, two pairs of which are situated in the lower and middle reaches of the tower with another band near the summit. There are crenellations on the summit of the minaret, coated with white plaster, a custom found in many parts of the region.

On the south-west side of the *ṣaḥn* is the prayer-hall which is now entirely closed off as a result of the insertion of screening walls between the columns of the prayer-hall facade. In these added walls air-conditioners have been inserted to cool the interior. Before it was

al-Māḍī mosque, Burayda. Minaret, south-west side.

screened off, the prayer-hall must have been similar to that of the Ḥuwayza mosque, with rows of high columns bearing simple capitals and supporting the level roof. Like the Ḥuwayza mosque and other mosques in Burayda, the Māḍī mosque has a *khalwa*. A staircase from the *ṣaḥn* leads to the roof of the prayer-hall on the south-east side of the enclosure and this roof is surrounded on all sides by a low parapet. The *miḥrāb* is a curved projection on the exterior surface of the *qibla* wall, rising to its full height so that there is a *miḥrāb* recess on the roof for those praying there.

1 Ṣafar 1403/18 November 1982

al-Māḍī mosque. North-east facade of the prayer-hall with the ṣaḥn *in the foreground.*

Western Nejd

al-Batrā' and al-Rawḍa

These two small towns are situated in the more westerly part of Nejd, beyond al-Rass, in al-Qaṣīm. They have *jāmiᶜs* in traditional Nejdi style, of a design which is so close in many respects that they are described together. Both are built of mud-brick and are plastered over with mud. Their appearance suggests that neither mosque is particularly old. They are both well maintained and typify a mosque style which was once widespread. Of the two, that at al-Rawḍa has a stone foundation visible at the foot of the wall, but this does not appear in the mosque at al-Batrā', although it probably exists under the mud-plaster.

Both mosques are sizeable structures with particularly deep open courtyards on the north-east side and correspondingly large prayer-halls. Access to the mosques is through simple rectangular doorways into the *ṣaḥn*, while in the mosque at al-Batrā' there are entrances in the sides of the prayer-hall as well. The size of the prayer-hall in each case means that a number of colonnades are required to support the roof. At al-Batrā', plain columns with simple capitals support the level roof directly, without intervening arches. The design used is the same as that employed further north-east in Burayda. In consequence of the size of the prayer-hall at al-Rawḍa, there are five lateral windows in the walls of the mosque to illuminate the interior of the covered part of the building. In both mosques the *miḥrāb* is a large curved projection in the centre of the exterior surface of the *qibla* wall.

The minarets of the two mosques adhere to the same design, differing only in their positions: that at al-Batrā' is situated on the north-west side against the *ṣaḥn* wall, while at al-Rawḍa the minaret is set on the south-east side of the courtyard, once again against the *ṣaḥn* wall. The design of a high, slightly tapering rectangular tower is one found in central Nejd but far more rarely in al-Qaṣīm to the east. The minarets are approached by staircases from the *ṣaḥn* which pass through the body of each. Above the passage stands the upper part of the tower proper, entered by means of a diminutive exterior staircase from the prayer-hall roof, which runs spiral-fashion around the exterior of the tower to give access to its summit. Both minarets are ennobled by a crenellation of stepped merlons which have been accentuated by white plaster.

7 Rabīᶜa I 1403/23 December 1982

Mosque, al-Batrā'.

Mosque, al-Rawḍa.

Uqlat al-Ṣuqūr

Uqlat al-Ṣuqūr is a small town on the road from al-Qaṣīm to al-Madina al-Monawarah. On the north side of the road through the town is a mosque which is probably of recent construction, for the exposed parts of the fabric are concrete blocks. Much of the mosque is covered with white plaster which effectively conceals the building material, although it is likely that it is in fact entirely concrete. The interest of the mosque lies not in its antiquity but in the manner in which modern building materials have been used to produce a mosque close in design to traditional architectural forms.

The prayer-hall is simple in the extreme, a shallow rectangle preceded by a *ṣaḥn* to the north-east and a central curved *miḥrāb* projection in the *qibla* wall. The main distinguishing feature of the building is the rectangular minaret built against the exterior surface of the north-west wall of the prayer-hall. Access to the minaret is by means of a staircase in the *ṣaḥn*, running along its north-west side, while a second staircase, quite narrow, leads from the roof of the mosque to the summit of the minaret. The minaret is terminated by a crenellated balustrade.

7 Rabīᶜa I 1403/23 December 1982

Mosque, Uqlat al-Ṣuqūr.

Shaqrān

Shaqrān is a small settlement on the road from al-Qaṣīm to al-Madina al-Monawarah, near the town of al-Ḥanākiyya. The mosque is of quite recent construction and there is a second mosque under construction nearby. Although the building material has been obscured by a covering of white plaster, it is probably concrete like the mosque currently being built. The mosque illustrated consists of a simple walled *ṣaḥn* to the north-east, and a prayer-hall to the south-west, towards the *qibla*. There are only two entrances to the mosque: one in the centre of the north-east wall to the *ṣaḥn*, opposite the *miḥrāb*, and a second on the north-west side also leading into the *ṣaḥn*. There are three doorways, set symmetrically, from the *ṣaḥn* into the prayer-hall, the central doorway being on line with the *miḥrāb* in the prayer-hall. A single slender square minaret is set at the north corner of the prayer-hall, culminating above in an elongated dome-like structure. It cannot be ascended and has no staircase. Its role, in effect, is purely symbolic and it is one of several such minarets in this area, all of which are of fairly recent date, it seems. The *miḥrāb* of the mosque is a curved projection in the centre of the *qibla* wall, terminating in a half-dome a little below the summit of the *qibla* wall. Two rectangular windows on either side of the *miḥrāb* illuminate the interior from this direction. The mosque can be compared with the southern mosque at Thamad, between al-Madina al-Monawarah and Khaybar.

21 Ṣafar 1403/8 December 1982

Mosque, Shaqrān.

Central Nejd

al-Jāsir mosque, Zilfī

Zilfī lies north of the district of Sudayr and is the last town before the road crosses the high sand dunes that precede al-Qaṣīm to the north-west. It is now largely rebuilt as a modern town but nevertheless there are still some mosques in traditional style in the old quarters.

The Jāsir mosque is a large building with a very big courtyard on the north-eastern side and a shallow prayer-hall with a level roof on the south-western (*qibla*) side. There is an entrance in the south-east side of the mosque enclosure leading directly to the *ṣaḥn*.

al-Jāsir mosque, Zilfī. Minaret and the north-east wall of the ṣaḥn

This entrance has a simple wooden door and is situated very close to the east corner. The door is interesting inasmuch as it has a wooden lock of a type once found throughout central Arabia.

In the north corner of the courtyard is a somewhat stumpy circular minaret on a high tapering square socle, entered from the south-east side. Above this socle the minaret shaft also tapers, in the style of the minarets of Sudayr and al-Qaṣīm. Also like other minarets of this style, the shaft of the minaret is divided into segments that indicate the phases of its construction. Each segment is marked by one or two slightly raised ridges running around the circumference, one just over half-way up, and another immediately beneath the summit. The summit of the minaret is given a turret-like aspect by the addition of decorative merlons, once plastered white.

The prayer-hall on the south-west side of the *ṣaḥn* recalls those of Burayda: it has a flat roof supported by high columns without arches, a system found in several mosques there. The spaces between the columns have been closed off by concrete walls, but it is quite clear that they were originally open. On the north-west side of the *ṣaḥn* is a broad staircase to the roof of the prayer-hall. Unfortunately, the *miḥrāb* is concealed by neighbouring buildings.

1 Ṣafar 1403/18 November 1982

ᶜAlawiyya mosque, Zilfī

Although the dominant type of minaret in Zilfī and the rest of Sudayr and al-Qaṣīm is circular, nevertheless the square minaret is found in the ᶜAlawiyya mosque. This is a rather fine building in the older part of Zilfī, built of mud-brick and coated with mud-plaster. It is a rectangular structure with a *ṣaḥn* on the north-east side, entered by a doorway at the northern extremity of the north-east wall. The flat-roofed prayer-hall on the south-west (*qibla*) side is an interesting structure inasmuch as the facade proper is preceded by a colonnade of ten arches resting on columns and running parallel to the *qibla* wall. I am unfamiliar with any similar system elsewhere in the area, of such a portico built in front of the mosque facade.

Running up the north-west side wall of the *ṣaḥn* on the inner face, is a staircase to the roof, over the head of which is set a rectangular minaret with a passage through, allowing access to the prayer-hall roof. This in turn leads to a small staircase to the upper part of the tower. This type of minaret is common further south in the neighbourhood of Riyadh, although it is also found in Burayda, in al-Qaṣīm, where it is regarded as a more recent introduction.

1 Ṣafar 1403/18 November 1982

ᶜAlawiyya mosque, Zilfī, from the north-east.

Jāmiᶜ, Majmaᶜa

Majmaᶜa is a large town in the northern part of the Sudayr district and is of some considerable antiquity. The town was already prominent before the rise of the first Saudi state. When Shaykh Muḥammad b. ᶜAbd al-Wahhāb went to al-Madina al-Monawarah some time before 1135/1723, he met there a *qāḍī* from Majmaᶜa, Shaykh ᶜAbd

Allah b. Ibrāhīm b. Sayf Al Sayf of the then ruling family of Majma^ca. Shaykh ^cAbd Allah was gathering together a large collection of books in al-Madina al-Monawarah which he planned to send back to Majma^ca as a gift to his fellow citizens.

By 1395/1975 Majma^ca had already undergone modernisation, a process which has continued since, but within the town there still survived a large *jāmi^c* built in the local traditional style in mud-brick. It stood next to a *sūq* which itself was of a type once common in the towns and villages of central Arabia, with a series of small booths set up behind a covered arcade of keel-arches, surrounding a small square and protecting shoppers from the sun. The keel-arches of the *sūq* were identical to those of the neighbouring *jāmi^c*. The proximity of *sūq* and mosque is a characteristic local arrangement, parallels for which occur elsewhere in Arabia as well as in the wider Islamic world.

The *jāmi^c* had an enclosure wall with an entrance in its longer eastern side, and a long shallow courtyard with the prayer-hall built along the western (*qibla*) side. There was a further entrance to the mosque in the *qibla* wall for the *imām* to enter, a feature which is common in Nejd and is of great antiquity in the Islamic world as a whole. The flat roof of the prayer-hall rested on six arcades on columns, all running parallel to the *qibla*. In contrast to the mud-floor of the courtyard, the prayer-hall of the mosque was paved. Running across the central area of the mosque floor, between the column bases and parallel to the *qibla* wall, was a series of low ridges, serving as back rests. There was no use of white plaster to enliven the interior of the mosque, but the lower parts of the columns were coloured grey. Small ledges projected from the columns and served as shelves for the Holy Qur'ān.

Jāmi^c, *Majma^ca, in 1975, with the arcades of the* sūq *in the foreground.*

Jāmi^c, *Majma^ca.* Ṣaḥn *and east facade of the prayer-hall.*

In the south-east corner of the mosque courtyard stood a minaret with a circular base which extended beyond the confines of the mosque into the street. Its sides tapered steeply so that the diameter of the minaret contracted markedly at the summit. The minaret was subdivided horizontally by four bands, each decorated with V-shaped motifs in slightly raised relief, one of the most common decorative forms in central Arabian architecture. Each ring appeared to mark the successive addition of the segments that constitute the minaret shaft. The entrance to the minaret was set high in the side and was approached by a staircase from the *ṣaḥn*, although a doorway was built half-way up the staircase to restrict access to the minaret. The staircase ascended beyond the minaret entrance to reach the roof of the prayer-hall to the west. Freestanding circular minarets of this type are common in Sudayr, but the relationship of the minarets to the overall plan of the mosque varies.

1394/1974
11 Muḥarram 1403/28 October 1982

Jāmiᶜ, *Majmaᶜa. The minaret from the south-east.*

Jalājil

Jalājil is situated in the district of Sudayr, and, like the rest of the villages in the area, it is an agricultural settlement. Today a modern town has been built to the west of the old town and the latter is still preserved in excellent condition, although no longer inhabited. As a consequence of this concern to preserve the older buildings, Jalājil constitutes a particularly valuable record of the local architectural tradition. The settlement is clearly ancient and was the home town of the famous historian of Nejd, ᶜUthmān b. Bishr, who indicates the local prominence already achieved by Jalājil before the rise of the first Saudi state; the town continued to play a quite prominent role in the subsequent history of Nejd.

The old *jāmiᶜ* of Jalājil has recently been replaced. A new *jāmiᶜ* occupies the same site as the old *jāmiᶜ* which I had photographed in 1394/1974 on the east side of the town square, opposite an old *qaṣr*. The old *jāmiᶜ* was built of mud-brick and was plastered with mud on the exterior. The high enclosure walls of the *ṣaḥn* and the prayer-hall were slightly banked in a manner rather unusual for the area generally. In the course of my brief visit in 1394/1974, I examined the entrance on the north side giving on to the *ṣaḥn*. It is likely that there were further entrances in the east and the south walls leading to the *ṣaḥn*. Within the rectangular mosque enclosure there were arcades to the east of the *ṣaḥn* and similar arcades forming a deeper prayer-hall on the western (*qibla*) side. All of these arcades had keel-arches and ran parallel to the *qibla* wall of the mosque. There is a similarity in the arrangement of these arcades on either side of the *ṣaḥn* with the organisation of both the old *jāmiᶜ* of Ḥuraymilā' and the old *jāmiᶜ* of Imām Turkī in Riyadh.

A most striking feature of the old *jāmiᶜ* at Jalājil was the minaret, built at the north-east corner of the prayer-hall at the point at which the *ṣaḥn* met the prayer-hall facade. The base of the minaret was circular in plan and projected into the street somewhat. In its position within the mosque as a whole, the minaret recalls that of the old *jāmiᶜ* of Ḥuraymilā', although the shapes differ overall. The minaret at Jalājil was a curiously flimsy-looking structure, a series of elongated segments each overlapping slightly the one beneath and together forming a tapering shaft. Although this minaret was related to others in Sudayr and in al-Qaṣīm to the north-west, its particular form was nonetheless unusual. So too was the *miḥrāb*, which formed a three-faceted projection set in the centre of the *qibla* wall, quite unlike the usual curved *miḥrāb* which is found throughout the district.

1394/1974
11 Muḥarram 1403/28 October 1982

New jāmiᶜ, *Jalājil.*

Old jāmiᶜ, *Jalājil, in 1394/1974.* Qibla *wall from the exterior.*

Two small mosques, Jalājil

Western mosque, Jalājil. View of ṣaḥn *and qibla* riwāqs.

On the western side of the old village of Jalājil is a mosque lacking a minaret and rather unusual in the shallowness of its *ṣaḥn* in relation to the prayer-hall. The *ṣaḥn*, entered by a single rectangular doorway in the centre of the east wall, is a very shallow open space defined by a wall of varying height, built like the rest of the building in mud-brick. By contrast with the shallow *ṣaḥn*, the rectangular prayer-hall on the west side is an extremely deep, flat-roofed structure and unusual in its proportions and the height of its walls. The prayer-hall is open only on the east side, where it has a facade of five keel-arches resting on columns; these are surmounted by a high wall. This facade is relieved from complete plainness in its upper part by a raised horizontal ridge running immediately above the crowns of the arches. In the sides of the mosque are larger rectangular windows, closed by wooden shutters. Deep plastered grooves cut vertically in the mud walls provide channels to carry off rainwater from the roof.

Another mosque in Jalājil has a high enclosure wall around the building, although it is lower on the east side. Within the *ṣaḥn* on the east side, there is a staircase to the

Small mosque, Jalājil. Prayer-hall from the south.

roof of the prayer-hall: this staircase is built against the inner face of the south wall of the enclosure. In the south side of the prayer-hall an entrance and lateral windows illuminate the mosque interior. The most striking feature of the mosque is the bulky, tapering *miḥrāb* in the centre of the *qibla* wall, which forms a curved projection terminating a short distance below the summit of the wall. An entirely independent *miḥrāb* in the form of a curved salient serves those praying on the roof of the prayer-hall, recalling the arrangement in the old *jāmiʿ* in Ḥuraymilā', further south.

11 Muḥarram 1403/28 October 1982

Small mosque, Jalājil. Miḥrāb.

A small mosque, Jalājil

In the old area of Jalājil I was shown a small mosque, apparently no longer in use. It is built amidst a group of houses and, like other buildings in Jalājil, the mosque is constructed of stone and mud-brick with wall-surfaces smoothed with plaster. The entrance to the mosque, most unusually, is in the *qibla* wall, to the west, and is closed by a simple wooden door, leading to a covered passage. At the eastern end, this passage reaches the rectangular *ṣaḥn* on the east side of the prayer-hall; the *ṣaḥn* is delimited on its eastern side by a *khalwa* chamber. On the right-hand side of the passage giving access to the mosque (i.e. the south) there is a double water basin made of stone with a drain plug. This receptacle is one of several that I saw in Jalājil, all made of stone. When filled with water, removal of the drain plug allows the water to flow out so that ablutions can be performed in running water.

The prayer-hall on the west side of the *ṣaḥn* has two arcades running parallel to the *qibla* wall to support the flat roof. The keel-arches of the colonnades rest on plastered pillars with rests for the Holy Qur'ān projecting from them. The columns have been whitened and contrast with the plain mud-plaster of the arches and their spandrels. The substantial back-rests for those sitting in the mosque, which are fixed to the floor

Disused mosque, Jalājil. Water tank for ablutions.

Disused mosque, Jalājil. Qibla riwāqs.

Disused mosque, Jalājil. Miḥrāb *in the* khalwa.

Disused mosque, Jalājil. Qibla riwāq.

parallel to the *qibla*, are also coated with white plaster. The *miḥrāb* in the centre of the *qibla* wall is a curved recess with a keel-arch that is stressed by a white painted frame around it.

The low *khalwa* prayer-hall on the east side of the *ṣaḥn* has a doorway in the southern end of its *qibla* wall. At the north end there is a staircase to the flat roof of the *khalwa*. There is also a lower, curved *miḥrāb* projection serving the enclosed *khalwa* in the centre of the chamber's *qibla* wall, and a second *miḥrāb* above it for those praying on its roof.

11 Muḥarram 1403/28 October 1982

*Jāmi*ᶜ*, al-Rawḍa*

Al-Rawḍa (not to be confused with the town of the same name further to the west, see page 130) is one of several towns in the agricultural district of Sudayr whose houses and mosques in traditional mud-brick, stone and plaster remain largely intact; even though modern houses have been built nearby it is still possible to gain an idea of the past character of the area from the defensive watch-towers, the walled farms and gardens, and the older houses that survive.

The *jāmi*ᶜ of al-Rawḍa stands in the centre of the old town and consists of a *ṣaḥn* surrounded by a low-walled courtyard entered through a door in the south-east corner. The prayer-hall has two rows of keel-arches parallel to the *qibla* wall which serve to carry a level roof. The facade of this prayer-hall is distinctive with a band of small, dentil-like rectangles in low relief running across the full width of the building and set within a band somewhat recessed from the surface of the rest of the wall. The rectangles are the projecting ends of the roof beams. Similar articulation was formerly found in the *jāmi*ᶜ of the neighbouring village of al-ᶜAwda but, within central Arabia as a whole, the motif appears to be rare. Above the relief is a balustrade from which wooden piping projects a little to drain off rainfall from the mosque roof. The roof of the prayer-hall is reached by a staircase on the north side of the *ṣaḥn*, while a freestanding minaret is situated in the north-east corner of the courtyard, on the opposite side from the prayer-hall.

Jāmiᶜ, *al-Rawḍa,* Qibla *wall.*

The *miḥrāb* is marked on the exterior of the mosque as a curved projection that tapers very slightly and runs the full height of the *qibla* wall. Two shallow grooves subdivide it horizontally, the upper marking the level of the prayer-hall roof. The *miḥrāb* is of a type found throughout the locality and further south towards the Riyadh area, as well as north-west into al-Qaṣīm.

The freestanding minaret in the courtyard is in the local style with a circular base and steeply tapering walls. It is subdivided into segments horizontally, with each segment tapering and narrowing slightly at its summit in comparison with the base of the segment that succeeds it. This overlapping effect may well reflect the construction technique of the minarets of the region, so that each segment was completed and left to dry out before the succeeding segment was added, tapering as it ascended, to ensure the stability of the tower as a whole. Several of the overlapping ridges that subdivide the body of the minaret are further accentuated by inverted V-shaped mouldings in relief. The staircase in the *ṣaḥn* divides, turning east to serve the minaret and west to reach the

Jāmiᶜ, *al-Rawḍa. Minaret in the* ṣaḥn, *from the south.*

roof of the prayer-hall. The construction of minarets of this type in the district of Sudayr is particularly graceful, and they are clearly related to the minarets of al-Qaṣīm and Ḥā'il. The Sudayr style of minaret tends to be narrower than those further north-west and westwards and that at al-Rawḍa is notably elegant in its lines and proportions.

1394/1974

Jāmi^c, al-^{c}Awda

Al-^{c}Awda is the southernmost village in Sudayr, and the *jāmi^c* in its central square was very closely related to the old *jāmi^{c}s* of the neighbouring towns, especially that of nearby al-Rawḍa. By 1403/1982, the old mosque of al-^{c}Awda had been rebuilt in modern style.

The original *jāmi^c* of al-^{c}Awda, like the rest of the buildings in the old town, was built of unfired mud-brick resting on stone foundations, with mud-plaster smoothing the wall surfaces. Walls of varying height surrounded the courtyard, while the prayer-hall

Jāmi^c, *al-^{c}Awda (1403/1982).*

Jāmi^c, *al-^{c}Awda. Minaret at the north-east corner (1394/1974).*

roof, which was level, rested on arcades with keel-arches running parallel to the west (*qibla*) wall. The facade of the prayer-hall had the same dentil-motif in shallow relief that ran across the facade of the *jāmi^c* at al-Rawḍa.

In the north-east corner of the *ṣaḥn* of the al-^{c}Awda *jāmi^c* was a freestanding, round minaret whose tall body tapered and whose base projected into the street, due both to its diameter and to the difficulty of accommodating such minaret forms in rectangular courtyard systems. The minaret was subdivided horizontally into eight segments, with the transition between the segments marked by slight ridges decorated with inverted V-shaped mouldings in relief, a common feature in the mud-built structures of Nejd. The form, style and quality of construction of the minaret and the mosque as a whole was so close to that of the *jāmi^c* in nearby al-Rawḍa as to make it extremely likely that both mosques were the work of the same architect.

1395/1974
2 Ṣafar 1403/19 November 1982

Malham

Malham lies north-west of Riyadh in the district of al-ᶜĀriḍ, situated in an ancient agricultural area. There seems to have been a settlement in this neighbourhood at least as early as the 6th/12th century, for Yāqūt al-Ḥamawī refers to a Malham in the region of al-Yamāma. In 1394/1974, the old village and farms of Malham had been largely abandoned, with scattered residences of the settlement strung out along the floor of the Wādī Ḥuraymilā' valley. A mosque lay on the southern side of the settlement: it was a simple mud-brick structure plastered externally with mud, although finer white plaster was used to decorate the interior. The building was rectangular with a courtyard surrounded by a low wall which was empty but for a staircase to the roof of the prayer-hall. The prayer-hall lay on the western side of the courtyard with two rows of arcades

Mosque, Malham. Qibla *wall.*

running parallel to the western (*qibla*) wall; keel-arches and the usual plastered stone columns supported a level roof. Particularly striking and substantial stone capitals were set on top of the columns to carry the keel-arches. Low masonry ridges were laid across the floor of the prayer-hall, running parallel with the *qibla* wall between the column bases of the arcades; these ridges were also set at the threshold between the courtyard and the prayer-hall. This internal subdivision of the mosque floor with raised ridges is found in many mosques in Nejd, and is explained as providing a back rest for people listening to the *imām's* address to the mosque.

The *miḥrāb* of the Malham mosque was in the form of a deep curving niche in the centre of the *qibla* wall: seen from within the prayer-hall it consisted of a vaulted niche with a keel-arch, whose form echoed that of the roof-supporting arcades, while the diminutive stepped capitals below the springing of the *miḥrāb* arch recalled the heavier capitals of the arcades. Seen from the exterior, the position of the *miḥrāb* was marked by a curved projection that continued all the way to the roof of the mosque, where its upper part constituted a secondary *miḥrāb* for those standing on the roof of the prayer-hall. The arrangement of the *miḥrāb* recess inside the prayer-hall gave no hint that it was a part of the continuous projection that became visible on the exterior surface of the *qibla* wall.

Contrasting with the plainness of the rest of the mosque, the wooden entrance door had painted decoration; this was more restrained than the painted doors of

Mosque, Malham. Qibla *wall and* miḥrāb.

houses elsewhere in the area, but nevertheless this rather fine door was unusual inasmuch as the entrances to most of the other mosques I have seen are without decoration or have been replaced with later doors. Other decoration inside the mosque was in plaster: the principal features of the *miḥrāb* and of the arcades were picked out in white plaster, which gave a visual unity beyond that created by the architectural forms. Thus the columns of the arcades and the raised ridges on the floor were plastered white, as were the column capitals, while the profiles of the keel-arches were also picked out in plaster. The *qibla* wall had a white dado of plaster covering its lower half which extended to the side walls of the prayer-hall. The upper edge of this dado rose to frame the small niches in the otherwise plain mud-plaster of the upper part of the *qibla* wall; these niches, like others found in central Arabian mosques, were probably intended for placing copies of the Holy Qur'ān. Rising in the centre of the dado, the entire *miḥrāb* recess was plastered white and its framing keel-arch was also in white, although the spandrels of the arch were left as a pair of unpainted triangles, the colour of the underlying mud-plaster. Running across the top of the *miḥrāb* was a white plaster band containing the inscription "*la ilāha ilā Allah, Muḥammad rasūl Allah*" ("There is no deity but God, Muḥammad is the Messenger of God"), and the date of the work, 1371/1951-2. This date may however refer to the plastering rather than to the date of construction of the mosque. If it is indeed the date of construction then it is of particular interest, for it underlines how recently the indigenous style of traditional architecture flourished in central Arabia. The mosque adhered in all respects to the local style of building and showed no other influence whatever; to this extent, despite its late date, the mosque may be taken as a model example of the local tradition.

Old jāmi^c, Ḥuraymilā'

Ḥuraymilā' is a town of al-Mahmal in Nejd, and is associated with the early career of Shaykh Muḥammad b. ᶜAbd al-Wahhāb. The Shaykh first taught in Ḥuraymilā' his doctrine of returning the practice of Islam to that which had pertained in the days of the Prophet (ṣ) and the first four Caliphs. Subsequently, the Shaykh was compelled to depart to nearby ᶜUyayna to continue his mission.

The old *jāmiᶜ* of Ḥuraymilā', which was built in mudbrick and stone, has now been demolished and replaced by a modern mosque. This old mosque was a large building with several interesting features, not least of which was its size, apparently not much less than that of the old *jāmiᶜ* in Riyadh of Imām Turkī b. ᶜAbd Allah Al Saᶜūd, to judge by photographs of the latter. The Ḥuraymilā' *jāmiᶜ* lay on the south side of a large town

Old jāmiᶜ, *Ḥuraymilā', from the north-west, with* qibla *wall and north side of* jāmiᶜ.

square with buildings obscuring it somewhat from the south, north and east, but with a clear view of the western (*qibla*) wall. The exterior of the mosque was unadorned, with a high enclosure wall on all four sides around the *ṣaḥn* and the prayer-hall. On the north side of the mosque was a staircase giving access to the roof. The minaret of the mosque, built against the exterior of the north wall, was a curiosity. It stood at just about the point at which the prayer-hall and the *ṣaḥn* met, although its base was hidden by the buildings clustered about it. It formed a half circle on its north side, but the minaret was entirely flat in the upper part of the side that touched the mosque, a curious arrangement which seems to have been unique: I have seen no other minaret like it. The minaret tapered as it rose and was subdivided horizontally by slightly projecting rings running around the body of the tower. Although flat on its south side, the minaret can nevertheless be related to the minaret style of Sudayr and al-Qaṣīm to the north-west, rather than to the style of the Nejdī mosques to the south.

Old jāmiᶜ, *Ḥuraymilā'.* Ṣaḥn, *looking towards the* qibla *wall.*

I examined only a single door to the mosque in the east wall, opposite the principal *miḥrāb*. The various buildings constructed against much of the exterior of the enclosure made it difficult to ascertain whether there were any other entrances. Internally the mosque was subdivided into three areas: a *riwāq* on the eastern side, a rectangular *ṣaḥn* lying to the west, and, beyond the *ṣaḥn* and against the western *qibla* wall, a deep prayer-hall roofed with four rows of arcades running parallel to the *qibla* wall. By contrast, the eastern *riwāq* had only

Old jāmiᶜ, *Ḥuraymilā'.* Qibla *wall.*

two arcades parallel to the *qibla* wall. In the presence of a second *riwāq* on the east side, the *jāmi*ᶜ of Ḥuraymilā' recalled others in Nejd, including the old *jāmi*ᶜ of Imām Turkī in Riyadh and those in Jalājil and ᶜUnayza.

Whereas the exterior of the Ḥuraymilā' mosque was plain, covered only by dun-coloured mud-plaster, the courtyard and the porticoes of the interior were covered with a fine white plaster. Within the *ṣaḥn* were two curved *miḥrāb*-like forms, one very low, like a balustrade, the other under two metres high and set close to the facade of the prayer-hall. The principal *miḥrāb* in the centre of the *qibla* wall projected on the exterior, but unlike other *miḥrābs* in the immediate area, it reached only a short way up the height of the wall before terminating in a simple canopy, somewhat like that of the *miḥrāb* of the Saᶜd mosque of the Al Saᶜūd at Ṭurayf in al-Dirᶜiyya. At the summit of the *qibla* wall, directly above the principal *miḥrāb*, was another *miḥrāb* projecting in a curve from the balustrade around the roof and designed to serve those praying on the roof of the mosque.

1394/1974

*Jāmi*ᶜ*, Sudūs*

The town of Sudūs in al-ᶜĀriḍ is one of the best preserved small walled settlements in Nejd, with its defensive towers and walls intact. It is surrounded by the gardens and palm-groves of the oasis with a number of outlying mansions and modern houses nearby. The fortified settlement has closely packed houses, a citadel and a mosque, the latter built in two storeys as an integral part of the town complex. As a result of the manner of its incorporation into the walled town, the mosque is virtually without an exposed wall except on the south side where it is built against the enclosure wall of the town. On the other three sides it is closely hemmed in by buildings. A doorway in the town wall gives access to a ground-floor mosque which stands immediately beneath the prayer-hall of the upper mosque and serves as a *khalwa*. A row of columns supports the roof of the *khalwa* and these columns continue upwards to serve as the colonnades in the upper prayer-hall. The *miḥrāb* was blocked with stones in the lower enclosed prayer-hall when I visited it but it was originally a curved niche that continued upwards to become the *miḥrāb* recess in the upper prayer-hall. Access to the upper mosque was by means of a staircase built within the lower prayer-hall. *Khalwas* of various types are found throughout central Arabia.

The upper prayer-hall of the Sudūs mosque repeats the lower mosque in its essentials, although it has a *ṣaḥn* built towards the east like a terrace, and the upper prayer-hall is more elaborate than that below. The *ṣaḥn* is surrounded on three sides by walls and to the west it is

Jāmiᶜ, *Sudūs.* Ṣaḥn, *with east facade of* qibla riwāq.

bordered by the upper prayer-hall of the mosque. In the north-west corner of this *ṣaḥn* is a staircase running up to the roof of the upper prayer-hall and to the minaret at the head of the staircase. Running parallel to the *qibla* wall across the floor of both the *ṣaḥn* and the upper prayer-hall alike are low ridges or copings: that in the *ṣaḥn* is of no great length but inside the prayer-hall these ridges run between the column bases in some cases and in others merely flank the sides of the columns for a short distance. These are found elsewhere in the area and serve, it is said, as back-rests for people listening to the recitation of the Holy Qur'ān or the address of the *imām*. Also in the *ṣaḥn*, built against the outer face of a column in the arcade that forms the facade of the prayer-hall, there is a platform, like a fixed *minbar*, reminiscent of a far more elaborate, recessed structure in the *ṣaḥn* of the old *jāmi*ᶜ of Huraymilā'. The block-like structure at Sudūs is in the form of a chair with a foot-rest.

In the upper prayer-hall at Sudūs, three colonnades run parallel to the *qibla* wall, just as they do in the enclosed mosque below, on whose columns these upper columns rest. The treatment of the upper *qibla* wall is especially interesting. The *miḥrāb* recess is a deeply curved, broad niche in the centre of the *qibla* wall, directly above the *miḥrāb* in the *khalwa* beneath. On the exterior, the *qibla* wall of the upper mosque is exposed and the *miḥrāb* is visible, showing itself as a curved projection running up to the summit of the wall. However, only the southern (left-hand) half of the recess is the *miḥrāb* proper, as seen from within the mosque, for a central column divides the southern and the northern halves; a pair of keel-arches spring from the column and emphasise the subdivision by creating a separate arched frame to each half of the double niche.

Jāmiᶜ, *Sudūs*. Miḥrāb *and* minbar.

The northern half of the niche has a large two-stepped platform filling it, constituting a fixed *minbar*. Although fixed *minbars* occur in various parts of Arabia, the particular form taken by the *miḥrāb* and *minbar* in the Sudūs mosque is unusual. The arrangement of the position of the fixed *minbar* at Sudūs accords with general Islamic practice whereby the *miḥrāb* is positioned to the right of the *imām* when the *khutba* is delivered from the *minbar*. To the south of the *miḥrāb-minbar* recess is a doorway providing access to the mosque from the exterior on that side; an entrance directly into the prayer-hall through the *qibla* wall is a common feature in mosques of the area, and indeed, in the wider Islamic world from early times. The arrangement allows the *imām* access to and egress from the area in front of the people gathered to pray.

The exterior surfaces of the Sudūs mosque are left the buff colour of mud-plaster, whereas the interior columns, the capitals and the profiles of the arches are emphasised with white plaster. The lower half of the *qibla* wall inside the mosque prayer-hall is also coated with a white plaster dado, while the interior of the *miḥrāb-minbar* recess is covered entirely in plaster. Around the top of this niche a rectangular frame is

Jāmiᶜ, *Sudūs*. Miḥrāb *and* minbar.

picked out and inscribed with the words *"la ilāha ilā Allah"* ("There is no deity but God"); there is no other inscription in the mosque. As elsewhere in the area, the stressing of certain major features of the prayer-hall in white plaster has the effect of unifying architectural elements that would otherwise be without visual connection. This decoration emphasises the severe simplicity of the lines of the mosque and is in keeping with the overall character of the local building tradition, with nothing superfluous to the mosque's architectural or liturgical needs. The only other significant features in the interior of the upper prayer-hall are the bracket-like shelves that project from the columns and which are used for resting copies of the Holy Qur'ān. Straw carpets cover the floor and in the *minbar* side of the *miḥrāb-minbar* recess there is a small window, closed by a wooden shutter.

The minaret that stands at the northern end of the mosque, at the head of the staircase from the *ṣaḥn*, allows access to the prayer-hall roof through a broad passage in its base, occupying its entire lower part. From the roof a diminutive staircase gives access to the tapering upper part of the rectangular minaret which consists of a square spiral staircase which is not roofed in any way. The *mu'adhdhin* ascends the staircase and gives the prayer-call with his body projecting out of the top of the minaret tower. Square or rectangular minarets of this type, constructed at the head of steps and in virtual suspension between prayer-hall and stairs are a traditional element throughout this area of Nejd.

Jāmi^{c}, *Sudūs. Minaret.*

Jāmi^{c}, *Sudūs. Minaret, with the staircase to the prayer-hall roof.*

The roof of the prayer-hall provides a further *miḥrāb* which is immediately above that of the prayer-hall below. This roof *miḥrāb* is again a curved recess, being in fact the summit of the *miḥrāb* projection which has already been described as extending the full height of the *qibla* wall. In this roof *miḥrāb* recess is yet another fixed platform-like *minbar* of two steps, recalling the *minbar* in the *miḥrāb* of the principal prayer-hall beneath, and also echoing the stepped *minbar*-chair in the *ṣaḥn*.

When photographed the mosque was still in use and was kept in a correspondingly good condition, despite the fact that the rest of the walled town had been abandoned and the people had moved out to the new village.

1393-4/1973-4

Mosque, Ḥazwa

Ḥazwa is a small settlement in Wādī Salbūkh, just to the east of the walled town of Sudūs, to the north of Riyadh. The diminutive mosque among the plantations at Ḥazwa is typical of the simpler mosques of Nejd. A low wall surrounds the courtyard on the east side while a single arcade along the west side of the *ṣaḥn* has the usual keel-arches supporting the roof of the mosque. This arcade, parallel to the *qibla*, illustrates well how broad, stone capitals resting on columns are used to reduce the space to be spanned by the triangular keel-arches, allowing them to remain stable. It can be seen elsewhere from keel-arches of this type that have collapsed that they are formed of two long stones, resting against each other at the apex of the triangle. The *miḥrāb* of the mosque is a simple curved recess that projects on the exterior surface of the *qibla* wall and extends the full height of the wall to provide a *miḥrāb* on the roof. The roof is reached by a staircase from the *ṣaḥn* built on the south side. Mosques in this simple style, lacking a minaret, are scattered throughout the area.

1393/1973

Mosque, Ḥazwa. Ṣaḥn *and prayer-hall.*

*al-Dir*ᶜ*iyya and its environs*

Al-Dirᶜiyya is a town on the banks of the Wādī Ḥanīfa, to the north-west of Riyadh. The neighbourhood of al-Dirᶜiyya is distinguished by its palm groves and gardens, indicating the agricultural nature of the ancient settlement, which relied for its water supply on wells. The town is the ancestral seat of the Al Saᶜūd and their residence there goes back to the 9th/15th century. In *c.* 1158/1745, the *amīr* of al-Dirᶜiyya, Muḥammad b. Saᶜūd, welcomed Shaykh Muḥammad b. ᶜAbd al-Wahhāb to the town after the Shaykh had departed the town of ᶜUyayna, further north; the *amīr* accepted Ibn ᶜAbd al-Wahhāb's call to revitalise Islam and to return to the practice of the Prophet Muḥammad (ṣ). In succeeding years, the power of al-Dirᶜiyya spread through Arabia until the first Saudi state encompassed much of the peninsula. Simultaneously, al-Dirᶜiyya itself grew, as evidenced by the great mud-brick mansions on the citadel of al-Ṭurayf, overlooking the Wādī Ḥanīfa. The entire site was defended by a very extensive line of walls and towers which exploited the topography of the *wādīs* and the landscape around al-Dir^c^iyya.

Today, old al-Dir^c^iyya lies in ruins as a result of the assault on the town by Ibrāhīm Pasha in 1233/1818 which brought about the end of the first Saudi state. Much of the damage to the palaces, houses and mosques can be attributed to the Pasha's policy of razing the town as he evacuated Nejd a year later. Today these ruins are a protected national monument, while a modern town of al-Dir^c^iyya has grown on the opposite bank of the Wādī Ḥanīfa.

Mosque of Imām Muḥammad b. Sa^c^ūd, al-Dir^c^iyya

After the establishment of the accord between Imām Muḥammad b. Sa^c^ūd and Shaykh Muḥammad b. ^c^Abd al-Wahhāb in *c.* 1158/1745, Imām Muḥammad ruled the expanding first Saudi state until his death in 1179/1765. The mosque of Imām Muḥammad stands on the west bank of the Wādī Ḥanīfa, just below the citadel of al-Ṭurayf, where the ruined palaces of al-Dir^c^iyya still survive. The mosque is of historical interest, although little remains of the original building. It is reduced to a row of arches to the east of a mosque of far more recent

Mosque of Imām Muḥammad b. Sa^c^ūd, al-Dir^c^iyya. View towards the east.

Khalwa roof of modern mosque next to remains of mosque of Muḥammad b. Sa^c^ūd.

date. These arches have the keel form that is found in many mosques in central Arabia and they rest on columns of stone. The building material of the walls and arcades is mud-brick. The mosque is in the traditional style of Nejd and shows the continuity between later mosques in central Arabia and those of the period of the first Saudi state. The destruction of this early mosque is presumably related to the demolition of al-Dir^{c}iyya that Ibrāhīm Pasha ordered in Sha^{c}bān 1234/ June 1819, a year after he took the town.

The mosque to the west of the remains of Imām Muḥammad's mosque is of a late date although it has many features of Nejdi design. It forms a rectangular enclosure with entrances in the lateral walls. On the east side of the rectangular *ṣaḥn* is a *khalwa*, occupying the entire eastern end of the mosque. This *khalwa* has a staircase to its roof at both ends leading up from the *ṣaḥn*, and in its western (*qibla*) wall is a curved *miḥrāb* projection. The main prayer-hall of the modern mosque is on the west side with a flat roof on concrete columns. The *miḥrāb* is a simple recess that projects on the exterior of the *qibla* wall, while there is a curious low tower at the north-west corner of the prayer-hall which serves to carry the loud-speaker for the prayer call. This tower cannot be ascended.

1393/1973

Sa^{c}d mosque, al-Ṭurayf, al-Dir^{c}iyya

Sa^{c}d mosque, al-Ṭurayf. Miḥrāb *before restoration.*

The Sa^{c}d mosque stands among the old residences of members of the Al Sa^{c}ūd in the Ṭurayf area of the former capital of the Saudi state, al-Dir^{c}iyya. The palaces that surround the mosque are all in ruins, and, indeed, it was among the worst damaged buildings in this part of the old town until it was excavated and partly restored in recent years by the Department of Antiquities.

The mosque is built against the exterior wall of a palace to the south, the Qaṣr Sa^{c}d. Like many of the buildings of al-Dir^{c}iyya, it is built of mud-brick coated in mud-plaster, although its walls had mostly collapsed before the restoration. The mosque had an entrance in the east wall of the rectangular enclosure that it formed in ground-plan, but there appear to have been no other entrances. Within the enclosure is a *ṣaḥn* to the east and a prayer-hall to the west, of which only the bases of columns remain, marking the positions of the five arcades that once supported the roof. Prior to the restoration, the entire floor of the prayer-hall was covered with mud-plaster. The points at which the arcades were anchored to the lateral walls of the mosque can still be identified, and it is clear that the arches were keel-shaped, the form seen in Nejd generally. Of the *qibla* wall, before the restoration, little remained except for the shell of the curved *miḥrāb* recess in the centre, opposite the entrance in the east wall. This *miḥrāb*

Saᶜd mosque, al-Ṭurayf. Ṣaḥn *and remains of prayer-hall colonnades after restoration.*

formed a curved projection on the exterior surface of the *qibla* wall, and sufficient remained of the original *miḥrāb* to see that it did not reach the summit of the *qibla* wall. In the *ṣaḥn* of the mosque the traces of a staircase could be identified, built against the interior of the north wall, leading to the prayer-hall roof. The foundations were clear and so too was the line of a staircase on the surface of the west wall of the *ṣaḥn*. Such staircases are commonly found in Nejdi mosques.

As to the date of the Saᶜd mosque, like all else in al-Dirᶜiyya, it falls within the period of the town's efflorescence after the establishment of the first Saudi state and the support of the state for Shaykh Muḥammad b. ᶜAbd al-Wahhāb from *c.* 1158/1745, and before the fall of al-Dirᶜiyya to Ibrāhīm Pasha in 1233/1818. The following year, along with the rest of the buildings of the town, the mosque was demolished by the Pasha before he withdrew from Nejd.

1393/1973

Wādī Ḥanīfa, al-Dirᶜiyya

Mosque in the Wādī Ḥanīfa Ṣaḥn *and* qibla riwāq.

There are a number of mosques scattered along the Wādī Ḥanīfa among the farms, plantations and palm groves that extend north and south of al-Dir^{c}iyya; these seem to have been built for the people working in the plantations outside the main settlement. There are many parallels for such small mosques throughout the country and especially in Nejd itself, and the small mosques in the Wādī Ḥanīfa are noteworthy for their particularly fine construction. As is normal for such mosques in the area, there are no minarets and, instead, they have either a staircase to the roof of the prayer-hall or are without even this feature. The mosques are all constructed in the usual local materials of limestone (used for the foundations and the construction of columns), with mud-brick for the walls and mud-plaster.

A mosque, without a staircase, stands on the west bank of the Wādī Ḥanīfa. It has a single arcade before the *qibla* wall to support the level roof. The prayer-hall is marked off from the *ṣaḥn* by a raised back-rest ridge running parallel to the *qibla* wall across the floor of the prayer-hall, between three of the columns. Within the walled *ṣaḥn* the ground surface is scattered with gravel. The facade and keel-arches of the shallow prayer-hall are plastered white, but around the column bases and along the *qibla* wall a dado with grey plaster is used instead. Another similar mosque nearby (not illustrated here) has a single arcade parallel to the *qibla* wall, and a *ṣaḥn* within an enclosing wall, with a staircase to the roof. On the exterior of the *qibla* wall, the *miḥrāb* projects as a curved structure extending to the summit of the wall, while the same wall has a small rectangular doorway for the *imām*.

1392/1972

al-Ghaṣība

Al-Ghaṣība is a ruined site on the east bank of the Wādī'l-Ḥanīfa, just to the north of al-Dir^{c}iyya. Ancient al-Ghaṣība is in far more ruinous a state than al-Dir^{c}iyya itself. One of its most prominent features is a mosque set on the very edge of the cliff overlooking the Wādī Ḥanīfa channel. The outline of the enclosure walls and the courtyard of the mosque can barely be traced today, and indeed, the limit of the mosque on its east side is rather unclear. Parts of the prayer-hall can be identified and it would seem that its arcades ran parallel to the *qibla* wall, as is usual in Nejd. The *qibla* wall marking the western limit of the mosque is far better preserved, built to straddle and face the cliff side. Originally the superstructure of the mosque was unfired mud-brick, but this has been nearly completely eroded, leaving only the stone foundations of the *qibla* wall against the side of the *wādī*.

The *qibla* wall with its lower courses of cut limestone descends the cliff for several courses, with the *miḥrāb* set in its centre. The *miḥrāb* proper which rested on this foundation was a curved projection, recessed internally, whose upper parts were of unfired brick. Although conventional enough in its form, the al-Ghaṣība mosque is most remarkable for its striking cliff-top position and the curious construction of the remains of its western (*qibla*) wall.

16 Sha^{c}bān 1402/9 June 1982

Mosque, al-Ghaṣība.

ᶜArqa

ᶜArqa is a village on the west bank of the Wādī Ḥanīfa between Riyadh and al-Dirᶜiyya. It figured in the early history of the Saudi state, and, although taken and destroyed by Ibrāhīm Pasha during his campaign against Nejd in 1233/1818, ᶜArqa briefly served Imām Turkī b. ᶜAbd Allah as a base before he established Riyadh as his capital in 1240/1824. Until recently ᶜArqa was quiet and picturesque with its gardens and palm plantations guarded by conical towers in mud-brick. Its older mud-brick houses built on the rocky cliff side above the Wādī Ḥanīfa overlooked the houses of the modern inhabitants, with the settlement defended from the west by a wall reinforced by towers. In recent years, ᶜArqa has changed greatly but in 1392/1972 there were still several mosques in traditional building material and style scattered through the village.

View of ᶜArqa, with old jāmiᶜ *in the background.*

Of these mosques, the old *jāmiᶜ* was the most striking, situated just at the entrance to the village, a little to the west of the bridge across the Wādī Ḥanīfa; since that time, it has been replaced by a modern mosque on the same site. The *jāmiᶜ*, as it stood in 1392/1972, was typical of the style of mosque once common in and around Riyadh. It had a rectangular *ṣaḥn* on the east side, surrounded by a low stone wall that was probably later than the rest of the mosque, which was of mud-brick resting on roughly cut stone foundations. On the west side of the *ṣaḥn*, against the *qibla* wall, was a prayer-hall with a level roof resting on three arcades which ran parallel to the *qibla* wall. These arcades were very regular and well built, with keel-arches and capitals resting on columns. At the southern end of the courtyard was a broad staircase to the roof of the mosque, while at the northern end a second staircase led up to the roof and also provided support for a square minaret with tapering sides that was built to stand forward from the facade of the prayer-hall itself. The lower part of this minaret, suspended between the staircase and the roof, was an open passageway from the head of the staircase on to the mosque roof. The upper part of the minaret above this passage was reached from the roof of the mosque by a smaller staircase. Inside this minaret superstructure was a further narrow spiral staircase and the *mu'adhdhin* would stand inside the upper part of the body of the tower to give the call to prayer, with his head and shoulders projecting from the open summit of the minaret.

The east facade of the mosque and the colonnades had been given a unifying coating of light plaster, creating a contrast with the dun-coloured mud-plaster of the rest of the building. On the exterior of the *qibla* wall, the only relief from the plain mud plaster was the curved projection of the *miḥrāb* niche which reached the full height of the *qibla* wall. At the summit, it provided an upper *miḥrāb* for those praying on the roof of the prayer-hall. The staircase system, the minaret, the use of light-coloured plaster to cover the interior of the prayer-hall, and the shape of the *miḥrāb*, as well as the overall distribution of the *jāmiᶜ*, are all indigenous architectural features in this area of central Arabia, but the *jāmiᶜ* of ᶜArqa was a particularly well proportioned and well maintained example of the type.

Of the other mosques scattered around ᶜArqa, one

still stands (in 1405/1985) on the *wādī* bank. It is a simple mud and stone building consisting merely of a courtyard with an enclosure wall and a single arcade parallel to the *qibla* wall supporting the roof. The mosque has no minaret. Simple mosques of this type, as opposed to the more elaborate *jāmi*ᶜ, are spread throughout the region.

19 Dhū'l-Qaᶜda 1392/25 December 1972

Old jāmiᶜ, *ᶜArqa, in 1392/1972. North wall and* qibla *wall.*

Old jāmiᶜ, *ᶜArqa, in 1972, from the east.*

Riyadh

Like other towns of central Arabia, the origin of the Saudi Arabian capital Riyadh goes back to mediaeval times, when the settlement was one of several small agricultural villages built of mud brick and scattered along the sides of the Wādī'l-Ḥanīfa. Riyadh was a place of some importance by the time of the rise of the first Saudi state in Nejd and is often mentioned in accounts of the period. With the fall of the first Saudi capital, al-Dirᶜiyya, to Ibrāhīm Pasha in 1233/1818 the former capital was abandoned. By 1238/1823, Imām Turkī b. ᶜAbd Allah Al Saᶜūd had returned to Nejd to begin to lay the foundations of the second Saudi state. After establishing himself at ᶜArqa, north of Riyadh, he expelled the Turkish garrison that had occupied Riyadh. In 1240/1824 Riyadh became Imām Turkī's capital. The town was to be developed under Al Saᶜūd rule and it is fortunate that we have descriptions of it during the heyday of the second Saudi state under Imām Fayṣal b. Turkī, as a result of the visits to Riyadh of W.G. Palgrave and Lewis Pelley at the end of the *imām's* reign.

It was the mud-brick town, surrounded by palm plantations, that was taken by the late King ᶜAbd al-ᶜAzīz Al Saᶜūd in 1319/1902. Following the recapture of Riyadh, Al Saᶜūd power was re-established in Nejd and Ibn Saᶜūd initiated the process which culminated in the re-unification of Arabia and the foundation of the Kingdom. There are several descriptions of Riyadh in the early years of the late King ᶜAbd al-ᶜAzīz. Of particular importance are photographs of the town, mainly by Philby, Rihani and Weiss: among these are photographs of the old *jāmiᶜ* of the town. Today, and especially in the last decade or so, Riyadh has transformed completely into one of the most modern cities of the Middle East and little trace remains of the mud-brick town that was described by visitors early in the century.

Jāmiᶜ, Riyadh

The present *jāmiᶜ* in the main square of the city, al-Dīra, dates only from the 1370s/1950s; it was preceded by a large mosque in mud-brick and stone that was built by Imām Turkī b. ᶜAbd Allah, according to Philby.(1) After Imām Turkī had expelled the last of the Ottoman forces from Riyadh in 1240/1824, he established the town as his capital and proceeded to rebuild the walls, to construct a *jāmiᶜ*, and to build a residence for himself. It was this *jāmiᶜ* which W.G. Palgrave saw in 1279/1862 and of which he wrote a brief description.(2) Some sixty years later, Philby (1917)(3) and Rihanī (1922-3)(4) saw the same mosque and added more detailed information which disagrees in some respects with that of Palgrave; more importantly, Philby, Rihani and Weiss(5) all photographed the mosque.

In its essentials, Imām Turkī's *jāmiᶜ* was closely related to the other mosques of the district although it was distinguished by its greater size, as befitted the *jāmiᶜ* of the capital of Nejd. Rihani estimated that the mosque was about 125 by 100 feet (about 38 by 30 metres), although Philby reckoned it to be about 50 feet longer in each direction. The mosque was constructed in the usual materials of the area, mud-brick, stone and a covering of mud-plaster, with wood and presumably palm-thatch for the level roofing of the building. It was entered through doorways in each of the north, east and south sides, while a further door was situated in the west (*qibla*) wall, near the *miḥrāb*. Rihani entered the mosque through the south door which he says was approached between the shops of the *sūq* that clustered close against it: such a relationship between *jāmiᶜ* and *sūq* is one that is encountered throughout the Islamic world from the earliest times. The south doorway of the mosque gave on to the courtyard which was covered by a pebble pavement and occupied about a quarter of the area of the entire mosque. The rest consisted of two roofed porticoes, one at the east side and a far deeper portico at the western (*qibla*) end, constituting the prayer-hall proper. The roofs of the two porticoes were level, resting on arcades with keel-arches supported by stubby round columns, no more than three metres in total height to the crown of the arch. The portico on the eastern side of the *ṣaḥn* was three arcades deep, but that in front of the western *qibla* wall had ten arcades running parallel to the *qibla* wall with 25 columns in each arcade, giving a total of 325 columns. According to Rihani, these columns were constructed of stone or of rubble, and then rendered smooth with plaster. There is a disagreement between Rihani's account and that of Palgrave on this point, for Palgrave referred to square, wooden pillars in the Friday Mosque which had been plastered; nevertheless, Rihani's account is supported by his photograph. Reconstruction of the porticoes may have taken place between the visit by Palgrave and that of Rihani some eighty years later but there are enough errors of detail in Palgrave's book for him to have misrecorded the shape of the colonnades in Imām Turkī's *jāmiᶜ*.

In view of the number of columns in the mosque, Rihani was to some extent justified in comparing their effect with the forest of columns in the Umayyad Great Mosque of Cordoba in Spain, although the parallels go no further. Certainly in central Arabia sixty years ago, the *jāmiᶜ* of Riyadh must have provided a remarkable contrast with the smaller mosques that Rihani would have seen on his journey to Riyadh. The *jāmiᶜ* of Riyadh was especially large, yet it was nevertheless duplicated by a further prayer-hall beneath the first, the *khalwa*, for use in winter or in wet weather; the system of an underground or covered mosque is found with some variation in other old mosques in Arabia, and indeed, the present Friday Mosque of Riyadh, which replaced Imām

Jāmi^c, *Riyadh in 1337/1917, from the* Amara.
The mosque was built by Imām *Turki b. ^cAbd Allah.*
(H. St. J. Philby)

Jāmi^c, *Riyadh, from the roof of the* amāra. *(1403/1983)*

Turkī's *jāmi*ᶜ, has a *khalwa* beneath, approached by stairs on the east side of the *ṣaḥn*.

In the main, the old *jāmi*ᶜ of Riyadh seems to have been left the colour of the mud-plaster that coated it, but as elsewhere the columns of the *qibla riwāq* (all that is visible in Rihani's photograph of the interior) were distinguished by a light plaster that must have both unified the colonnades visually and created an atmosphere of sparseness and restraint. Running around the courtyard was a parapet resting on the roofed porticoes; supporting this parapet was a series of stepped projections, one above each column and a shorter one above each arch-crown, which had the effect of a rhythmic articulation across the facade of the prayer-hall; I have not seen such a system on the wall-surfaces of other mosques in the area.

Above the columns there were also a number of small shelves projecting from the facade, one to each column: in other mosques, such shelves (*rāfa*) are used to rest copies of the Holy Qur'ān, but in the case of this mosque they seem to have been somewhat high.

The minaret of the *jāmi*ᶜ stood at the north end of the prayer-hall, at the head of a staircase approached from within the north *riwāq*, rather than from the *ṣaḥn*, which is the case usually in Nejd. The minaret was typical of the immediate area. It had a square base, a tapering body and a rectangular passageway through the lower part giving access from the staircase to the roof of the mosque; the upper part was entered by a doorway in the south side, reached by a small staircase. Philby mentions another raised platform on the roof against the *qibla* wall, above the *miḥrāb*. There were also higher walls at the south-east corner of the mosque, as Philby's photograph shows. Of the *miḥrāb* itself, Philby says that it was "a slight projection" on the exterior surface of the *qibla* wall: I have seen no photograph that records its exact shape.

In his account of the mosque, Palgrave mentions a passage above the street which led from the palace. Imām Fayṣal b. Turkī b. ᶜAbd Allah made use of this passage for the sake of security at the time of Palgrave's visit. Such a construction is reported as early as the 3rd/9th century in Umayyad Cordoba, where it linked the *jāmi*ᶜ with the palace of the *amīr*. The passage to the Riyadh *jāmi*ᶜ is not visible in the photographs published by Rihani and Philby.

19 Shaᶜbān 1403/31 May 1983

Jāmiᶜ, *Riyadh. Prayer-hall.*

Jāmi^c, *Riyadh in 1341/1922-23 showing the* ṣaḥn *and the east facade of the prayer-hall. The* jāmi^c *was built by* Imām *Turki b.* ^c*Abd Allah. (Ameen Rihani)*

Jāmi^c *Riyadh.* Ṣaḥn *and facade of the prayer-hall. (1403/1983)*

Ghaṭ Ghaṭ

Ghaṭ Ghaṭ was one of the most important *ḥijras* or settlements of the *ikhwān* established in central Arabia after the beginning of the *ikhwān* movement in Nejd in about 1330/1912. These *ḥijras* were encouraged by the late King ᶜAbd al-ᶜAzīz b. ᶜAbd al-Raḥmān Al Saᶜūd and Ghaṭ Ghaṭ, lying west of Riyadh, was one of the earliest, settled by members of the al-ᶜUtayba tribe under their shaykh, Sulṭān b. Bijād. The *ḥijras*, with their newly settled beduin inhabitants, became a mainstay of the Saudi forces that unified the country in campaigns before the establishment of the Kingdom's present boundaries. Each of these *ḥijras* included a mosque, small houses for the settlers, and agricultural land for cultivation. The settling beduin were assisted by the government with grain and technical advice while the religious authorities ensured their spiritual welfare.

Old Ghaṭ Ghaṭ is now abandoned and a more recent town stands a short distance away from the original *ḥijra*. The mosque of old Ghaṭ Ghaṭ was built, presumably, about 1330/1912 at the time of the foundation of the settlement. It still survives, although badly ruined, and is by far the largest building of the old *ḥijra*. It is a long shallow structure measuring some 31 by 14 metres, in which the *qibla* wall is the best preserved part. The course of the enclosure walls around the *ṣaḥn* can easily be traced although they have fallen, and it is quite clear that the original mosque consisted of a rectangular *ṣaḥn* to the east with a prayer-hall to the west, against the *qibla* wall. The building material throughout is mud-brick, and the vanished roof was probably of wood and palm-thatch: the columns are of stone, similar to those seen elsewhere in Nejd. Remains of these columns indicate the position of the single arcade of keel-arches which once ran parallel to the *qibla* wall to form the prayer-hall; however, the arcade has now fallen for the most part and the roof which it supported has entirely disappeared. A low balustrade separated the prayer-hall from the *ṣaḥn*. There are a number of small recesses set into the *qibla* wall and the side walls of the prayer-hall, which served as places to rest copies of the Holy Qur'ān.

Mosque, Ghaṭ Ghaṭ. Qibla *wall from the south-west.*

The well preserved *miḥrāb* is an exceptionally large, deeply curved niche forming a projection on the exterior, tapering as it rises; indeed the *miḥrāb* is the most prominent feature of the mosque. There is no indication that there was either a staircase to the roof of the prayer-hall or a minaret.

1393/1973

Mosque, Ghaṭ Ghaṭ. Miḥrāb.

Southern Nejd

The country south and south-west of Riyadh, as far as Wādī'l-Dawāsir, is treated here as southern Nejd. The settlements lie mainly to the east of the Jabal Ṭuwayq escarpment, although this is not the case in the far south. The landscape of al-Ḥawṭa and al-Ḥarīq does not differ greatly from that of the more northerly areas around Riyadh and Sudayr, with deep *wādī beds cutting through the plateau as rocky gorges. In these gorges the agricultural land and palm groves are stretched out along the valley floor, with the settlements strung along the line of the wādī*, rather than closely grouped together. It is apparent from the ruins of walls that this fertile area has been settled since distant times. Further south in al-Aflāj the country is different. It is far more level, with settlements clustered together amidst plantations scattered across the sandy landscape, somewhat reminiscent of al-Aḥsā'. Agriculture here is very ancient, supported formerly by a sophisticated irrigation system. Only in the extreme south is the wall of the Jabal Ṭuwayq broken by the Wādī'l-Dawāsir channel, beyond which the Ṭuwayq escarpment continues into the desert, finally to fade out in the western part of the Empty Quarter. Beyond the Wādī'l-Dawāsir, the next significant settlement if Najrān.

The southern area of Nejd was a major source of support for the first Saudi state and, after the fall of al-Dir^{c}iyya to the Egypto-Turkish forces of Ibrāhīm Pasha in 1233/1818, the southern region of Nejd suffered the reverses of the rest of the country. With the restoration of Al Sa^{c}ūd authority by Imām Turkī b. ^{c}Abd Allah and his son and successor, Imām Fayṣal, these areas enjoyed the revival of stability that came to the rest of central Arabia. When the late King ^{c}Abd al-^{c}Azīz Al Sa^{c}ūd regained Riyadh in 1319/1902, the south quickly gave him support and a major encounter with the Al Rashīd was fought out at al-Dilām.

The south of Nejd was visited in the past by few travellers who left records of their journeys, although Palgrave claimed to have made an expedition to al-Aflāj in 1279/1862, while he was sojourning in Riyadh. However, Philby doubted the veracity of Palgrave's confusing account. Whatever the truth, Philby produced the first carefully observed description of the terrain, made during his own expedition to Wādī'l-Dawāsir in 1336/1918.(1) However, he gave no information about the mosques of the district. In the al-Aflāj area some archaeological survey work has been carried out(2), while at al-Faw an important archaeological excavation has been undertaken at the foot of the southern extremity of Jabal Ṭuwayq.(3)

al-Kharj

Al-Kharj is a large town to the south of Riyadh, the centre of a very extensive agricultural area which has developed greatly in recent years. The district as a whole was one of settled agricultural communities long before the modern period. The entire region of which al-Kharj is now a major town is a part of the historical district of al-Yamāma. A visitor to the area in the 4th/10th century, Nāṣir-i Khusraw, wrote of the running water, subterranean canals and dates of Yamāma, and the number of cavalrymen that the district could support. A widely travelled individual, well-acquainted with the finest Islamic architecture of his day, it is interesting that Nāsir-i Khusraw should also have commented on the beauty of the main mosque of al-Yamāma.(1) Unfortunately, no trace of this mosque remains.

In 1392/1972 a vast old mosque in traditional style built of mud-brick still stood intact in al-Kharj, although it has now vanished and I can no longer identify its site. It had one of the largest *ṣaḥns* of any mosque in the region and yet the prayer-hall was of no great depth. Its broad facade on the *ṣaḥn* side was formed by nine slightly irregular keel-arches, resting on columns. At the north end of the prayer-hall, stretching forward into the *ṣaḥn*, was a staircase running from the courtyard to the mosque roof. There was no minaret. At least two mosques of similar design, although not of such scale, could be seen in Riyadh itself a decade ago before the city was modernised.

1392/1972

Old mosque, al-Kharj, in 1392/1972.

Old jāmi^c, al-Ṣaḥanā'

In 1394/1974 I photographed a large mosque in al-Ṣaḥanā', although by 1402/1982 this had been replaced by a modern *jāmi^c*. The old *jāmi^c* was an unusual building, partly for its size, but more particularly for its minaret. There was a *ṣaḥn* on the east side with quite a high enclosure wall around it which rose sharply to the summit of the much higher walls of the prayer-hall on the west side. The building material throughout was apparently mud-brick, resting on foundation courses of stone. An entrance in the north side gave access to the mosque at the point at which the prayer-hall and the *ṣaḥn* met, while there was a further entrance to the mosque on the east side of the *ṣaḥn*. The flat-roofed prayer-hall was particularly deep and was illuminated from the *ṣaḥn* itself and from the lateral walls. There were therefore a number of rectangular windows framed in white plaster to relieve the lack of light in the interior of the prayer-hall.

The minaret stood in the south-east corner of the *ṣaḥn* and it was unlike any other I have seen in central Arabia, inasmuch as it was a freestanding and rectangular tower with slightly banked walls. It was unadorned and had rectangular windows in the summit. I am reluctant to hypothesise how this departure from tradition appeared in al-Ṣaḥanā'.

1394/1974

Old jāmiᶜ, *al-Saḥanā', from the north (1395/1975).*

Two small mosques near al-Ṣaḥanā'

On the south-western side of al-Ṣaḥanā' is an extensive area of farm-land. There are two small mosques within a kilometre of each other which are interesting examples of the smaller mosques of the district as a whole, displaying features which are characteristic of more southerly districts of Nejd.

Of these two mosques, the southern is a small building in mud-brick covered in the usual mud-plaster. It has a rectangular courtyard surrounded by a low wall, entered by a single door at the north extremity of the east wall; this allows those entering the prayer-hall to approach it from the right hand. The raised frame of the door to the *ṣaḥn* serves to emphasise the entrance, although the work is somewhat irregular. Doorways of this design are found in many Arabian mosques.

The prayer-hall lies on the western side of a featureless *ṣaḥn*. It is in the form of a rectangular building with a level roof, entered by two small entrances at either end of the east facade. The light passes into the shallow prayer-hall from these two doorways to supplement that entering through small rectangular windows in each of the short side walls of the building. However, the west (*qibla*) wall is without windows. The *miḥrāb* is indicated on the exterior surface of the *qibla* wall by a curved projection which does not reach the summit of the wall. While the mosque is a severely simple building, it is

Small mosque near al-Ṣaḥanā'.

relieved from a harsh starkness by stepped finials at each of the four corners, while an open triangle crowns the east wall on axis with the *miḥrāb*. There is also a finial on the summit of the *miḥrāb*.

The second mosque in the agricultural outskirts of al-Ṣaḥanā' is a somewhat larger structure than the preceding mosque. Once again the building material is unfired mud-brick, made smooth with plaster. The overall ground-plan is essentially the same, with an open *ṣaḥn* and a somewhat deeper flat-roofed prayer-hall on the *qibla* side. The only entrance is at the south end of the east wall, giving on to the *ṣaḥn* directly. An interesting feature of this and the previous mosque in al-Ṣaḥanā' is the sloping stretch of wall that forms a transition on either side between the lateral walls of the *ṣaḥn* and the facade of the prayer-hall itself.

Another striking aspect of the building is the row of seven steep keel-arches, resting on columns and capitals. The profiles of these arches are rather different to those of keel-arches seen further north in Nejd. The level roof of the prayer-hall is supported by yet another row of columns and keel-arches running parallel to the *qibla* wall. The east facade of the prayer-hall has been walled up partially, with concrete blocks between the columns. This work is obviously quite recent. Although the large arches in the east wall provide adequate illumination for the interior, the lateral walls of the prayer-hall are also lit by a pair of narrow windows on each side. The *miḥrāb* of the mosque is in the centre of the *qibla* wall and forms a curved projection just reaching the summit of the wall. The mosque lacks decoration of any sort.

14 Jumāda II 1402/8 April 1982

Small mosque near al-Ṣaḥanā', from the east.

Mosque between al-Ḥilwa and al-Ḥawṭa

In 1395/1975 I photographed a mosque in the region between al-Ḥawṭa and al-Ḥilwa which is either of recent construction or a restoration, to judge by the excellent finish of the mud-plaster surfacing the exterior. This small mosque illustrates the quality of building achieved in the Nejdi tradition in terms of line and construction in the materials locally available. It consists of a *ṣaḥn* to the east and a flat-roofed prayer-hall to the west. A foundation of some seven courses of shaped limestone provides the footing for mud-brick walls which are somewhat banked, an effect which relieves the overall cube-effect of the building. As elsewhere in southern Nejd, the mosque has a rectangular projecting *miḥrāb*, contrasting in this respect with the mosques of similar character further north in Nejd, where *miḥrābs* tend to be curved.

1395/1975

al-Ḥawṭa (al-Ḥawṭa Banī Tamīm)

Al-Ḥawṭa is a settled agricultural district of considerable extent in the broad gorge of Wādī'l-Ḥawṭa, south of Riyadh. There are relatively large areas of long-established fields in these valleys as well as old well-heads, ruined field-walls and traces of disused ancient fields, all emphasising the fact that this has been an agricultural and settled area of Nejd for a long period. The town of al-Ḥawṭa Banī Tamīm is spread out along the course of the *wādī* beneath steep rocky cliffs; on the cliff tops above it is overlooked by watchtowers.

In the more northerly part of the town are thick palm plantations and several old mosques. One of these, on the south side of the valley, presses up close to the foot of the cliff, while on the opposite side of the road is an interesting small mosque amidst gardens. It is built of mud-brick on stone foundations, and, as with other buildings in the area, the brick-work of the *qibla* wall is exposed, with no plaster attached. The mosque is a rectangular building with a *ṣaḥn* to the east, through whose east wall it is entered. The prayer-hall on the west side has a flat roof resting on four keel-arches parallel to the west (*qibla*) wall. There is a staircase to the roof on the south side of the *ṣaḥn*, the steps distinguished by white plaster. A side entrance gives directly on to the prayer-hall, but the most interesting aspect is the *miḥrāb*, a square projection in the centre of the *qibla* wall. This type of *miḥrāb* is found elsewhere in al-Ḥawṭa and southern Nejd, as well as beyond, at al-Aflāj and as far south as Najrān.

14 Jumāda II 1402/8 April 1982

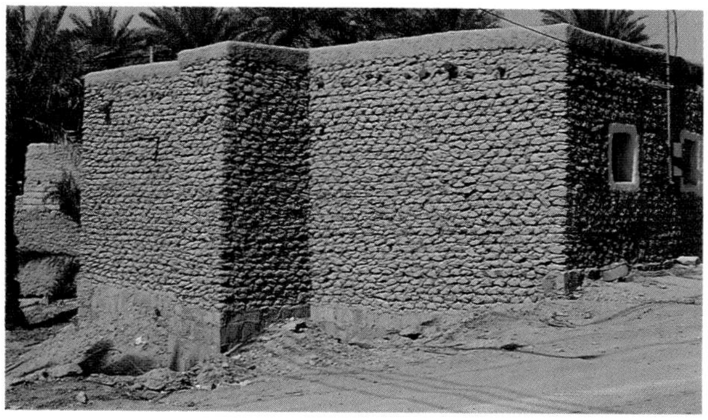

Mosque, al-Ḥawṭa, from west of the qibla *wall.*

Mosque, al-Hawṭa. Qibla *wall in 1395/1975.*

Mosque, al-Hawṭa. Ṣaḥn *wall with prayer-hall beyond (1395/1975).*

Mosque, Naᶜām

Naᶜām is a farming settlement situated in a valley between cliffs in a particularly beautiful district lying between al-Ḥawṭa and al-Mufayjir, towards al-Ḥarīq. South of the asphalt road through the district, at the time of my first visit to Naᶜām in 1402/1982, was a mosque in traditional materials. It was built of mud-brick covered with mud-plaster and was quite a large building. To the east of the prayer-hall was the *ṣaḥn*, enclosed by high walls. The prayer-hall on the west side had a level roof supported by arcades with keel-arches running parallel to the *qibla* wall. A staircase led to the roof, built against the southern wall of the enclosure; it was greatly eroded, although usable. The windows in the side walls of the mosque were of a form common in central Arabia, all consisting of high, steep apertures of triangular shape. A number had been blocked up.

The *miḥrāb* of the mosque was a particularly large example of the square projecting type found in the more southerly parts of Nejd. It rose the height of the western (*qibla*) wall and dominated the wall in a manner and degree striking even in this region, where *miḥrābs* tend to be large and prominent. The *miḥrāb* had a small wedge-shaped window in the centre of its west wall, but it had been blocked. On the summit of the *miḥrāb*, in the centre, was a small triangular motif formed by two bricks leaning against each other, similar to the motif on the top of the *miḥrāb* of a mosque outside al-Ṣaḥanā' (page 163). When I returned to Naᶜām in 1404/1984, the old mosque had been replaced by a new mosque.

14 Jumāda II 1402/8 April 1982
11 Rajab 1404/12 April 1984

Mosque, Naᶜām.

New mosque, Naᶜām.

al-Aflāj

An unusually precise reference to a mosque in al-Aflāj in early times is recorded by the Persian *hajji*, Nāṣir-i Khusraw, who was compelled to return to Basra from Makkah al-Mukarramah via al-Ṭā'if, al-Aflāj, al-Yamāma and al-Aḥsā' in 443/1051. His great detour to the south of Nejd was dictated by the chronic insecurity of central Arabia in the period. While in al-Aflāj for four months, awaiting a caravan to carry them onward, the pilgrims of his company were reduced to penury. Nāṣir was able to earn payment in dates to relieve his difficulties by decorating the mosque of al-Aflāj:

"Nous logions dans la mosquée; comme j'avais un peu de vermillon et de bleu minéral, je traçai, sur la muraille, un distique que j'encadrai d'une branche chargée de feuilles, en mettant une autre feuille (pour séparer les hémistiches). La vue de cette peinture émerveilla les gens du château qui se rassemblèrent pour venir la regarder. 'Si tu consens, me dirent-ils, à orner de peintures le mihrab de la mosquée, nous te donnerons cent men de dattes.' Une pareille quantité représente à leurs yeux une valeur considérable."(1)

He continues:

"Je décorai le mihrab conformément à l'engagement qui avait été pris vis-à-vis de moi, et je reçus les cent men de dattes qui furent pour nous un secours dans la détresse à laquelle nous étions réduits."(2)

This mosque has been lost, although the remains of many old *qaṣrs* still exist on the outskirts of Layla, the main town of al-Aflāj. Layla itself is a modern settlement with little architecture of any age. However, on the north-eastern outskirts of the town, there is a mosque in traditional style in mud-brick. Its *qibla* wall, facing north-westwards, has been repaired in concrete where it has collapsed. The most important feature of the mosque is the square *miḥrāb* projection, reaching to very little less than the full height of the *qibla* wall.

To the north of Layla is the village of Usayliya, among whose traditional houses is a mud-brick mosque with a walled *ṣaḥn* on the south-east side and a flat-roofed prayer-hall on the north-west. The mosque is far wider than it is deep on its *qibla* axis. On the north-east of the *ṣaḥn*, in the corner, is a staircase to the roof, passing through a square minaret at the head of the staircase. This is similar to the type of minaret found in other parts of Nejd to the north. The *miḥrāb* is a rectangular projection in the centre of the *qibla* wall and resembles not only those of southern Nejd but also the *miḥrābs* of Najrān to the south-west.

11 Rajab 1404/12 April 1984

III

The Eastern Province

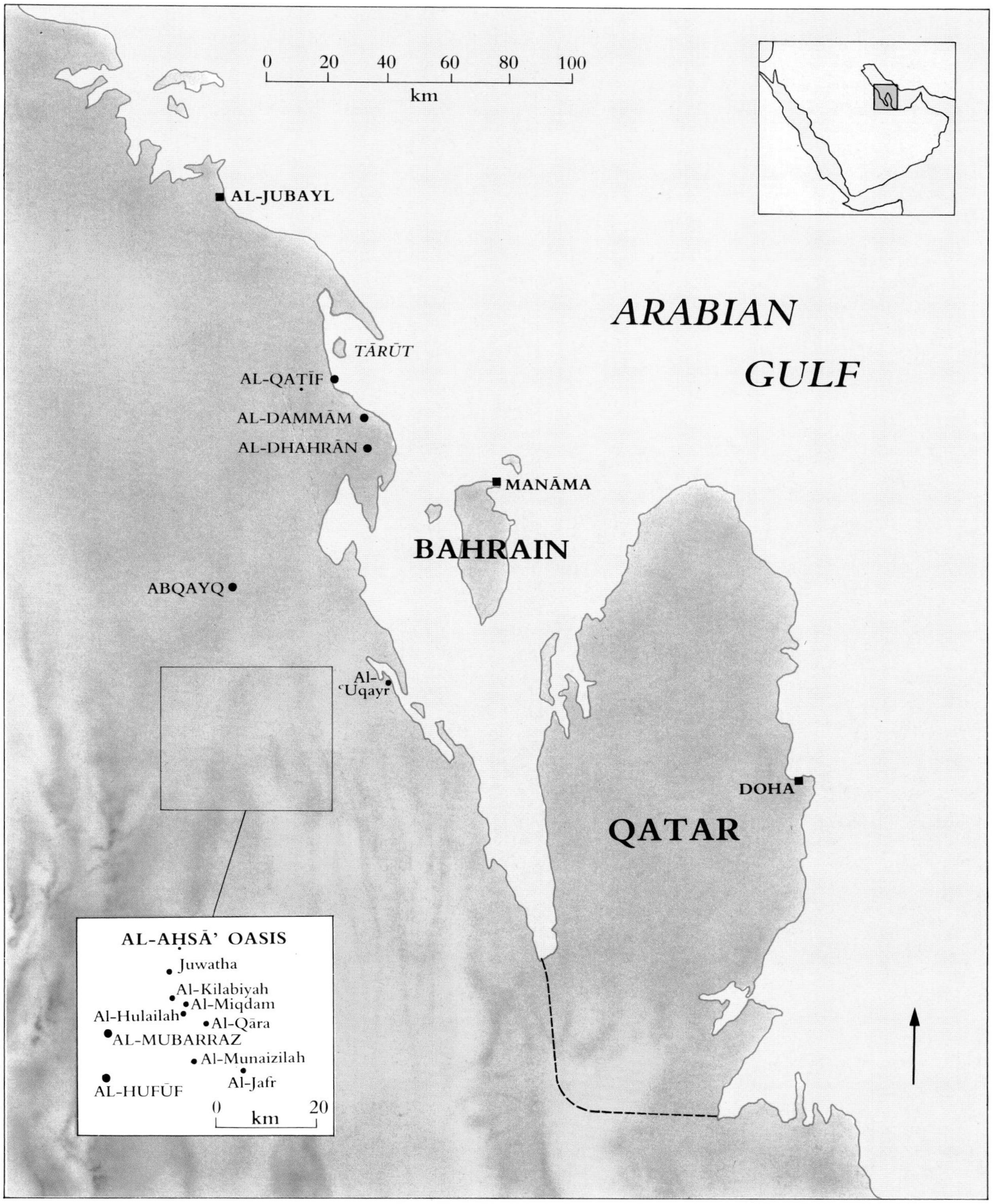

The Eastern Province of Saudi Arabia is today the centre of oil production in the Kingdom. The main inland settlement area is the great oasis of al-Aḥsā', on the east side of the al-Dahnā' sands. The principal city of the al-Aḥsā' oasis is al-Hufūf Al-Mubarraz is another major town, which today has become linked with al-Hufūf; there are also a number of other towns and villages scattered through the oasis. The agriculture of al-Aḥsā' has been the basis of the district's prosperity since antiquity and this is made possible by the copious supplies of sweet water available beneath the ground. There are extensive palm groves and farms throughout the oasis.

Apart from agriculture, al-Aḥsā' has long been important for trade from the Gulf coast to inner Arabia. There are several ports for the area – al-Jubayl, al-Qaṭīf, al-Dammām and al-ᶜUqayr. Although the ports of al-Jubayl and al-Dammām are the results of modern development programmes, they were preceded by small harbours which were important elements in the traditional commerce of the east Arabian coast. The wealth of eastern Arabia was sufficient long before oil was discovered to make it a worthwhile economic and strategic objective for the Ottomans. They twice held the area, with their inland base at al-Hufūf, from 959/1552 until 1080/1668-9, and from 1288/1871 until 1331/1913.

The climate of al-Aḥsā' oasis is not so different from the surrounding desert but along the coast the atmosphere is one of hot and heavy humidity, like the Red Sea. This has resulted in the same concern in traditional architecture to ensure means of cooling the interiors of buildings by ventilation as much as possible.

The building materials of eastern Arabia vary. In al-Aḥsā', stone and mud is used, reflecting the fact that al-Aḥsā' is an inland oasis and to this extent shares some features of central Arabian architecture. However, a most important aspect of al-Aḥsā' architecture is the use of carved plaster decoration that has its origin in the buildings of the Arabian Gulf. This east Arabian tradition of fine decoration in plaster affects mosques and houses alike, and is found throughout the settlements of the Aḥsā' oasis. Ornamental plaster is also found in the coastal towns of eastern Saudi Arabia; however, on the coast, the building material changes to coral aggregate, as on the coast of the Red Sea. In al-Jubayl, al-Qaṭīf and ᶜUqayr, this is the principal building material, and is then finished on the exterior and the interior wall-surfaces with finely worked plaster decoration.

Jawātha mosque, al-Aḥsā'

Jawātha mosque, al-Aḥsā'. Arches on the east side.

The mosque of Jawātha is considered one of the oldest in Saudi Arabia. It is said to have been founded in the time of the Prophet Muḥammad (ṣ) by al-ᶜAlā' b. al-Ḥaḍramī or by a man of ᶜAbd Qays, who had converted to Islam at al-Madina al-Monawarah when he met the Prophet (ṣ) there. He then returned to his own people in al-Aḥsā', establishing a mosque on the site occupied by the present mosque of Jawātha.

The Jawātha mosque is situated in a sandy area known as al-Qilabiyya and is near the villages of Miqdam and Halayla.(1) In older photographs, the mosque appeared engulfed by sand dunes, but now the area around the building has been cleared and a modern park with trees has been established in its vicinity. The mosque itself stands in the centre of a walled enclosure approached by steps. As a result of clearing the sur-

Jawātha mosque, al-Aḥsā'. Qibla *wall.*

rounding sand in modern times, the remains of the ancient mosque are now situated on a freestanding platform about one metre above ground level. A protecting roof on concrete piers covers the entire mosque. The ancient building is constructed of stone in a mud mortar, and then plastered, a combination of building materials found elsewhere in the oasis of al-Aḥsā'. The mosque is reduced to the remains of an arcade of two pointed arches lying parallel to the fragments of the *qibla* (western) wall. The pointed arches once continued to either side of the present remnants which are plastered white on their intrados. The *qibla* wall is the most substantial surviving part of the mosque, consisting of two keel-arches on each side of a broader keel-arch: this central arch is blocked by an ancient wall in all but the uppermost part and forms the *miḥrāb*. The *miḥrāb* is marked by a rectangular projection on the exterior surface of the *qibla* wall. In the arch to the south of the *miḥrāb* are wooden shelves for the Holy Qur'ān. The floor of the mosque is covered with carpets and mats, all of recent date.

23 Jumāda II 1403/7 April 1983

Mosque of Ibrāhīm, al-Hufūf

The mosque of Ibrāhīm in al-Hufūf is also referred to locally as Masjid al-Qubba (the Mosque of the Dome). It is situated in the south-west corner of the great Qaṣr Ibrāhīm. The present mosque is dated to the second half of the 10th/16th century[1] and the strong Ottoman influence which so greatly affects its design must be seen in context of the fact that, by 959/1552[2], an Ottoman garrison was stationed in al-Aḥsā'. Although Ottoman mosque design is the principal inspiration of the mosque of Ibrāhīm, nevertheless, other more local influences have also made their presence felt, particularly in the decoration.

The mosque is coated in plaster, on the exterior and the interior, but enough of the underlying building material is visible to show that it is built of baked brick and stone. There is also decoration in plaster around the doors and the pierced window screens. The mosque is a square building on a platform slightly higher than the courtyard of the *qaṣr*, and it stands close to the *qaṣr* walls on the south and west (*qibla*) sides; only the east and north walls of the mosque are exposed to view. On these exposed sides there is a portico running around the exterior, with bulky circular columns which support small domes, five to each portico. The arches that spring from the columns vary in their design: those on the east side are all pointed, with the sole exception of the arch on axis with the east entrance to the mosque and the main *miḥrāb* in the *qibla* wall of the prayer-hall. This arch alone is accentuated by ornamental lobes, as if stressing the *qibla* direction. The north portico is different, with pointed arches alternating with lobed arches. At the north-east and the south-east corners of the porticoes are buttresses which are similar in form to those at the corners of the *qibla* wall of the Jabrī mosque nearby in al-Hufūf. At the *qibla* end of the north portico there is a small *miḥrāb*, a curved recess with a pointed arch, but devoid of decoration. There is another external *miḥrāb*, a large freestanding structure east of the mosque.

Mosque of Ibrāhīm, al-Hufūf, from the north.

Mosque of Ibrāhīm, al-Hufūf. Portico on the north side.

The minaret stands at the north-east corner of the prayer-hall, forming a curved salient in the porticoes. It is entered through a small pointed archway from the east portico. The shaft is plain as far as the base of the single *shurfa*, at which point it has ranks of diminutive *muqarnaṣ* supporting the balcony. A wooden parapet with elegant arches supporting the roof of the balcony recalls mosques of the eastern Islamic world, as opposed to the Ottoman style that prevails in the prayer-hall. The uppermost part of the minaret, emerging above the balcony, is a narrow tapering structure, terminated by a small dome and a *hilāl*.

The domed prayer-hall has only two entrances: one in the centre of the east wall, opposite the main *miḥrāb*, and a second in the centre of the north wall. The east entrance is the principal access and is emphasised by an ornate extrado in carved plaster, slightly recessed around the pointed arch of the doorway. The stylised scroll patterns and geometrics seem to belong to the repertoire of eastern Arabian plaster ornament, rather than to any external influence. Above the entrance is an inscription panel of 977/1569-70.

The great dome that vaults the prayer-hall rests on a zone of transition consisting of four large, plain squinches, an unusual structural form in Saudi Arabia. These squinches are each surmounted by a diminutive dome, visible from the exterior; these are an uncommon feature in comparable domed mosques. The interior of the prayer-hall is lit at ground-level by rectangular

Mosque of Ibrāhīm, al-Hufūf. Minaret.

Mosque of Ibrāhīm, al-Hufūf. Miḥrāb *and* minbar.

windows with wooden shutters, all set back in the thick walls of the mosque. There is a window on either side of the east entrance to the prayer-hall and the same arrangement flanks the north entrance. There is also a single window on each side of the *miḥrāb* in the west (*qibla*) wall. On the south side are three windows, all rendered redundant by the proximity of the *qaṣr* wall. There are other windows high up in the walls of the prayer-hall with plaster screens pierced with geometric patterns. Windows of the same design stand above each squinch and in the lateral walls. All are pointed, with the exception of a single round-headed window on the south side. There is also a window with a keel-arch above the *miḥrāb*. The carved plaster screens recall once more the tradition of decorative plaster which is found throughout the Arabian Gulf.

On the western side of the prayer-hall a low platform distinguishes the floor preceding the *qibla* wall from the rest of the mosque. The *miḥrāb* in the centre of the west wall is in the form of a curved niche with a pointed arch. The upper part of the *miḥrāb* canopy has an elegant, ornate *muqarnaṣ* motif, more complex than that beneath the balcony of the minaret. To the north of the *miḥrāb* is a fixed *minbar* of three steps built against the *qibla* wall. Its design differs from others in Saudi Arabia, yet the fixed *minbar* in various forms is a feature of many mosques in the country as a whole, and its presence here may reflect a specifically Arabian tradition.

23 Jumāda II 1403/7 April 1983

al-Jabrī mosque, al-Hufūf

The Masjid al-Jabrī is situated to the west of the Qaṣr Ibrāhīm in al-Hufūf, amidst a number of traditional-style houses. The mosque is distinguished by its very large size and is dated to 820/1417.(1)

The building material is cut stone, as it is in other buildings in al-Hufūf, but this masonry is covered over by a thick coat of hard plaster which gives the exterior of the mosque an ochre tinge. The exterior of the mosque is generally plain and devoid of decoration. There are a number of doors in the north and the south sides of the mosque, although I examined the interior only from the doors giving on to the *ṣaḥn* from the south. A further doorway is built into the projecting *miḥrāb*, a rectangular construction in concrete against the exterior surface of the west (*qibla*) wall. In contrast with the plainness of the other exterior wall surfaces, there is a certain amount of articulation on the exterior surface of the *qibla* wall of the mosque, where shallow buttresses at regular intervals project from the wall on either side of the *miḥrāb*. At the extremities of the *qibla* wall are narrow corner towers: that at the south-west corner is terminated by a curious grooved, fluted cone. Although not emphasised in the same way, the south-east corner of the mosque enclosure is bevelled to protect it from buffeting by traffic in the street.

Inside the mosque enclosure, there is an open *ṣaḥn* at the east end, with *riwāqs* on the north and south sides of the *ṣaḥn* formed by pointed arches on rectangular piers. On the east side there are rooms which have the effect of concealing the base of the circular minaret in the south-east corner.

On the west side of the *ṣaḥn* are a series of three or four arcades of keel-arches running parallel to the *qibla* wall, in the traditional and elegant pointed style of the Arabian Gulf. While some of the piers are rectangular, others have substantial round piers with rectangular pilasters projecting from the east and west faces. The rounded piers recall Sassanian and early Islamic architectural forms in the east: for example, the *jāmiᶜ* of al-Hajjāj at al-Wāsiṭ (*c.* 83-6/702-5), the Tārīkh Khān mosque in Damghān (*c.* 132-70/750-86) or, far further

al-Jabrī mosque, al-Hufūf. Prayer-hall riwāqs.

afield, the Masjid-i Tārīkh in Balkh, of the 2nd-4th/8th-10th century, where the thick circular Sassanian-style piers are a major feature. This form of pier persists in architecture in the eastern Islamic world at least until the 4th/10th century: it may be that the piers in the al-Jabrī mosque represent a survival of a tradition from earlier Islamic times. Not all the piers in the Jabrī mosque are of this circular form, however, for other plain arches around the *ṣaḥn* rest on rectangular or square piers.(2)

In contrast to the plain arches around the *ṣaḥn*, those of the prayer-hall on the *qibla* side are more complex. They are set within rectangular frames in relief that rise from the supporting piers and separate the spandrels of the arches; the frames terminate just below the wooden roof-beams of the prayer-hall. A number of the arches are stepped back from these frames. The *miḥrāb* in the centre of the *qibla* wall is treated in the same way and consists of a rectangular recess with a pointed arch south of a fixed *minbar* recess which is approached by two steps. The *minbar* recess is reminiscent of recessed fixed *minbars* in other parts of Saudi Arabia. The arches of the aisle on axis with this *miḥrāb* are differently treated, being pointed but with a lobed profile.(3) This method of accentuating the aisle preceding the *miḥrāb* is found elsewhere in al-Hufūf: in the Ibrāhīm mosque an exterior arch on axis with the *miḥrāb* is stressed by lobed ornamentation of the arch profile. A similar decoration was used to accentuate the aisle leading to the *miḥrāb* of the old *jāmiᶜ* of al-Jubayl on the Arabian Gulf.

The entire prayer-hall of the mosque and the *riwāqs* on the courtyard are coated with a fine hard white plaster, contrasting with the ochre plaster on the exterior of the building. The overall effect of the interior of the Jabrī mosque is one of great elegance, enhanced by the rows of carpets running along the aisles between the arcades, parallel to the *qibla* wall. An additional covered area in the *ṣaḥn* is provided by a modern, roofed construction against the facade of the prayer-hall.

The minaret of the Jabrī mosque is an unusual and striking structure. It is situated, as already noted, in the south-east corner of the mosque enclosure and is apparently built of stone, coated with white plaster. The shaft is circular, with its lower part concealed within the rooms on the east side of the *ṣaḥn*. An arched entrance to the minaret can be seen in its north face, giving on to the flat roof of these rooms. The upper part of the minaret has four arched windows, one towards each of the cardinal points. Just below the level of the windows is a narrow platform around the shaft, supported by wooden beams that project like the spokes of a wheel. As the balcony lacks a guard rail, it seems a dangerous place from which to call the prayer, in its present state. However, its presence may be customary rather than practical. The minaret has a narrow roof resting on wooden beams projecting in a ring around the tower. The roof is in the form of a conical cap surmounted by a *hilāl*.

23 Jumāda II 1403/7 April 1983

al-Jabrī mosque. Minaret at the south-east corner.

al-Fātiḥ mosque, al-Hufūf

al-Fātiḥ mosque, al-Hufūf. The portico from the east.

The al-Fātiḥ mosque in al-Hufūf is commonly known as Masjid al-Dibs[1] and it lies just to the west of the Qaṣr Ibrāhīm. Adjoining the mosque on the south side is a house in traditional Hufūf style which had been the residence of Amīr Saᶜd b. Jilūwī. On this side, therefore, the exterior of the mosque is concealed from view, as it also is on the west (*qibla*) side and the north. Only the eastern facade is exposed, facing a street. This has undergone major alterations. The five pointed arches which once formed an open portico preceding the mosque on this side have all been partly closed off by screening walls of concrete. In the original design, the portico had no screening between the thick circular columns that support the arches. It appears that there was a passageway along the south side of the mosque, accessible through a door at the south end of the facade, but this is now closed off from the portico by a wall which I take to be recent. Above this southern entrance is a small window with a trefoil profile: the motif of the lobed window is one of long standing in the region, flourishing in ᶜAbbāsid ornament from the 3rd/9th century, and clearly still a vital motif in al-Hufūf in much later times. As a result of the modern alterations, the only entrance to the Fātiḥ mosque today is a wooden doorway in the screen closing the central archway of the portico, opposite the doorway to the prayer-hall that lies to the west. The portico is roofed by five domed vaults, supported by five arches that spring at right angles to the prayer-hall wall from the portico columns.

The prayer-hall itself has two doors, one on axis with the entrance to the portico from the street and also on axis with the central *miḥrāb* in the *qibla* wall of the mosque; the second doorway is just south of the first. Both doors are rectangular and of wood, with shallow blind niches above them. Inside the prayer-hall, the *miḥrāb* takes the form of an arched curved recess coated

al-Fātiḥ mosque, al-Hufūf. The portico looking south.

in white plaster like the rest of the interior. Above the *miḥrāb* is a rectangular inscription panel which has been painted, giving the date of the mosque as 963/1555-6.

The design of the mosque, preceded by its portico and without a *ṣaḥn*, is unusual in Arabia. The idea of a portico preceding the prayer-hall, or forming a facade to a mosque, is known elsewhere, however. It occurs first in the Bū Fatāta mosque in Sūsa, Tunisia in 223-6/838-41, and in 555/1160 in Cairo in the mosque of al-Ṣāliḥ al-Ṭalāᶜi. During Ottoman times, the portico preceding the prayer-hall was to become a common feature of mosques.

23 Jumāda II 1403/7 April 1983

al-Sharafiyya mosque, al-Hufūf

This small mosque stands in the central part of al-Hufūf, to the east of the main street through the *sūq* and to the south-east of the Qaṣr Ibrāhīm. It is built of roughly finished stone and mortar with thick white plaster covering the entire exterior, the minaret and the interior. I examined the Sharafiyya mosque only from the exterior where the minaret forms part of a salient on the western (*qibla*) side. The base of the minaret is square with a doorway in the south side; the shaft above the base is a circular structure with tapering sides, which terminates at the summit in a dome. This dome is not separated by any differentiating articulation from the shaft; rather, the tapering walls of the minaret grow directly into the dome. Close to the summit of the minaret are four small arched windows, one at each of the cardinal points. On top of the minaret is a *hilāl*.

al-Sharafiyya mosque, al-Hufūf, from the west.

Minarets of this type have been noted elsewhere. There is a minaret of a very similar form, as far as its upper shaft is concerned, in the Maghlūth mosque in al-Mubarraz, near al-Hufūf, for instance. Many years ago, J.B. Mackie [1] mentioned a small mosque with a minaret in the same style in al-Hufūf, which he rather curiously termed a "Small Turkish Mosque". There was little of Turkish design in the mosque he illustrated, but it was very close in the design of its minaret to the Sharafiyya mosque. Unfortunately, Mackie's mosque had vanished by 1393/1973. Minarets of this type in Saudi Arabia appear to be confined to the oasis of al-Aḥsā', and specifically to al-Hufūf, although there are apparently minarets of similar form in other Arab Gulf states.

23 Jumāda II 1403/7 April 1983

al-Sharafiyya mosque, al-Hufūf. Minaret from the north.

*Jāmi*ᶜ *of Imām Fayṣal b.Turkī, al-Hufūf*

In al-Hufūf, the principal mosque is the recently rebuilt *jāmi*ᶜ of Imām Fayṣal b. Turkī, completed in 1401/1981. It is a building in the same general style as the modern mosque of Imām Fayṣal in al-Mubarraz.(1) The new *jāmi*ᶜ of Imām Fayṣal in al-Hufūf replaces an earlier mosque, but I have seen no illustration of the older building. W.G. Palgrave wrote of a mosque of Imām Fayṣal in the Na'āthil quarter of al-Hufūf, whose "Moresco arches, light porticoes, smooth plaster and mat-spread floor" he admired.(2) This mosque, which he saw in 1279/1862, appears from his cursory remarks to have been in the style of eastern Arabian architecture which is still preserved in al-Hufūf and elsewhere in the eastern province of the Kingdom.

23 Jumāda II 1403/7 April 1983

*Jāmi*ᶜ *of Imām Fayṣal b. Turkī, al-Mubarraz*

Jāmiᶜ *of Imām Fayṣal b. Turkī, al-Mubarraz, from the east.*

Al-Mubarraz has now grown to become a part of the city of al-Hufūf, although in the past it had a separate existence. It still has a number of interesting traditional buildings and mosques. Among the historical mosques of al-Mubarraz is that of Fayṣal b. Turkī, a large modern mosque which was completed in 1398/1978. The former mosque was built by Imām Fayṣal during the second Saudi state's dominance in eastern Arabia. W.G. Palgrave visited al-Mubarraz in 1279/1862[1] and mentioned the mosque that Imām Fayṣal had constructed. According to Palgrave, the mosque was the main building of al-Mubarraz and was noteworthy for its size and elegance.

23 Jumāda II 1403/7 April 1983

al-Maghlūth mosque, al-Mubarraz

al-Maghlūth mosque, Mubarraz. Minaret.

In al-Mubarraz is situated the Maghlūth mosque, its exterior walls obscured by the numerous shops which surround it. The most ancient part of the mosque, I was told, is the minaret. It is visible from outside the mosque and stands on a high square socle; the upper part has a circular shaft with a single round-headed window in the western face for the *adhān* and for illumination of the staircase. The summit of the minaret is terminated by a dome which grows from the sides of the shaft in the same way as the roof of the minaret of the Sharafiyya mosque in al-Hufūf (pages 175-6). However, the minaret of the Maghlūth mosque differs inasmuch as a decorative raised band forms a ring visually separating the dome from the minaret shaft.

23 Jumāda II 1403/7 April 1983

Mosque, al-Munayzila, al-Aḥsā' oasis

Al-Munayzila is a village in the oasis of al-Aḥsā'. Its mosque is interesting inasmuch as it has elements of the repertoire of the eastern Arabian tradition, although the mosque is of no great age. It is a simple structure with a prayer-hall on the west side, a level roof and a high walled *ṣaḥn* on the east. The *ṣaḥn* has an entrance in the south wall. At the south-east corner of the *ṣaḥn* is a rectangular minaret with a canopy on top, opened on four sides by round-headed arches; the minaret is capped by a dome.

There are high rectangular windows in the sides of the prayer-hall, set into shallow blind niches with round-headed arches. The exterior surface of the *qibla* wall is articulated by regular rows of round-headed blind arches, all very shallow, flanking the rectangular *miḥrāb* projection in the centre. Such shallow recesses are a widespread feature of traditional Islamic architecture in eastern Arabia.

25 Jumāda II 1402/20 April 1982

Mosque, al-Munayzila, from the south-west, al-Aḥsā' oasis.

Mosque, al-Jafr, al-Aḥsā' oasis

In the village of al-Jafr in the Aḥsā' oasis is a *jāmiᶜ* of no great age. It has a whitewashed, rather plain prayer-hall with a level roof and windows in the sides providing ventilation and light. The *miḥrāb* in the centre of the west (*qibla*) wall is a rectangular projection with a pair of arched vaults covering it, a most unusual arrangement. The entrance to the mosque is in a salient projecting from the *ṣaḥn* enclosure wall. The high wall of the *ṣaḥn* effectively conceals the interior.

The most prominent feature of the mosque is the square minaret on the east side of the *ṣaḥn*, with an open window in each face of its wall. There are crenellations at the top of the tower, which is terminated by a dome bearing a finial. This type of minaret seems to be confined to eastern Arabia. The mosque in al-Jafr is similar to others in the oasis of al-Aḥsā'.

25 Jumāda II 1402/20 April 1982

al-Jafr, al-Aḥsā' oasis.

Old mosque, al-Qāra, al-Aḥsā' oasis

In 1393/1973 I photographed a mosque near al-Qāra which had long before fallen in ruins. Such as remained of this building showed that it had been a mosque of some elegance with features related to the local style of eastern Arabia in general and of al-Aḥsā' in particular. The ruined mosque was built of stone fixed in mortar, with stabilising wooden beams laid horizontally at regular intervals. The mosque had originally been plastered externally and internally, while the decoration had been executed in carved plaster. On the exterior, only a little of this plaster remained intact, although the interior was in better condition. The roof of the mosque was level, and constructed with cleft palm trunks covered by matted palm thatch. All that could be ascertained of the ground-plan was that the prayer-hall had originally been a wide, shallow rectangular chamber with a single arcade parallel to the *qibla* wall, serving to support the roof. The arches of this arcade were semicircular, resting on substantial circular columns. Each of these had a square impost block. Between every two arches was a simple ornamental pilaster with a notional rectangular capital in relief. The arches and the intervening pilasters were reminiscent of the facade of the mosque at al-ᶜUqayr on the Arabian Gulf.

The most striking feature of the ruined mosque in al-Qāra was the principal *miḥrāb* in the centre of the *qibla* wall, a deep rectangular recess with a pointed arch, whose depth was such that it probably projected on the exterior. A succession of ornamental bands in carved plaster accentuated the outline of the *miḥrāb*. Of these, the innermost had a row of V-motifs; the next band was broader with floral motifs (akin to those around the doorway to the mosque of Ibrāhīm in al-Hufūf); finally, the outermost extrado band around the arch profile was of blind lobed arches. The *miḥrāb* was framed by a slightly raised rectangular frame with stylised floral discs in the spandrels, although the later insertion of a recess had cut into the plaster decoration. Above the *miḥrāb* was an inscription panel in plaster which I had no opportunity to read. A second blind niche, shaped like a *miḥrāb*, appeared on the exterior surface of the east wall of the mosque, with an elongated scalloped canopy above a shallow rectangular recess.

Ramaḍān 1393/October 1973

Remains of mosque, al-Qāra. Qibla *wall in 1393/1973.*

Mosque remains, al-Qāra, in 1393/1973.

The coast

al-Rajihiyya mosque, al-Qaṭīf

The Rajihiyya mosque is one of two old mosques in the town of al-Qaṭīf, both of similar type.[1] It is situated within the confines of the narrow streets and high buildings of the old town, where houses of two storeys and more provide shade for the streets below. It stands on the south side of a street through the old quarter and its only entrance is from this side, it seems. The building material is coral aggregate reinforced with wood, the material used for traditional architecture in all old buildings in al-Qaṭīf and the Saudi Arabian Gulf coast. The mosque is clearly visible only on its north side, from the street. In plan it is a rather irregular structure, doubtless because of the restrictions on space in the old city and because of the need to ensure the correct orientation of the *qibla* wall. There is a courtyard entered from the north, from the single doorway on the street; bordering it on the west side are the prayer-halls in two storeys. On the eastern side of the *ṣaḥn* are rooms and there is a staircase in the north-east corner.

Although the exterior of the mosque is otherwise plain, the entrance to the courtyard has decoration that distinguishes it from other doorways in the street. The entrance itself is rectangular with an elegant carved wooden door in a style found along the length of the Arabian Gulf coast. This door is set back within a shallow rectangular recess which is framed by a stilted blind arch decorated with lobes. In the tympanum of this blind arch, as well as in the spandrels of the panel, are carved geometric motifs.

al-Rajihiyya mosque, al-Qaṭīf. Entrance from the street on the north side.

Inside the enclosure wall, the lower prayer-hall on the ground floor is approached from the *ṣaḥn* and the arrangement of its arcades, parallel to the *qibla* wall, duplicates the prayer-hall on the upper storey, directly above. The upper prayer-hall is reached by a staircase on the south side, while a staircase already mentioned on the east side of the courtyard gives access to the roofs of buildings adjacent to the mosque. The upper prayer-hall is preceded by an open terrace to the east and has two arcades running nearly parallel to the west (*qibla*) wall. Five stilted, pointed arches form the facade of the upper prayer-hall; each arch is supported by a thick hexagonal column, all quite short. A narrow floral band in plaster provides a sort of capital to each column, and resting on each is a square impost block, the base from which the arches spring. Accentuated by shallow recessed extrado bands which follow the arch profiles, the arches are set in rectangular frames which are also recessed very slightly from the plane of the wall. In the upper corners of each spandrel are rectangular openings with pierced plaster screens, decorated with geometric motifs. The uppermost part of the wall forms a parapet which is plain on the east side and rests on small corbels. These corbels are very carefully positioned so that one stands directly above each column and two above each arch. It is a small point but an instance of the attention to detail that characterises the careful design of the mosque. In the north lateral wall are rectangular windows with plaster screens decorated with pierced geometric motifs. These small windows have the advantage of allowing the circulation of air to provide some degree of cooling in the humidity that prevails in al-Qaṭīf. In the centre of the *qibla* wall is a recessed *miḥrāb* in carved plaster. It culminates in a shell motif in its half-dome, recalling a similar *miḥrāb* at a mosque in al-Qāra, in the al-Aḥsā' oasis (see page 178).

12 Jumāda I 1403/25 February 1983

al-Rajibiyya mosque, al-Qaṭīf. Upper prayer-hall, from the east.

Mosque in the oasis, al-Qaṭīf

Mosque in the oasis, al-Qaṭīf, from the north-east.

Mosque, al-Qaṭīf oasis, from the east (1393/1973).

Mosque, al-Qaṭīf oasis. View from the ṣaḥn *towards the* qibla *wall (1393/1973).*

In the oasis north of al-Qaṭīf is a simple but distinctive mosque of a type which once may have been more common in the area. This small mosque stands west of the road from al-Qaṭīf to al-Jubayl and is constructed of coral aggregate like other buildings in al-Qaṭīf and on the Arabian Gulf coast. The mosque is a very open building, reminiscent of the upper prayer-hall of the Rajihiyya mosque in al-Qaṭīf itself.

The oasis mosque is rectangular with a high wall around the *ṣaḥn* and an elegant prayer-hall on the western (*qibla*) side. A doorway gives access to the *ṣaḥn* from the south, the only entrance to the mosque. The lintel of the doorway is raised somewhat above the level of the enclosure wall, a characteristic treatment of mosque doorways in many parts of Saudi Arabia. The *ṣaḥn* is empty and gives access to the prayer-hall on the west side. The prayer-hall has two rows of arcades parallel to the *qibla* wall, with three arches to each arcade. The arches spring from bulky circular columns that taper somewhat. A stylised capital is indicated by a slightly raised band around the summit of each column, and rectangular impost blocks complete the support for each stilted arch. These arches resting on the columns are set in shallow recessed rectangular frames in the same way as those in the Rajihiyya mosque, while rectangular windows in the spandrels of all the arches also recall similar opening in the Rajihiyya. The north wall of the prayer-hall has two pairs of arched windows resting on single stumpy columns, in the same general style as the columns of the arcades of the prayer-hall. The *miḥrāb*, in the centre of the *qibla* wall, is a simple arched recess, which makes no projection or other indication of its presence on the exterior of the *qibla* wall.

Ramaḍān 1393/October 1973
12 Jumāda I 1403/25 February 1983

al-ᶜUqayr

Al-ᶜUqayr is a small port on the east coast of Saudi Arabia, to the south of al-Dammām and al-Dhahrān. There is no town as such, only a *qalaᶜ*, a ruined and abandoned "*khān*", a mosque and some modern buildings. Al-ᶜUqayr was the site of negotiations between His Late Majesty King ᶜAbd al-ᶜAzīz Al Saᶜūd and British officials during the early days of the third Saudi state.

Of the buildings standing at al-ᶜUqayr, the *qalaᶜ* is probably the oldest, constructed originally as a free-standing fortress reinforced by towers. The extensive "*khān*", as earlier travellers describe it(1), was probably built next, while the mosque and the *majlis* (or reception room) of which it is a part, was apparently built last. In al-ᶜUqayr I was informed that the late King ᶜAbd al-ᶜAzīz built the mosque some time after he had won eastern Arabia from the Ottomans in 1331/1913. The strange manner in which the mosque is sited in relation to the rest of the buildings suggests strongly that it was inserted in a previously existing complex.

The building material of the mosque, as well as of the *majlis* and the *khān*, is plastered coral aggregate. The construction is reinforced with wooden beams, and the roof is also of wood with palm thatching, like the rest of the complex. The humid climate has had a very destructive effect on the fabric of the older buildings, and the good state of preservation of the mosque reflects its relatively recent date and the attention paid to its upkeep.

Mosque, al-^{c}Uqayr.

Mosque, al-^{c}Uqayr. Prayer-hall.

The mosque is constructed as a single continuous unit with the *majlis*, while beyond to the north-west is the *qala^{c}*. Within the structure, the *qibla* wall of the mosque runs at an angle; given the orientation of the pre-existing buildings, the architect was compelled to turn the *qibla* wall towards the direction of Makkah al-Mukarramah in such a manner that the ground-plan of the mosque acquired a curious trapezoidal shape.

The entrance to the mosque is in the east wall, leading directly to the *ṣaḥn*; the wall in which the door is set runs on to form the facade of the neighbouring *majlis*. Apart from the entrance, which is preceded by a low flight of steps, there is also in this wall a series of round-headed windows, with wooden frames for shutters and metal grilles, that give on to the *ṣaḥn* from the street. All of these windows are lower than the east doorway to the mosque. This window system continues beyond the mosque to articulate the exterior of the *majlis* in the same way and thus unifies the entire eastern side of the two structures.

On the other sides, the trapezoid *ṣaḥn* is surrounded by high walls, and to the south-west it is bordered by the prayer-hall. The roof of the prayer-hall, which is level, is supported by two rows of arcades running parallel to the *qibla* wall. The arches rest on thick octagonal columns, each surmounted by a square capital. The round-headed arches are set back slightly within shallow rectangular frames. At the top of the facade of the prayer-hall there is a low parapet. Cut through this wall, directly above the columns, are spouts to cast rainwater into the *ṣaḥn*.

The *qibla* wall is emphasised by a series of blind-arched panels, some trilobed and others with round-headed arches, all extremely shallow. The central panel constitutes the *miḥrāb*.

16 Jumāda II 1403/31 March 1983

al-Jubayl

In 1392/1972 several traditional mosques still stood in the Arabian Gulf port of al-Jubayl in the Eastern Province. At that time, al-Jubayl was still only a small commercial and fishing port and the vast petro-chemical complex that later transformed the town into a major industrial centre had not yet had any visible effect. Subsequently, the entire site was reconstructed and most of the old buildings, including the mosques, were replaced with modern structures. Before al-Jubayl was developed, there were at least three old mosques, one of which had long fallen into ruin and disuse by 1392/1972; all the older mosques which I saw in al-Jubayl at that time were of considerable size and were finely constructed, reflecting the town's economic role in the pre-oil period as one of the more important ports serving eastern and central Arabia, as well as indicating the quite sizeable population concentrated there. There were numerous traditional-style houses at al-Jubayl still intact in 1392/1972, as well as a customs house at the harbour which was said to have been Ottoman. The only building material in use at that time was coral aggregate carved from offshore which had been carved up and formed into building blocks described as *ḥajar al-baḥr*. The same building material is found around all of the Arabian coast, and is generally reinforced with wooden beams. Wood was also used for roofs; some of this was imported as part of the area's traditional trade with India and East Africa. The wall surfaces of these buildings were usually plastered on the exterior as well as on the interior, and delicate and complex patterns were carved in the plaster, often as window grilles and ornamental panels. The pliability of the Gulf building materials allowed an elegance of decorative form which is not encountered outside the immediate area, although parallels exist between the architecture of the Gulf, the Indian Ocean littoral and the Red Sea. The traditional building material of the area is fragile and none of the buildings in old al-Jubayl or in other coastal towns seems to have been of very great antiquity.

Old *jāmi*ᶜ, al-Jubayl

The old *jāmi*ᶜ was the most prominent mosque in al-Jubayl, with an unusual staircase minaret and elegant decorative motifs in the local style of the Gulf; it was still intact as late as 1393/1973, but was subsequently demolished and rebuilt. The *jāmi*ᶜ was particularly large, with a walled *ṣaḥn* to the east, a prayer-hall to the west, and a level roof resting on arcades parallel to the west (*qibla*) wall. The entire building was constructed on a "pier and panel" principle whereby the structure of the enclosure wall and the prayer-hall was provided by small rectangular piers; between these piers were slightly recessed panels designed to form a screen rather than to support any weight. The system is used elsewhere in the Gulf and in regions where coral aggregate is employed. It has the advantage that the panels can be pierced by windows and doors without any difficulty since all structural weight is supported by the intervening piers. In the *jāmi*ᶜ of al-Jubayl, the possibilities inherent in this system were exploited to provide a continuous wall around the courtyard with the side-walls of the prayer-hall built on the same principle, but with the panels between the structural piers opened up

Old jāmiᶜ*, al-Jubayl. Prayer-hall, from the south west (1392/1972).*

Old jāmi^{c}, *al-Jubayl, from the south-east (1392/1972).*

Old jāmi^{c}, *al-Jubayl. East facade of the prayer-hall in 1392/1972.*

to provide windows for internal ventilation. Air circulation was a primary consideration in all Gulf and coastal Arabian traditional architecture; in contrast to central Arabia, there is not such a variation between winter and summer, and, instead, architects in the past seem to have concentrated on methods of providing a free circulation of cooling breeze in order to ameliorate the heavy humidity and heat which prevails at most times of the year. Considerations such as these seem to have led to the particularly open design of the lateral walls of the old *jāmi*^{c} of al-Jubayl.

The only entrance in the south wall of the mosque was a rectangular doorway leading into the courtyard and it was given particular emphasis by a complex blind arch forming a decorative tympanum above it, with ogees, lobes and angles. Similar lobed and broken arches framed a series of windows in the sides of the prayer-hall, each set above a larger rectangular window which was fitted with a wooden frame and double shutters, and which could be closed when necessary. A very similar system is found in houses of the rest of the Gulf region as well as elsewhere around the coasts of Arabia.

The facade of the prayer-hall giving on to the courtyard was treated somewhat differently: the arcades that supported the level roof were set parallel to the *qibla* wall, and seem to have numbered seven in all. The arches of the prayer-hall were predominantly of the pointed type found in old al-Jubayl and elsewhere in eastern Saudi Arabia and its vicinity, and were supported

Old jāmi^{c}, *al-Jubayl. Doorway in the south wall of the* ṣaḥn.

Old jāmi^c^, *al-Jubayl. South wall of the prayer-hall in 1392/1972.*

by rectangular piers. In contrast with the other arches, the central aisle of arches on axis with the *miḥrāb* was different, with more complex decoration used to emphasise this direction and serving to denote on the facade the direction of the *miḥrāb* within the mosque. This is a device frequently found in Islamic architecture generally, whereby the area leading to the principal *miḥrāb* is stressed either by additional ornament, as in this case, or by some other means. Parallels for the decorated axis of al-Jubayl's old *jāmi*^c^ can be found as far west as Morocco and as far east as India. In Saudi Arabia, other examples of this decorative attention to the *miḥrāb* axis are encountered in the mosque of the Qaṣr Ibrāhīm and the Jabrī mosque in al-Hufūf, south-west of al-Jubayl in the al-Aḥsā' oasis. I had no opportunity to examine the *miḥrāb* of the al-Jubayl *jāmi*^c^, although on the exterior it appeared as a curved projection in the centre of the *qibla* wall. The parapet that ran round the other three sides of the mosque roof continued around the summit of the *miḥrāb*.

Access to the roof and to this continuation of the *miḥrāb* recess on the roof was provided by a staircase set in the corner of the mosque courtyard, against the south side; this led to the level roof of the prayer-hall. At the top of the staircase was a rectangular tower-like structure, built forward from the prayer-hall facade and reminiscent in its design of some of the rectangular staircase minarets of central Arabia. However, unlike central Arabian minarets of this type, that of the *jāmi*^c^ of al-Jubayl could not actually be ascended and was little more than an elaborate structure framing the way to the roof, with a complicated ornamental archway vaulting the staircase proper.

Ramaḍān 1393/October 1973

Old jāmi^c^, *al-Jubayl. Windows in the south wall of the prayer-hall in 1392/1972.*

Old jāmi^c^, *al-Jubayl. Staircase to the prayer-hall roof, 1392/1972.*

Old mosque, al-Jubayl

A mosque reduced to mere fragmentary arcades still survived in al-Jubayl in 1392/1972, although the arches illustrated here had vanished by the following year. The mosque itself had already been replaced by another mosque a little further to the east. All that remained of the old mosque were two elegant arcades which originally had run parallel to the vanished *qibla* wall. These finely plastered arches, built of coral aggregate, had once belonged to a mosque of considerable size and distinction, judging both from the remains themselves and the area which the mosque had apparently occupied. These remaining pointed arches were in the local style and rested on rectangular pillars; the outline of each arch was stressed by a shallow moulding, while a V-moulding ran in a band beneath the summit of the wall. To judge from the other mosques in al-Jubayl, this ruined mosque would have had a level roof and an open *ṣaḥn* on the east side, but at the time of my visit no trace of the *qibla* wall, minaret or *miḥrāb* remained, and in the absence of anything but sporadic traces of the enclosure wall, it was impossible to estimate precisely the overall dimensions of the mosque.

Shaᶜbān 1392/September 1972

Old mosque, al-Jabayl in 1392/1972. Riwāqs, looking east.

Mosque, al-Jubayl

To the east of the fragmentary remains of the above mosque was a second, still extant in 1401/1982, of more recent construction and apparently intended as a replacement. Although not especially distinguished, it is a type common in eastern Arabia. The newer mosque is a rectangular structure whose *ṣaḥn* is surrounded by an enclosure wall; the unadorned prayer-hall has a level roof and the *miḥrāb* forms a curved projection with a half-dome. There are two windows in the *qibla* wall, while the *miḥrāb* has further small windows. The entire structure is covered with white plaster. Mosques of similar stark simplicity occur elsewhere in the Eastern Province.

Shaᶜbān 1392/September 1972

Mosque on the seashore, al-Jubayl

In 1392/1972 a large mosque stood by the shore at al-Jubayl, similar in most respects to the old *jāmi*ᶜ, although it lacked a minaret. The mosque was built of coral aggregate and was plastered; its construction was on the same "pier and panel" principle as described for the old *jāmi*ᶜ of al-Jubayl. The mosque had a large rectangular *ṣaḥn* surrounded by an enclosure wall, and on the south side structures were built against the exterior wall. The prayer-hall to the west had a level roof supported by arcades parallel to the *qibla* wall. The arches of this arcade were of the pointed form that prevailed in al-Jubayl, with the exception of the arcade on line with the *miḥrāb* in the *qibla* wall; here, lobes and angles were used to distinguish the arch. The sides of the prayer-hall of the mosque repeated the design of the *jāmi*ᶜ of al-Jubayl to some degree, with rectangular windows below closed by pairs of wooden shutters; above were openings, vaulted by slight ogee arches. Although the mosque by the seashore followed the general form and design of the *jāmi*ᶜ of al-Jubayl, its finish was poorer and less ornately decorated. Nevertheless, the mosque was consistent with a particular repertoire of design and ornament peculiar to the Gulf area of Arabia in the past.

Shaᶜbān 1392/September 1972

Mosque on the seashore, al-Jubayl, from the south.

Saudi Arabian mosques and the Islamic architectural tradition

The diversity of mosque architecture in the Kingdom is self-evident from the material gathered in this survey; faced with this diversity, it is practical to indicate only some general antecedents and parallels for the styles of mosque within Saudi Arabia. Certain types of Saudi Arabian mosque are related to Islamic architectural traditions which have arisen outside the peninsula whereas other mosques seem to derive from an indigenous Arabian tradition of building. It may well be that these indigenous Arabian mosque traditions preserve very early Islamic forms that perhaps have undergone little evolution over centuries. However, only further investigation of Islamic archaeological sites in the Kingdom can determine the validity or otherwise of this hypothesis. The King Saud University excavations, directed by Dr S.A. al-Rāshid at al-Rabadha on the Darb Zubayda – the ancient *hajj* route from Iraq to Makkah al-Mukarramah – have revealed two early mosques which are important for illustrating Arabian mosque types of considerable antiquity(1); other investigations along the Darb Zubayda have identified the remains of ancient mosques(2), and it is to be hoped that these recent researches will eventually be supplemented by excavation at Islamic archaeological sites in other parts of the Kingdom. There are, of course, a number of very early mosques in the Kingdom, apart from those of the *ḥaramayn*. However, as we have seen, the original mosques of Makkah al-Mukarramah, al-Madina al-Monawarah, al-Aḥsā', Tabūk and Dūmat al-Jandal, have been rebuilt, sometimes on several occasions, and their earlier forms are difficult or impossible to determine. These ancient mosque sites are thus of limited help in identifying the forms of Arabian mosques in early times. Excavations therefore acquire great importance for the future study of the development of the mosque in Arabia.

As we have seen, the documentation of the mosques of the Holy Cities of Makkah al-Mukarramah and al-Madina al-Monawarah is particularly thorough, and the design of the Mosque of the Prophet (ṣ) from the earliest period is well known. It formed the model for subsequent mosques throughout the Islamic world in its combination of basic elements – a rectangular, walled enclosure with a roofed prayer-hall on the *qibla* side, a *miḥrāb*, and an open *ṣaḥn*, with the *minbar* from which to deliver the *khutba* to the right of the *miḥrāb*. These are the essentials of the design of the mosques of Saudi Arabia, as they are elsewhere in Islam. However, there are also specific architectural features of the Mosque of the Prophet (ṣ) and of other mosques of early date in Islam which are retained in mosques in Saudi Arabia. Among these features of design is the construction of prayer-halls with level wooden roofs resting directly on colonnades or piers. This is found in mosques in al-Wajh, Khaybar, Dūmat al-Jandal, Burayda, al-Zilfī and in various parts of south-western Saudi Arabia. This is the form of the Mosque of the Prophet (ṣ) as Ibn Jubayr described it in 580/1184, when it still retained the design it had acquired in the Umayyad period. In the days of the Prophet (ṣ), it seems certain that the palm-trunks that supported the roof of the *qibla riwāq* and the *suffa* of his mosque also bore the roof directly, without any intervening vaulting.

This type of colonnaded prayer-hall was that adopted in Iraq in early mosques built by the Muslims, who may be expected to have looked back to familiar Arabian traditions when designing mosques. The *jāmiᶜ* of Kūfa as rebuilt in 50/670 was of this type, as was the mosque of ᶜAmr b. al-ᶜĀṣ in al-Fusṭāṭ, rebuilt in 53/673. So too was the *jāmiᶜ* of the ᶜAbbāsid Caliph al-Manṣūr in Baghdad, dated 145-9/762-7. The *jāmiᶜ* of Wāsiṭ in south-eastern Iraq, built by the Umayyad governor, al-Ḥajjāj b. Yūsuf, in 83-6/702-5, possibly had the same relationship between its columns and its roof. This system was still being used in Iraq when the ᶜAbbāsid Caliph al-Mutawakkil built a *jāmiᶜ* at Sāmarrā' in 234-7/848-52. Dr. R. Lewcock has pointed out that in Bahrayn, in the mosque of Sūq al-Khamīs, reconstructed in 740/1339-40, the roof rested on columns, and that this tradition persisted in Kuwayt in traditional mosques.(3) There would seem to be some reason, therefore, for regarding the Saudi mosques with a level roof borne on columns without intervening arches as a tradition in Islamic architecture in Arabia and the vicinity, and of very ancient origin.

A commonly encountered design of prayer-hall in Saudi Arabia consists of arcades running parallel to the *qibla* wall. Mosques in Jidda, the Tihāma, the whole of Nejd, al-Aḥsā', al-Qaṭīf and al-Jubayl all share this characteristic; nor is the arrangement of arcades parallel to the *qibla* wall confined to the mosques of Saudi Arabia, for the *jāmiᶜ* of Ṣanᶜā' has the same ground plan, as have other mosques in the city(4) and in Zabīd.(5) The tradition of building mosques with prayer-halls in which the colonnades run parallel to the *qibla* wall is found from very early times in the Islamic world. The *jāmiᶜ* of Damascus, as constructed by the Umayyad Caliph al-Walīd b. ᶜAbd al-Malik in *c.* 85-96/*c.* 705-15, is the earliest example remaining intact, and it is known that the Umayyad reconstruction of the mosque of ᶜAmr b. al-ᶜĀṣ in al-Fusṭāṭ, dated 92-3/710-12, included arcades parallel to the *qibla* wall in the prayer-hall. In Egypt this tradition was to recur in later times in the mosque of Aḥmad b. Ṭūlūn as a result of the influence of the mosque of ᶜAmr. In Syria, the construction of arcades parallel to the *qibla* wall persisted throughout the Umayyad period, with examples of this plan occurring in Palestine and Syria in a number of mosques: at Qaṣr al-Minyā near Lake Tiberias, at Khirbat al-Mafjar in the Jordan Valley, at ᶜAnjār in Lebanon, at Qaṣr al- Ḥayr al-Sharqī in Syria, and in the last *jāmi*ᶜ built by the Syrian Umayyads, that of Ḥarrān, now in southern Turkey. Thus, the plan of arcaded mosques, which is so ubiquitous in Saudi Arabia in mosques of more recent times, preserves an Islamic architectural tradition of very ancient origin.

There are also a number of mosques in the vicinity of Saudi Arabia dated to the 3rd-4th/9th-10th centuries, that is, to the early ᶜAbbāsid period, which display the characteristics of mosques in the peninsula: Sāmarrā', the ᶜAbbāsid capital on the Tigris, has simple mosques in the Jawsaq al-Khāqānī palace (after 221/836) and the Qaṣr al-Balkuwarra, dated between 235/849 and 245/859.[(6)] The excavated remains of these small mosques suggest an affinity with the mosque tradition that survives in Arabia, in the prayer-hall type with arcades parallel to the *qibla*. An indication of the persistence of this mosque plan that manifests itself in Saudi Arabia can also be seen in a group of small mosques excavated at the early Islamic town site of Sirāf, on the Iranian shore of the Arabian Gulf.[(7)] The mosques at Sirāf display the essential features of mosques in many parts of Saudi Arabia in their general design – walled *ṣaḥns*, the level-roofed prayer-hall, arcades parallel to the *qibla* wall, and rectangular, projecting *miḥrābs*. However, most significant of all is the fact that several of the small mosques found at Sirāf have staircases from the *ṣaḥn* to the prayer-hall roof. This is a very important parallel with mosques in many parts of Saudi Arabia, where staircases to the roof from the *ṣaḥn* are found with and without a minaret situated at the head of the flight of steps. David Whitehouse has tentatively dated the group of small mosques at Sirāf to the early ᶜAbbāsid period, to 232/847, and to as late as the second half of the 4th/10th century.

The staircase to the roof of the prayer-hall varies in its treatment in different parts of Saudi Arabia, but as an element of mosque design it is a basic feature in all parts of Nejd, in Najrān, in the south-western mountains near Abhā, in the Tihāmat ᶜAīr and at al-Jubayl, on the Gulf. In Nejd, the Tihāma and al-Jubayl the staircases in many mosques are also accompanied by rectangular minarets, built at the head of the steps. The existence of the tradition of the staircase minaret in the Islamic world was first discussed in the context of Upper Egypt and Anatolia.[(8)] In Egypt, staircases to the prayer-hall roofs are surmounted by rectangular minarets in the area of Aswan, Edfu, Luxor and Zagazig. These examples are undated village mosques, although their concentration and persistent adherence to a particular form argue for a conscious loyalty to a certain model. In Anatolia they also appear to indicate a conservative survival of an early tradition. Joseph Schacht, who first drew attention to these minarets, suggested that they may be related to the design of the very first minaret built in Egypt in the mosque of ᶜAmr b. al-ᶜĀṣ during reconstructions in 53/673. If Schacht's hypothesis is correct and the staircase minarets of Upper Egypt and Anatolia are the survivals of a very early minaret form in Islam, then the examples in various parts of Saudi Arabia must also be reckoned as evidence of the persistence of this little-studied Islamic tradition.

In the northern parts of central Nejd, north of al-Ḥuraymilā', in Sudayr, in much of al-Qaṣīm, and formerly in Ḥā'il, the normal style of minaret is circular, and with no similarity to the rectangular staircase minarets of areas of Nejd to the south. The square minaret in Islamic architecture is considered to derive from Syria and persists to this day in the western Islamic world. By contrast, the circular minaret appears initially in ᶜAbbāsid Iraq with the famous helicoidal minarets of Sāmarrā' of the mid-3rd/9th century. Circular minarets gradually came to dominate the eastern Islamic world and, as a result, this tradition affected Iraq as well as the Arabian Gulf. It could be that these eastern minarets influenced the circular minarets of northern Nejd; acquaintance with eastern Islamic architecture is quite possible on the part of Nejdi architects, given the widespread activities of merchants, like those of al-Qaṣīm. However, another alternative must be considered, that the minarets' design stems from an indigenous Arabian tradition of building conical watch-towers, and that the circular Nejdi minarets are developments from these antecedents.

Other types of minaret are found in Arabia, of more obvious origin. In the Holy Mosques of the *ḥaramayn*, in Jidda, al-Ṭā'if, al-Wajh and in al-ᶜUlā, the minarets all indicate a strong Ottoman influence, reflecting the dominance of the Turkish Sultans in the Hejaz from the 10th/16th century. It may well be that the prevalence of the Ottoman-style minaret in the Hejaz was a reflection of the presence of such minarets in the Holy Mosque of Makkah al-Mukarramah and in the Mosque of the Prophet (ṣ) in al-Madina al-Monawarah: the overwhelming importance and prestige of these two Holy Mosques encouraged the imitation of their minarets in other towns of the Hejaz.[(9)]

The styles of *miḥrāb* in traditional Saudi Arabian mosques are extremely interesting. The curved recessed *miḥrāb* is known to have existed in the Mosque of the Prophet (s) from 88-90/707-9, and became widespread during the Umayyad Caliphate, with a number of examples surviving still in Jordan, Palestine and Syria. This type of *miḥrāb* is found in many parts of Arabia, often indicated on the exterior surface of the *qibla* wall by a curved projection. Another early Islamic tradition which occurs in Arabian mosques is a rectangular *miḥrāb* recess, often forming a prominent rectangular projection on the exterior of the *qibla* wall; these are particularly prevalent in southern Nejd, in Najrān and in the mountainous areas of the south-west. The tradition of the rectangular *miḥrāb* recess is known from ᶜAbbāsid Iraq in the 2nd-3rd/8th-9th century, at Qaṣr al-Ukhayḍir, and in the mosques of Sāmarrā' on the Tigris. However, the size of the rectangular *miḥrābs* of southern Nejd and the south-west constitutes a quite remarkable architectural development of the form.

A most interesting feature related to *miḥrābs* that appears in many parts of Saudi Arabia – in the Hejaz, in Nejd and in the Eastern Province – is the fixed or built *minbar*, constructed either within or against the *qibla* wall and to the right (facing) of the *miḥrāb*. The fixed *minbar* is so widespread that it should be regarded as a major tradition of Arabian Islamic architecture, although very little studied. There is an affinity between the Arabian tradition of recessed, fixed minbars and the built *minbars* that have been noted by several scholars in East Africa.[10] The tradition is an area of architectural research in Arabia that deserves further detailed investigation; it may be the case that such *minbars* developed in the Arabian peninsula and then spread to areas in contact with it.

It is to be hoped that the information gathered in this volume will go some way toward enhancing scholarly interest in the historical mosques of Saudi Arabia, representing, as these do, a most important aspect of mosque design in the Islamic world. Given the range of mosque forms found in the Kingdom, from the stark simplicity of village mosques through to the grand and ornate forms of the major mosques of the *ḥaramayn*, the historical mosques of Saudi Arabia provide a remarkable picture of how local traditions shape mosque style, and how, at every level, the mosque is an integral part of the life of the community.

Notes

Introduction ***p. 11***

1. There are a growing number of studies of mosques in Yemen. Apart from other works on this subject mentioned elsewhere in the notes and in the bibliography, the following can be cited:

Barbara Finster, "Die Freitagsmoschee von Ṣan^{c}ā'. Vorläufiger Bericht, 1." *Baghdader Mitteilungen*, ix (1978), pp. 92-93.

Barbara Finster and Jürgen Schmidt, "Die Freitagsmoschee von Ṣan^{c}ā'. Vorläufiger Bericht, 2. Der Ostriwāq", *Baghdader Mitteilungen*, x (1979), pp. 179-92.

Barbara Finster, "Die Freitagsmoschee von Šibām-Kaukabān", *Baghdader Mitteilungen*, x (1979), pp. 193-228.

Barbara Finster, "Die Moschee von Ṣarḥa", *Baghdader Mitteilungen*, x (1979), pp. 229-42.

Barbara Finster, "Die Moschee von Hāu", *Baghdader Mitteilungen*, x (1979), pp. 246-8.

Jürgen Schmidt, ed., *Archäologische Berichte aus dem Yemen*, Deutsches Archäologisches Institut Ṣan^{c}ā', Mainz-am-Rhein, i (1982).

R.B. Serjeant and Ronald Lewcock, eds., *Ṣan^{c}ā'. An Arabian Islamic City*, London (1983).

2. Saad A. al-Rashid, "Lights on the history and archaeology of al-Rabadhah (Locally called Abu Salim)", *Proceedings of the 12th Seminar for Arabian Studies*, ix (1979), pp. 88-101.

Saad A. al-Rashid, *Al-Rabadhah: A portrait of early Islamic civilisation in Saudi Arabia*, London (1986).

3. Sa^{c}d A. al-Rāshid, "Darb Zubayda fī'l-^{c}aṣr al-^{c}abbāsī: dirāsa tā'rīkhiyya wa āthāriyya", *al-Dāra*, (Rabī^{c}a II, 1398/March 1978) year 4 no.1, pp. 8-31; "Darb Zubaydah in the ^{c}Abbasid period: historical and archaeological aspects", *Proceedings of the 11th Seminar for Arabian Studies*, viii (1978), pp. 33-45.

Saad A. al-Rashid, *Darb Zubaydah. The Pilgrim Road from Kufa to Mecca*, Riyadh (1980).

4. ^{c}Uthmān b. Bishr, *^{c}Inwān al-majd fī tā'rīkh Najd*, Riyadh (no date), i, p.6.

5. Carsten Niebuhr, *Travels through Arabia and other countries in the East*, trans. from the German by Robert Heron, Edinburgh (1792; reprinted Beirut, no date), ii, pp. 130-6.

6. G.F. Sadleir, *Diary of a journey across Arabia, 1819*, Byculla (1866; reprinted Cambridge, 1977), pp. 81-3, 90-1.

7. For a general historical survey of the Kingdom, see H. St. J. Philby, *Sa^{c}udi Arabia*, London (1955; reprinted Beirut, 1968). Philby has also written a number of books on general and specific aspects of Saudi history which are of interest to the general reader. An important and more recent study is R. Bayley Winder, *Saudi Arabia in the Nineteenth Century*, London and NY (1965). There are a number of major sources in Arabic including ^{c}Uthmān b. Bishr, *^{c}Inwān al-majd fī tā'rīkh Najd*, Riyadh (no date), and Ḥusayn b. Ghannām, *Tā'rīkh Najd, rawḍat al-afkār wa'l-afhām*, Riyadh (1368/1949). Recent studies which should be consulted are ^{c}Abd al-Rahīm ^{c}A. ^{c}Abd al-Rahīm, *Al-dawlat al-Su^{c}ūdiyyat al-ūlā, 1158-1233/1745-1818*, 2nd printing, Ma^{c}had al-baḥūth wa'l-dirāsat al-^{c}arabiyya (1395/1975); ^{c}Abd al-Fattāḥ H. Abū ^{c}Ulya, *Al-dawlat al-Su^{c}ūdiyyat al-thāniyya, 1256-1309/1840-91*, Riyadh (1394/1974); A.S. ^{c}Uthaimīn, *Nasha't amārat Āl Rashīd*, Riyadh (1401/1981); Shaykh ^{c}Abd al-Raḥmān b. ^{c}Abd al-Laṭīf Āl al-Shaykh, "Shaykh Muḥammad b. ^{c}Abd al-Wahhāb", *al-Dāra* (Rajab 1396/July 1976), year 2, no. 2, pp. 16-27.

The Honourable Ka^{c}ba and the Holy Mosque, Makkah al-Mukarramah ***p. 19***

1. Holy Qur'ān, *Sūra III, 96*.

2. al-Azraqī, *Akhbār Makkah*, ed. Rushdī al-Ṣāliḥ Malḥas, Makkah al-Mukarramah (1403/1983), i, pp. 46-74.

Ḥusayn ^{c}Abd Allah Bā Salāma, *Tā'rīkh al-ka^{c}ba al-mu^{c}aẓẓama*, 2nd printing, Jidda (1402/1982), pp. 23-44.

3. al-Azraqī, *op. cit.*, i, pp. 157-8.

Ibn Hishām, *al-Sīrat al-nabawiyya*, ed. A. al-Saqqā, Cairo (1399/1979), i, p. 117.

Bā Salāma, *Tā'rīkh al-ka^{c}ba, op. cit.*, p. 51.

K.A.C. Creswell, *Early Muslim Architecture*, Oxford (1969), i, part 1, pp. 1-2.

4. See especially *Sūra II, 144:*

'We see the turning
Of thy face (for guidance)
To the heavens: now
Shall We turn thee
To a Qibla that shall
Please thee. Turn then
Thy face in the direction
Of the sacred Mosque:
Wherever ye are, turn
Your faces in that direction.'

5. al-Azraqī, *op. cit.*, ii, pp. 68-9.

al-Balādhūrī, *Kitāb futūḥ al-buldān*, ed. M.J. de Goeje, 2nd ed., Leyden (1968), p. 46.

al-Ya^{c}qūbi, *Tā'rīkh*, ed. Th. Houtsma, Leyden (1883), ii, p. 170.

Bā Salāma, *Tā'rīkh ^{c}imārat al-masjid al-ḥarām*, 3rd printing, Jidda (1400/1980), p. 13.

Creswell, *op. cit.*, i, part 1, p. 27.

6. Bā Salāma, *Tā'rīkh al-ka^{c}ba, op. cit.*, pp. 244-97.

Aḥmad ^{c}Abd al-Ghafūr ^{c}Aṭṭār, *al-Ka^{c}ba wa'l-kiswa mundhu arba^{c}t ālāf sinna ḥatā al-yawm*, Makkah al-Mukarramah (1397/1977), 118 ff.

7. al-Azraqī, *op. cit.*, ii, p. 69.

al-Balādhūrī, *Futūḥ, op. cit.*, p. 46.

al-Ya^{c}qūbī, *Tā'rīkh, op. cit.*, ii, pp. 189-90.

al-Ṭabarī, *Annales*, ed. M.J. de Goeje *et al.*, Leyden (1893), series I, v, p. 2811.

Bā Salāma, *Tā'rīkh ^{c}imārat, op. cit.*, pp. 15-16.

Creswell, *op. cit.*, i, part 1, p. 40.

8. al-Azraqī, *op. cit.*, i, pp. 196-200, 201-21; ii, pp. 69-70.

al-Balādhūrī, *Futūḥ, op. cit.*, pp. 46-7.

al-Ya^{c}qūbī, *Tā'rīkh, op. cit.*, ii, pp. 309-10.

al-Ṭabarī, *Annales, op. cit.*, series II, i, pp. 537, 592.

Bā Salāma, *Tā'rīkh ^{c}imārat, op. cit.*, pp. 17-18.

Creswell, *op. cit.*, i, part 1, pp. 62-4.

9. al-Mas^{c}ūdī, *Murūj al-dhahab*, trans. into French from

the Arabic by C. Barbier de Meynard, Paris (1869), v, pp. 192-3.
Creswell, *op. cit.*, i, part 1, p. 63.
10. al-Azraqī, *op. cit.*, ii, p. 71.
al-Ṭabarī, *Annales*, *op. cit.*, series II, ii, p. 854.
Bā Salāma, *Tā'rīkh ^{c}imārat*, pp. 19-22.
11. al-Ya^{c}qūbī, *Tā'rīkh*, ii, pp. 339-40.
al-Azraqī, *op. cit.*, ii, pp. 71-2, observes that al-Walīd put crenellations on the walls of the mosque. The motif is an ancient one in the Near East and enjoyed widespread popularity in the Umayyad period in Syria and Palestine, as well as in Arabia.
Bā Salāma, *Tā'rīkh ^{c}imārat, op. cit.*, pp. 23-4.
12. al-Azraqī, *op. cit.*, ii, pp. 72-4.
Bā Salāma, *Tā'rīkh ^{c}imārat, op. cit.*, pp. 25-7.
13. al-Azraqī, *op. cit.*, ii, pp. 74-81.
Bā Salāma, *Tā'rīkh ^{c}imārat, op. cit.*, pp. 28-38.
14. Fawziyya Ḥusayn Maṭar, *Tā'rīkh ^{c}imārat al-ḥarām al-Makkā al-sharīf*, Jidda (1402/1982), pp. 146-53.
15. Bā Salāma, *Tā'rīkh ^{c}imārat, op. cit.*, p. 52.
16. *ibid.*, pp. 54-63.
17. *ibid.*, pp. 63-8.
18. Saad A. al-Rāshid, *Darb Zubaydah*, Riyadh (1980), p. 56.
19. Nāṣir-i Khusraw, *Sefer Nameh. Relation du Voyage de Nassiri Khosrau en Syrie, en Palestine, en Egypte, en Arabie et en Perse pendant les années de l'hégire 437-444 (1035-1042),* trans. from the Persian and annotated by C. Schefer, Paris (1881), pp. 194-210.
20. Vicenzo Strika, "A Ka^{c}bah picture in the Iraq Museum", *Sumer*, xxxii (1976), pp. 195-201.
idem, "A Ka^{c}ba picture from Mosul", *Studies in the History of Arabia, I; Sources for the History of Arabia*, part 1, Riyadh (1399/1979), pp. 145-8.
21. Bā Salāma, *Tā'rīkh al-ka^{c}ba, op. cit.*, p. 222.
22. Ibn Jubayr, *The Travels of Ibn Jubayr*, trans. from the Arabic by R.C.J. Broadhurst, London (1952), pp. 77-9.
23. *ibid.*, p. 96. There were four minarets in the Holy Mosque in the 5th/11th century according to Nāṣir-i Khusraw, *op. cit.*, p. 195.
24. Bā Salāma, *Tā'rīkh al-ka^{c}ba, op. cit.*, p. 139.
25. *ibid.*, pp. 140, 222-3. A Malik al-Muẓaffar built the Shāfi^{c}ī mosque in Jidda in 649/1251 (*q.v.*). E. von Zambaur, *Manuel de généalogie et de chronologie pour l'histoire de l'Islam*, Hanover (1927), p. 120, gives the full name as al-Malik al-Muẓaffar Shams al-Dīn Yūsuf I b. ^{c}Umar, 647-94/1249-95.
26. Bā Salāma, *Tā'rīkh al-ka^{c}ba*, *op. cit.*, p. 179.
27. *ibid.*, p. 179.
28. Bā Salāma, *Tā'rīkh ^{c}imārat, op. cit.*, pp. 69-75.
Sayyid ^{c}Abd al-Majīd Bakr, *Ashhar al-masājid fī'l-islām*, Jidda (1400/1980), pp. 21-2.
29. Bā Salāma, *Tā'rīkh al-ka^{c}ba, op. cit.*, p. 223.
30. *ibid.*, p. 179.
31. Bā Salāma, *Tā'rīkh ^{c}imārat*, *op. cit.*, pp. 75-8.
32. Bā Salāma, *Tā'rīkh al-ka^{c}ba*, *op. cit.*, pp. 138, 179.
33. Bā Salāma, *Tā'rīkh ^{c}imārat*, *op. cit.*, pp. 78-81.
34. *ibid.*, pp. 82-8.
35. Bā Salāma, *Tā'rīkh al-ka^{c}ba*, *op. cit.*, 92 ff.
^{c}Uthmān b. Bishr, *^{c}Inwān al-majd fī tā'rīkh Najd,* Riyadh (no date), i, pp. 36-40.
36. Bā Salāma, *Tā'rīkh al-ka^{c}ba*, *op. cit.*, p. 140.
37. Bā Salāma, *ibid.*,p. 141, records restoration to the roof of the Honourable Ka^{c}ba by Sultan Muḥammad IV in 1070/1659-60, and there is an inscription in the building of Aḥmad Bak, Shaykh al-Ḥarām, dated 1109/1697-8 (*ibid.*, p. 139).
38. Ibn Bishr, *^{c}Inwān al-majd, op. cit.*, i, p. 123.
39. Alī Bey (Domenico Badia y Leblich), *Travels of Ali Bey*, London (1816; reprinted, Farnborough, 1970), pp. 74-91.
40. *ibid.*, pp. 87-8.
41. J.L. Burckhardt, *Travels in Arabia,* London (1829; reprinted, 1968), pp. 134-5.
42. *ibid.*, p. 136.
43. ^{c}Abd al-Quddūs al-Anṣāry, "Tawsi^{c}āt al-masjidayn al-sharīfayn bi'l-Madina wa Makkah ^{c}abra al-tā'rīkh", *Qāfilat al-zayt,* (Rajab 1389/September-October 1969), xvii, no. 7, p. 12.
44. Bakr, *Ashhar al-masājid fī'l-islām, op. cit.*, pp. 86-8.

Other mosques of Makkah al-Mukarramah *p. 26*
1. Sayyid ^{c}Abd al-Majīd Bakr, "al-Biqa^{c} al-muqaddisa", *Ashhār al-masājid fī'l-islām,* part 1, Jidda (1400/1980): al-Rāya mosque (pp. 90-7), al-Jinn mosque (pp. 98-104), al-^{c}Ajāba mosque (pp. 105-11), Abī Bakr al-Ṣadīq mosque (pp. 112-17), Bilāl mosque (pp. 118-23), mosque of Ḥamza (pp. 124-29). Other mosques at ^{c}Arafat and elsewhere are also discussed (pp. 130-88).

Masjid Qubā', al-Madina al-Monawarah *p. 27*
1. Ibn Isḥāq, quoted by Ibn Hishām, *al-Sīrat al-nabawiyya,* ed. A. al-Saqqā, Cairo (1399/1979), ii, p. 313.
2. *ibid.*, ii, p. 313.
al-Samhūdī, *Wafā' al-wafā'*, ed. M.M. ^{c}Abd al-Ḥamīd, Cairo (1373/1954), i, 250 ff.
^{c}Abd al-Quddūs al-Anṣāry, *Āthār al-Madina al-Monawarah*, 3rd printing, al-Madina al-Monawarah (1393/1973), pp. 84-6.
Muḥammad Maḥmūd al-Dīb, "Nasha't al-Madina al-Monawarah wa qiyām al-masājid fīha", *al-Manhal,* part 2, (Sha^{c}bān 1395/August 1975), year 41, xxxvi, part 8, p. 570.
3. Ibrāhīm b. ^{c}Alī al-^{c}Ayyāshī, *al-Madina bayn al-māḍī wa'l-ḥāḍir*, al-Madina al-Monawarah (1392/1972), pp. 248-50, provides an important discussion of the foundation of the mosque at Qubā'. He suggests that the site, a former drying-floor for dates, was used for prayer by the first followers of the Prophet (ṣ) in al-Madina al-Monawarah, before the Prophet (ṣ) made his own *hijra*. The Prophet (ṣ) then prayed on the same spot, and with the place thus established by him as a mosque, it was marked out and subsequently a building constructed. The first direction of prayer on this site was, of course, Jerusalem, but it was subsequently altered to face Makkah al-Mukarramah.
4. al-^{c}Ayyāshī, *op. cit.*, p. 253-4, includes a plan of the mosque.
al-Anṣāry, *op. cit.*, pp. 81-7.
Sayyid ^{c}Abd al-Majīd Bakr, *Ashhar al-masājid fī'l-islām*, Jidda (1400/1980), part 1, pp. 190-8.
5. *al-Jazīra*, year 21, no. 4418 (9 Ṣafar 1405/2 November 1984).

The Mosque of the Prophet (ṣ), al-Madina al-Monawarah *p.27*

1. There is a very extensive bibliography for the Mosque of the Prophet (ṣ). The Arabic sources are listed by Creswell, *Early Muslim Architecture,* Oxford (1969), i, part 1, p. 142, note 6. To these should be added Ibn Shibh Abū Zīr ᶜUmar b. Shibh al-Numayrī al-Baṣrī, *Kitāb tā'rīkh al-Madina al-Monawara,* Jidda (no date). In more recent times other accounts have recorded the Mosque:

J.L. Burckhardt, *Travels in Arabia,* London (1829; reprinted, 1968), pp. 329-52.

Sir Richard Burton, *Personal Narrative of a Pilgrimage to el Medinah and Meccah,* 2nd ed., London (1857), i, pp. 292-325.

Ibrāhīm Rifaᶜat Pasha, *Mir'āt al-ḥaramayn*, Cairo (1344/1925).

Eldon Rutter, *The Holy Cities of Arabia*, London and New York (1928), ii, pp. 189-261.

Jean Sauvaget, *La Mosquée Omeyyade de Médine*, Paris (1947).

Aḥmad al-Khayārī, "Tā'rīkh al-masājid al-Madina al-Monawarah qadīman wa ḥadīthan", part 1, *al-Manhal*, (Dhū'l-Qaᶜda 1379/May 1960), pp. 622-4; part 2, *al-Manhal,* (Muḥarram-Ṣafar 1380/July-August 1960), pp. 69-71.

Emel Esin, *Mecca the Blessed, Madinah the Radiant,* London (1963).

ᶜUthmān Ḥāfiẓ, "Ma thar al-Madina", *Qāfilat al-zayt,* (Ṣafar 1385/June 1965), xiii, no. 2, pp. 2-6.

Ḥikmat Ḥassan, "al-Madina al-Monawarah, māḍīha wa ḥāḍirha", *Qāfilat al-zayt* (Ramaḍān 1387/December 1967), xv, no. 9, pp. 5-14.

K.A.C. Creswell, *op. cit.*, i, part 1, pp. 6-16, 142-9.

ᶜAbd al-Quddūs al-Anṣāry, "Tawsiᶜāt al-masjidayn al-sharīfayn bi'l-Madina wa Makkah ᶜabra al-tā'rīkh", *Qāfilat al-zayt* (Rajab 1389/September-October 1969), xvii, no. 7, pp. 7-12.

idem, Āthār al-Madina al-Monawarah, 3rd printing, al-Madina al-Monawarah (1393/1973).

Muhammad Hamidullah, *The Battlefields of the Prophet Muhammad*, Hyderabad (1392/1973). This shows a number of mosques in the city.

Muḥammad Maḥmūd al-Dīb, "Nasha't al-Madina al-Monawarah wa qiyām al-masājid fīha", part 1, *al-Manhal*, (Rabīᶜa II-Jumāda I 1395/May-June 1975), year 41, xxxv (*sic.* xxxvi), parts 4, 5, pp. 360-4; part 2, *al-Manhal*, (Shaᶜbān 1395/August 1975), year 41, xxxvi, part 8, pp. 569-72.

Ḥassan al-Bāshā, *Madkhal ila al-āthār al-islāmiyya*, Cairo (1979), pp. 119-25.

Ghazi Bisheh, *The Mosque of the Prophet at Madinah throughout the first century* A.H. *with special emphasis on the Umayyad Mosque*, University Microfilms International (1979).

Sayyid ᶜAbd al-Majīd Bakr, *Ashhar al-masājid fī'l-islām,* part 1, *al-biqāᶜ al-muqaddisa*, Jidda (1400/1980), pp. 200-26.

Farīd Maḥmūd al-Shāfᶜī, *al-ᶜImārat al-ᶜarabiyyat al-islāmiyya*, Riyadh (1402/1982), i, 166 ff.

Ministry of Information, Kingdom of Saudi Arabia, *The Holy Places*, London (no date), pp. 64-79.

2. Ibn Hishām, *al-Sīrat al-nabawiyya*, Cairo (1399/1979), ii, pp. 313-14.

3. Ibn Saᶜd, *Kitāb al-ṭabaqāt al-kabīr*, eds. E. Mittwoch and E. Sachau, Leyden (1917), i, part 2, pp. 1-2.
Ibn Hishām, *op. cit.,* ii, p. 314.

4. *ibid.*, ii, p. 401.
Ibn Saᶜd, *op. cit.*, i, part 2, pp. 3-5.
al-Ṭabarī, *Annales*, Series I, iii, pp. 1279-81.
al-Samhūdī, *Wafā' al-wafā'*, ed. M.M. ᶜAbd al-Hamīd, Cairo (1373/1954), i, pp 359-64.

5. al-Anṣāry, *Āthār al-Madina al-Monawarah, op. cit.*, p. 104.

6. Ibn Saᶜd, *op cit.*, i, part 2, pp. 9-11.
Aḥmad b. Ḥanbal, *Musnad*, Beirut (no date), iii, pp. 295, 324.

7. Ibn Saᶜd, *op. cit.*, i, part 2, pp. 9-10, 12.

8. al-Anṣāry, *Āthār al-Madina al-Monawarah, op. cit.*, p. 96.

9. *ibid.*, p. 106.

10. al-Samhūdī, *op. cit.*, ii, pp. 481-2.

11. al-Yaᶜqūbī, *Tā'rīkh, op. cit.*, ii, p. 191.
al-Ṭabarī, *op. cit.*, Series I, v, p. 2853.
al-Samhūdī, *op. cit.*, ii, pp. 501-3.

12. al-Balādhūrī, *Kitāb futūḥ al-buldān,* ed. M.J. de Goeje, Leyden, 2nd ed. (1968), p. 6.
al-Anṣāry, *Āthār al-Madinah al-Monawarah, op. cit.*, p. 104.

13. Ibn Saᶜd, *op. cit.*, i, part 2, p. 181; viii, p. 119.
al-Balādhūrī, *Futūḥ, op. cit.*, pp. 6-7.
al-Yaᶜqūbī, *Tā'rīkh*, ii, pp. 339-40.
al-Ṭabarī, *op. cit.*, series II, i, pp. 1192-4.

14. al-Balādhūrī, *Futūḥ, op. cit.*, p. 7.

15. *ibid.*, p. 7.

16. Ibn Jubayr, *The Travels of Ibn Jubayr*, trans. from the Arabic by R.C.J. Broadhurst, London (1952), p. 198.

17. *ibid.*, pp. 200-1.

18. *ibid.*, p. 202.

19. A ruler of Yemen of this name also restored the Holy Mosque in Makkah al-Mukarramah and the Shāfiᶜī mosque in Jidda.

20. al-Anṣāry, *Āthār al-Madina al-Monawarah op. cit.*, p. 105.

21. Sauvaget, *La Mosquée Omeyyade de Médine, op. cit.*, p. 44.

22. al-Anṣāry, *Āthār al-Madina al-Monawarah, op. cit.*,
p. 96.

23. *ibid.*, pp. 105-6.

24. Burckhardt, *Travels in Arabia, op. cit.*, pp. 330-1.

25. Burton, *Personal Narrative of a Pilgrimage, op. cit.*, i, pp. 319-20.

26. *ibid.*, i, p. 321.

27. Rutter, *The Holy Cities of Arabia, op. cit.*, ii, p. 192.

28. al-Anṣāry, *Āthār al-Madina al-Monawarah, op. cit* p.109.

29. Ministry of Information, Kingdom of Saudi Arabia, *The Holy Places, op. cit.*, p. 70.
Bakr, *Ashhar al-masājid, op. cit.*, pp. 219, 222.

30. *Arab News*, 7 Ṣafar 1405/31 October 1984.

Other mosques of al-Madina al-Monawarah *p34*

1. ᶜAbd al-Quddūs al-Anṣāry, *Āthār al-Madina al-Monawarah*, al-Madina al-Monawarah (1393/1973), pp.

62-3.
Sayyid ^{c}Abd al-Majid Bakr, *Ashhār al-masājid fī'l-islām*, Jidda (1400/1980), pp. 227-31.
Ibrāhīm al-^{c}Ayyāshī, *al-Madinah bayn al-māḍī wa'l-ḥāḍir*, al-Madina al-Monawarah (1392/1972), discusses numerous mosques in al-Madina al-Monawarah and its neighbourhood.
2. al-Anṣāry, *op. cit.*, pp. 88-90.
Bakr, *op. cit.*, pp. 232-7.
3. al-Anṣāry, *op. cit.*, pp. 94-5.
Bakr, *op. cit.*, pp. 238-43.
4. Bakr, *op. cit.*, pp. 244-52.

Jidda *p. 34*
1. Ibn Jubayr, *The Travels of Ibn Jubayr*, trans. from the Arabic by R.J.C. Broadhurst, London (1952), p. 70.
2. See p. 103 of this book.
3. ^{c}Abd al-Quddūs al-Anṣāry, *Mawsū^{c}a tā'rīkh madīna Judda*, i, 3rd printing, Cairo (1402/1982), pp. 429-30.
Angelo Pesce, *Jiddah, Portrait of an Arabian City*, London (1976), p. 125.
4. Ibn Baṭṭūṭah, *The Travels of Ibn Baṭṭūṭah 1325-1354*, trans. from the Arabic by H.A.R. Gibb, Cambridge (1962), ii, p. 361.
5. Nāṣir-i Khusraw, *Sefer Nameh, Relation du Voyage de Nassiri Khosrau en Syrie, en Palestine, en Egypte, en Arabie et en Perse pendant les années de l'hégire 437-444 (1035-1042)*, trans. from the Persian by Charles Schefer, Paris (1881), pp. 181-2. ("The *qibla* of the great mosque faces toward the east. Outside the town there are no buildings to be seen except for a mosque known as the Mosque of the Prophet.")

al-Mi^{c}mār mosque, Jidda *p. 34*
1. ^{c}Abd al-Quddūs al-Anṣāry, *Mawsū^{c}a tā'rīkh madīna Judda*, i, 3rd printing, Cairo (1402/1982), p. 428.
EI^2, "Djudda", R. Hartmann/Phebe Ann Marr, refers to the construction of a mosque in Jidda by the Grand Vizir Qāra Muṣṭafā Pasha during his period of office, 1087-94/1676-83.
Vicenzo Strika, "Studi saudiani. 1, Le moschee di Gedda", *Annali, Istituto Orientale di Napoli*, xxxv, new series, xxv, part 4 (1975), pp. 559-60.
See also: Carlo Alfonso Nallino, "L'Arabia Sa^{c}ūdiana", *Raccolta di Scritti Editi e Inediti*, Rome (1939), i, pp. 166, 181.
Angelo Pesce, *Jiddah, Portrait of an Arabian City*, London, revised ed., (1976), pp. 123-4.
2. Maurice Tamisier, *Voyage en Arabie. Séjour dans le Hedjaz – Campagne d'Assir*, Paris (1840), i, p. 79.
Unfortunately, J. L. Burckhardt, *Travels in Arabia*, London (1829; reprinted, London, 1968), p. 11, fails to give any details of the mosques of Jidda at the time of his visit in 1229/1814. He observes that no building in the city was of great age as a result of the deleterious effect on their coral fabric of the humid atmosphere of the city.
3. Strika, *op. cit.*, p. 560. ("The *miḥrāb* reveals nothing in particular; the *minbar*, on the other hand, juts out, although the staircase is parallel to the *qibla* wall, thereby avoiding the projecting pulpit which might have altered the relative importance of the *miḥrāb* and *minbar*.")

al-Ḥanīfī mosque, Jidda *p. 36*
1. Maurice Tamisier, *Voyage en Arabie*, Paris (1840), i, p. 79. Unfortunately Tamisier is not very descriptive: "... et vers le centre de la ville s'élève celle de Hanefi".
^{c}Abd al-Quddūs al-Anṣāry, *Mawsū^{c}a tā'rīkh madīna Judda*, i, 3rd printing, Cairo (1402/1982), p. 428.
Carlo Alfonso Nallino, "L'Arabia Sa^{c}ūdiana", *Raccolta di Scritti Editi e Inediti*, Rome (1939), i, p. 166. He refers to the mosque as Abī Ḥanīfa.
Vicenzo Strika, "Studi saudiani. 1, Le moschee di Gedda", *Annali, Istituto Orientale di Napoli*, xxxv, new series, xxv, part 4 (1975), pp. 558-9.
Angelo Pesce, *Jiddah, Portrait of an Arabian City*, London, revised ed., (1976), pp. 122-3.

al-Shāfi^{c}ī mosque, Jidda *p. 38*
1. ^{c}Abd al-Quddūs al-Anṣāry, *Mawsū^{c}a tā'rīkh madīna Judda*, i, 3rd printing, Cairo (1402/1982), pp. 425-7.
Also see: Carlo Alfonso Nallino, "L'Arabia Sa^{c}ūdiana", *Raccolta di Scritti Editi e Inediti*, Rome (1939), i, p. 166.
Vicenzo Strika, "Studi saudiani. 1, Le moschee di Gedda", *Annali, Istituto Orientale de Napoli*, xxxv, new series, xxv, part 4 (1975), pp. 557-8.
Angelo Pesce, *Jiddah, Portrait of an Arabian City*, London, revised ed., (1976), pp. 120-2.
2. E. von Zambaur, *Manuel de Généalogie et de Chronologie pour l'histoire de l'Islam*, Hanover (1927), p. 120, mentions al-Malik al-Muẓaffar. He gives the full name as al-Malik al-Muẓaffar Shams al-Dīn Yūsuf I b. ^{c}Umar.
3. Ḥusayn Bā Salāma, *Tā'rīkh al-ka^{c}bat al-ma^{c}aẓẓama*, 3rd printing, Jidda (1402/1982), p. 140.
4. Strika, *op. cit.*, pp. 557-8.
5. It is found in the Umayyad period in the *jāmi^{c}* of Damascus as well as in the design of smaller mosques of this period in Bilād al-Shām; the mosque of ^{c}Amr b. al-^{c}Āṣ in al-Fusṭāṭ also had arcades running parallel to the *qibla* wall in the Umayyad period.
6. al-Anṣāry, *op. cit.*, plate ج . See also plates أ و ب .

al-Bāshā mosque, Jidda *p. 39*
1. Carlo Alfonso Nallino, "L'Arabia Sa^{c}ūdiana", *Raccolta di Scritti Editi e Inediti*, Rome (1939), i, p. 166.
2. ^{c}Abd al-Quddūs al-Anṣāry, *Mawsū^{c}a tā'rīkh madīna Jidda*, i, 3rd printing, Cairo (1401/1980), pp. 428-9.
3. Angelo Pesce, *Jiddah, Portrait of an Arabian City*, Falcon Press, revised ed. (1976), p. 123.
4. Vicenzo Strika, "Studi saudiani. 1, Le moschee di Gedda", *Annali, Istituto Orientale di Napoli*, xxxv, new series, xxv, part 4, (1975), p. 559.
5. Maurice Tamisier, *Voyage en Arabie*, Paris (1840), i, pp. 78-9, records the following: "La première se nomme Gémaa-Soultan-Hassan. Elle est carrée et entièrement bâtie en pierre de corail bien équaries. A l'angle du sud s'élève isolément un minaret dont la partie supérieure penche considérablement." ("The first is called 'Gémaa-Soultan-Hassan'. It is square and built entirely of well cut coral. At the southern corner rises a detached minaret whose upper part leans considerably.")
6. Nallino, *op. cit.*, p. 166.
Strika, *op. cit.*, p. 559.
7. It is possible that the double register windows of the

al-Bāshā mosque represent a "vernacularisation" of Islamic forms from beyond the Red Sea area. Thus the heavily Cairene-Ottoman forms of the doorways and the windows of the Ḥanīfī and the Mi[c]mār mosques were transformed into a more indigenous arrangement in the old Bāshā mosque.
8. Strika, *op. cit.*, p. 559.

al-Ṭā'if *p. 41*
1. These early mosques have recently been studied in some detail; see Su[c]ād Māhir Muḥammad, "Al-Ṭā'if wa Waj wa mā bihā min āthār al-Nabī (ṣalā Allah [c]alayhi wa salam) wa'l-masājid al-āthāriyya", *al-Dāra,* (Jumāda II 1401/April 1981), no. 3, year 6, pp. 41-56.
Also Ḥikmat Ḥassan, "Al-Ṭā'if: yaqūta mu[c]allaqa fawq qimam al-jibāl", *Qāfilat al-zayt*, (Rabī[c]a II 1389/June-July 1969), xvii, no. 4, pp. 25-34, for a plate of an old mosque, [c]Utba Washiba, p. 27.
2. Nāṣir-i Khusraw, *Sefer Nameh. Relation du Voyage de Nassiri Khosrau en Syrie, en Palestine, en Egypte, en Arabie et en Perse pendant les années de l'hégire 437-444 (1035-1042),* trans. from the Persian by C. Schefer, Paris (1881), p. 215.
3. J.L. Burckhardt, *Travels in Arabia*, London (1829; reprinted, 1968), pp. 84-5.
4. Maurice Tamisier, *Voyage en Arabie*, Paris (1840), i, pp. 276-9.
5. C.M. Doughty, *Travels in Arabia Deserta*, London (1923), ii, p. 516.
H. St.J. Philby, *The Heart of Arabia*, London (1922), i, pp. 194-5.
Western Arabia and the Red Sea, Naval Intelligence Division, B.R. 527 (June 1946), p. 572 and plate 327 which includes the mosque in a general view of the town.
Muhammad Hamidullah, *The Battlefields of the Prophet Muhammad*, Hyderabad (1392/1973), p. 44, published a photograph of the mosque of [c]Abd Allah b. al-[c]Abbās as it was in 1358/1939; unfortunately it is very blurred.

al-Wajh *p. 42*
1. Sir Richard Burton, *Personal Narrative of a Pilgrimage to el Medinah and Meccah*, 2nd ed., London (1857), i, pp. 209-12.
2. D.G. Hogarth, *Hejaz before World War I: a handbook*, 2nd ed., with a new introduction by R.L. Bidwell, Falcon-Oleander (1978), p. 22.
3. Ameen Rihani, *Around the Coasts of Arabia*, London (1930), pp. 8-9.
4. Saleh M. al-Amr, *The Hijaz under Ottoman Rule, 1869-1914: Ottoman Vali, the Sharif of Mecca, and the Growth of British Influence*, Riyadh (1978), pp. 214-17.
5. *Western Arabia and the Red Sea*, Naval Intelligence Division, B.R. 527 (June 1946), pp. 539-40; fig. 285 shows al-Wajh with the minaret of the Ashrāf mosque in the foreground.

al-Ashrāf mosque, al-Wajh *p. 43*
1. *Western Arabia and the Red Sea*, Naval Intelligence Division, B.R. 527 (June 1946), fig. 285.

al-Budaywī al-Shaḥāta mosque, al-Wajh *p. 45*
1. H. St.J. Philby, *The Land of Midian*, London (1957), p. 243, refers to a prominent merchant family of al-Wajh called 'al-Budairi'.

The mosque of the Prophet (ṣ), Tabūk *p. 48*
1. [c]Abd al-Quddūs al-Anṣāry, *Bayn al-tā'rīkh wa'l-āthār*, 3rd printing, Jidda (1397/1977), pp. 313-14, refers to a mosque founded by the Prophet (s) outside Tabūk at Ṭarf al-Batrā'.
2. A. Jaussen and F. Savignac, *Mission Archéologique en Arabie (mars-mai 1907) de Jerusalem au Hedjaz, Medain-Saleh*, Paris (1909), i, p. 59.
3. H. St.J. Philby, *The Land of Midian*, London (1957), p. 122.
For another account of the mosque, see [c]Alī al Muḥammad al-[c]Amar, "Tabūk", *al-Manhal* (Rabī[c]a II 1391/ Haziran/June 1971), year 37, part 4, xxxii, p. 382.
4. Along the course of the *hajj* route there are several other fortresses in Jordan and in Saudi Arabia, including two further south, at Madā'in Ṣāliḥ and Qala[c] Mu'aẓzam. These were also refurbished by the Ottomans but may replace considerably older buildings. On Madā'in Ṣāliḥ, see A.R. al-Anṣāry, A.H. Ghazal, and G.R.D. King, *Muwāqi[c] āthāriyya wa suwar min haḍārat al-[c]arab fī'l-mamlikat al-[c]arabiyyat al-su[c]ūdiyya: al-[c]Ulā, al-Hijr*, Riyadh (1404/1984), p. 46.

Jāmi[c], al-[c]Ulā *p. 50*
1. A.A. Nasif, *An Historical and Archaeological Survey of al-[c]Ula with special reference to its irrigation system*, unpublished doctoral thesis, Manchester University (1981).
2. A. Jaussen and F. Savignac, *Mission Archéologique en Arabie*, Paris (1914), ii; *Atlas*, plate xviii. They mark the mosque on their plan of al-[c]Ulā of 1909.
Hamza Muḥammad Jābir, "Baldat al-[c]Ulā", *al-Manhal*, (Shawwāl 1388/January-Kanun II 1968), year 29, part 10, p. 1395.
G.R.D. King, "Notes on some mosques in eastern and western Saudi Arabia", *Bulletin of the School of Oriental and African Studies*, xliii, part 2 (1980), pp. 267-8.

Khaybar *p. 51*
1. H.St.J. Philby, *The Land of Midian*, London (1957), p. 33.

Mosque of the early Islamic period *p. 51*
1. Earlier travellers have recorded this mosque in varying degrees. Charles Doughty, *Travels in Arabia Deserta*, London (1923), ii, p. 76, refers to it as follows: "In the falling ground upon the left hand stands an antique four-square building of stone, which is the old mesjid from the time, they say, of Mohammed; and in the precinct lie buried the *Ashab en-Néby*". He refers to this mosque as "Mesjid Aly" in his sketch (p. 95). However, Philby, *The Land of Midian*, London (1957), pp. 32-46, does not describe the mosque. Shaykh Ḥamad al-Jāsir, *Fī shimāl gharb al-jazīra*, 2nd printing, Riyadh (1401/1981), pp. 218-19, and the late [c]Abd al-Quddūs al-Anṣāry, *Bayn al-tā'rīkh wa'l-āthār*, 3rd printing, Jidda (1397/1977) pp. 209-10, both associate the site with

the time of the Prophet (ṣ), and refer to it as a *jāmiʿ*. Al-Anṣāry refers to the site as "Arḍ al-Maʿarika", "the Battlefield". The local people refer to the mosque as that of ʿAlī b. Abī Ṭālib. However, the early geographers make no reference to this, nor does Dr Abdullah al-Wohaibi, *The Northern Hijaz in the Writings of the Arab Geographers 800-1150*, Beirut (1973).

Mosque of the ḥiṣn, Khaybar *p. 53*
1. ʿAbd al-Quddūs al-Anṣāry, *Bayn al-tā'rīkh wa'l-āthār*, Jidda (1397/1977), pp. 210-11.

al-Qunfudha *p. 55*
1. Adolf Grohmann, "Ḳunfuda", *EI*^{1}.
2. Carsten Niebuhr, *Travels through Arabia*, Edinburgh (1792; reprinted, Beirut, no date) i, p. 242.
3. The book of watercolours is held by the Royal Geographical Society, London, by whose courtesy the present plate is reproduced. Kirk was an Assistant Surgeon in the East India Company from 1830 and saw service in Afghanistan and Abyssinia. He eventually died in western India. I am indebted to Miss Philippa Copeman of the Map Room, RGS, for kindly providing this information.
4. Eldon Rutter, *The Holy Cities of Arabia*, London and New York (1928), i, p. 71.
5. H. St. J. Philby, *Arabian Highlands*, Ithaca, New York (1952), pp. 691-4.
6. I am most grateful to Dr Prochazka for showing me his pictures and for the information that he provided me with in 1976.
7. Kinahan Cornwallis, *Asir before World War I: a handbook*, Cambridge (1976), p. 34.
Western Arabia and the Red Sea, Naval Intelligence Division, BR 527 (June 1946), pp. 544-5.
8. Rutter, *The Holy Cities of Arabia, op. cit.*, i, p. 71.
9. G.R.D. King, "Notes on some mosques in eastern and western Saudia Arabia", *Bulletin of the School of Oriental and African Studies*, xliii, part 2 (1980), pp. 271-6.

Tihāmat ʿAsīr *p. 56*
1. H.St.J. Philby, *Arabian Highlands*, Ithaca, New York (1952), pp. 572-5.
2. M. Tamisier, *Voyage en Arabie*, Paris (1840), i, pp. 383-91.
3. Kinahan Cornwallis, *Asir before World War I: a handbook*, Cambridge (1976), p. 41.
Western Arabia and the Red Sea, Naval Intelligence Division, BR 527 (June 1946), p. 571.

ʿAlāwiyya mosque, Ṣabyā *p. 56*
1. H.St.J. Philby, *Arabian Highlands*, Ithaca, New York (1952) p. 474.
2. Eldon Rutter, *The Holy Cities of Arabia*, London and New York (1928), i, p. 51.

Old mosque, Ṣabyā *p. 59*
1. Kinahan Cornwallis, *Asir before World War I*, Cambridge (1976), p. 41: "Sabiyeh. About twenty miles inland, north-east of Jeizan. It is the Idrissi's capital and is a straw-built town with a two-storied 'palace' of mud, and a fine mosque..."
2. H.St.J. Philby, *Arabian Highlands*, Ithaca, New York (1952) p. 464.

Masjid, Abū ʿArīsh *p. 63*
1. Muḥammad Aḥmad al-ʿAqīlī, *al-Āthār al-tā'rīkhiyya fī mantiqa Jāzān*, Riyadh (1399/1979), facing p. 81.
2. H.St.J. Philby, *Arabian Highlands*, Ithaca, New York (1952), p. 573.
3. Philby, *ibid.*, p. 573, refers to a *jāmiʿ* in Abū ʿArīsh which was the principal mosque, built in the 11th/17th century by Imām Manṣūr b. ʿImad al-Dīn. It is not clear from Philby's text if this *jāmiʿ* was larger than the Ashrāf mosque.
4. al-Aqīlī's plate, *op. cit.* p. 82, seems to show a lower wall than is now to be seen.
5. Philby, *op. cit.*, fig. 55, facing p. 577.

Old Mosque, Abū ʿArīsh *p. 64*
1. H.St.J. Philby, *Arabian Highlands*, Ithaca, New York (1952), p. 575.

Muḥāyil *p. 65*
1. A similar but narrower *miḥrāb* is illustrated in a mosque in Rijāl al-Maʿ by Yaḥyā Ibrāhīm al-Almaʿī, *Riḥlāt fī ʿAsīr*, Jidda (no date), p. 74.

Jāmiʿ, Umm Farasān *p. 65*
1. ʿAbd al-Raḥmān Ṣādiq al-Sharīf, "Dirāsāt fī jughrāfiyyat al-Mamlikat al-ʿArabiyyat al-Suʿūdiyya; Juzā'ir Farasān", *Journal of the College of Arts,* King Saud University, vii (1980), pp. ٩-٨.

al-Nejdi mosque, Umm Farasān *p. 68*
1. I am indebted to Mr Yaḥyā Ibrāhīm al-Nejdī al-Tamīmī for the information that he gave me during my visit to Farasān regarding the mosque built by his father and his own house. Mr Yaḥyā al-Nejdī is *mu'adhdhin* of the mosque today.
2. Locally referred to as *ḥajar baḥrī* or *sukhūr baḥrī*.
3. Similarly emphatic treatment of mosque doorways occurs elsewhere in coastal Saudi Arabia at Jubayl on the Arabian Gulf, in the old *jāmiʿ*.

Mosque, Umm Farasān *p. 74*
1. The prayer-hall with six domes of the Muʿtabiyya mosque in Taʿizz of *c.* 796/1393 is of the same generic type. (See R.B. Lewcock and G.R. Smith, "Three Medieval Mosques in the Yemen: a preliminary report. Part II", *Oriental Art* xx, no. 2 (Summer 1974), pp. 202-3). There is a three-dome mosque of Zakariyya at Zabīd (see E.J. Keall, "Zabid and its hinterland: 1982 report", *Proceedings of the 16th Seminar for Arabian Studies*, xiii (1983), p. 67), and a mosque apparently of this type is recorded at Hays, Yemen (Fernando Varanda, *Art of Building in Yemen*, London and Cambridge, Mass. (1982), p. 61). A multi-domed mosque also occurs at Mocha in Yemen.
2. An interesting example of a six-dome mosque arranged in a three by two formation is found in al-Madina al-Monawara, in the Masjid al-Ghumāma: for a schematic plan, see Muḥammad Maḥmūd al-Dīb, "Nasha't al-Madina al-Monawara wa qiyām al-masājid

fīha", *al-Manhal*, (Rabīᶜa II-Jumāda I 1395/May-June 1975), year 41, nos. 3, 4, pp. 571-2. Al-Dīb gives the date of the last rebuilding as 1255-77/1839-60, preferring, however, to associate it on stylistic grounds with the mosques of Istanbul in the 9th-10th/15th-16th centuries.

Mosque, al-Qahaba, Banī Mālik *p. 77*
1. Philby visited al-Qahaba in 1355/1936 when the place was a police post. He refers to the village as 'al-Qahba': *Arabian Highlands*, Ithaca, New York (1952), p. 501. He makes no reference to this mosque in al-Qahaba, although he refers to the Banī Mālik mosques generally. However, he mentions an ᶜId mosque in al-Qahaba, an open space with "a low masonry structure with the usual Qibla niche and a rough seat for the preacher", *ibid.*, p. 504.

Mosque, Nīd al-Ḥaqū, Banī Mālik *p. 78*
1. H.St.J. Philby, *Arabian Highlands*, Ithaca, New York (1952), p. 506, mentions this settlement, but gives it the name "Najd Haqu".

The southern Hejaz and ᶜAsīr *p. 82*
1. Maurice Tamisier, *Voyage en Arabie. Séjour dans le Hedjaz – Campagne d'Assir*, Paris (1840), ii, p. 358.
2. J.L. Burckhardt, *Travels in Arabia*, London (1829), pp. 445-55.
3. Sir Kinahan Cornwallis, *Asir before World War I: a handbook*, Cambridge (1976), refers occasionally to mosques.
4. H.St.J. Philby, *Arabian Highlands*, Ithaca, New York (1952).
5. *ibid.*, p. 150.
6. W. Thesiger, "A journey through the Tihama, the ᶜAsir, and the Hijaz Mountains", *The Geographical Journal* cx, nos. 4-6 (October-December 1947), pp. 188-200.
Yaḥyā Ibrāhīm al-Amaᶜī, *Riḥlāt fī ᶜAsīr*, Jidda (no date).
G.R.D. King, "Notes on some mosques in eastern and western Saudi Arabia", *Bulletin of the School of Oriental and African Studies*, xliii, part 2 (1980), pp. 268-70.
7. Anon, "Bilād Ghāmid wa Zahrān", *Qāfilat al-zayt*, (Rabīᶜa I 1388/May-June 1968), xvi, no. 3, p. 49.

Jāmiᶜ, al-Suqā' *p. 83*
1. This use of large stepped crenellations over important points in the mosque is not confined to al-Suqā'. See the mosque of the village of Rijāl al-Maᶜ in ᶜAsīr, in Yaḥyā Ibrāhīm al-Almaᶜī, *Riḥlāt fī ᶜAsīr*, Jidda (no date), p. 82. The same type of decoration, but in rather different form, occurs east of Abhā and at Najrān.

al-Aṣfal mosque, Masqī *p. 93*
1. The use of wooden columns, found in this mosque and elsewhere in ᶜAsīr, is not confined to the area. They are found for instance in the *jāmiᶜ* at Harib in Yemen (Fernando Varanda, *Art of Building in Yemen*, London and Cambridge, Mass. (1982), p. 59).

Wādī Najrān *p. 99*
1. H.St.J. Philby, *Arabian Highlands*, Ithaca, New York (1952), pp. 226-319. Tchekof Minosa, *Najran, Desert Garden of Arabia*, Paris (1983).

Mosque of Muḥammad Manṣūr, Dahdha al-Ṣuqūr *p. 104*
1. The house is owned by Mr Manṣūr Muḥammad Manṣūr al-Ṣuqūr, and he attributes the building of the mosque to the time of his father or his grandfather.

Mosque of ᶜUmar b. al-Khaṭṭāb, Dūmat al-Jandal *p. 117*
1. G.A. Wallin, "Narrative of a Journey from Cairo to Medina and Mecca, by Suez, Arabá, Tawilá, al-Jauf, Jubbé, Háil and Nejd, in 1845", *Journal of the Royal Geographical Society*, xxiv (1854), pp. 141-2.
2. ᶜUthmān b. Bishr, *ᶜInwān al-majd fī tā'rīkh Najd*, Riyadh (no date), i, pp. 101-2.
3. Geoffrey King, "A mosque attributed to ᶜUmar b. al-Khaṭṭāb in Dūmat al-Jandal in al-Jawf, Saudi Arabia", *Journal of the Royal Asiatic Society*, no. 2 (1978), pp. 109-23.
4. Ḥamad al-Jāsir, *Fī shimāl gharb al-Jazīra*, 2nd printing, Riyadh (1401/1981), pp. 150-1.

Ḥā'il *p. 120*
1. Communication (1 Rajab 1403/14 April 1983) from H.R.H. Amīr Miqrin b. ᶜAbd al-ᶜAzīz Al Saᶜūd, Governor of Ḥā'il Region.
2. D.G. Hogarth, "Gertrude Bell's Journey to Hayil", *The Geographical Journal*, lxx, no. 1 (July 1927), pp. 1-21 and plate facing p. 12.
3. W.G. Palgrave, *Narrative of a Year's Journey through Central and Eastern Arabia (1862-1863)*, London and Cambridge (1865; reprinted Farnborough, 1969), i, "Plan of Ha'yel" facing p. 139.
4. *ibid.*, i, p. 180.
5. Carlo Guarmani, *Northern Najd*, trans. from the Italian by Lady Capel-Cure with introduction and notes by D. Carruthers, London (1938), pp. 44-5.

Mosque, Ḥarṭa al-Zubāra, Ḥā'il *p. 120*
1. Mr Khālid al-ᶜAlī al-Ṣāliḥ of Ḥā'il kindly showed me his photographs of the Wāṣiṭ mosque.

Jāmiᶜ, ᶜUnayza *p. 122*
1. Muhammad al-ᶜAbūdī, "Madina ᶜUnayza", *al-ᶜArab*, (Shaᶜbān-Rajab 1400/May-June 1980), parts 1-2, year 15, p. 17.
H. St. J. Philby, *Arabia of the Wahhabis*, London (1928), pp. 253-4, describes the minaret of this *jāmiᶜ*.
2. M.S. Mousalli, F.A. Shaker and O.A. Mandily, *An Introduction to Urban Patterns in Saudi Arabia: the Central Region*, London (1977), pp. 43, 56.

al-Mushayqaḥ mosque, Burayda *p. 125*
1. An alternative name given to me for this mosque was "*jāmiᶜ* of the old *sūq*".
H. St. J. Philby, *Arabia of the Wahhabis*, London (1928), pp. 198, 200, mentions the great mosque of Burayda and "about a dozen mosques in the city"; see also plan facing p. 196.
2. Muḥammad al-ᶜAbūdī, "Burayda, qā'ida bilād al-Qaṣīm", *al-ᶜArab* (Dhū'l-Qaᶜda-Dhū'l-Ḥijja 1399/October-November 1979), year 14, parts 5-6, p. 361.
3. The Burayda minarets discussed here are of the circular type. It seems that these represent an older tradition in Burayda and I understand that they are

locally regarded as such: the rectangular minaret is a more recent introduction in Burayda and is to be seen in several mosques, including the Mutawiᶜ mosque and the Ismaᶜīl mosque. The antiquity of the tradition of circular towers in al-Qaṣīm generally seems to be indicated by the survival of an ancient circular tower at al-Shanāna, near al-Rass, which is twenty-five metres high. See *ATLAL 4* (1400/1980), p. 121١٢٨.

Philby, *Arabia of the Wahhabis*, *op. cit.*, p. 198, seems to have regarded the circular minarets of Burayda as a development of more recent times. As Philby points out, Doughty, *Travels in Arabia Deserta*, London (1923), ii, p. 314, had mentioned a square minaret attached to the *jāmiᶜ* of Burayda forty years earlier.

al-Ḥuwayza mosque, Burayda ***p. 126***
1. Muḥammad al-ᶜAbūdī, "Burayda, qā'ida bilād al-Qaṣīm", *al-ᶜArab*, (Dhū'l-Qaᶜda-Dhū'l-Ḥijja 1399/October-November 1979), year 14, parts 5-6, p. 361.
2. A similar system occurs in al-Wajh on the Red Sea coast in the al-Budaywī mosque and al-Ashrāf mosque, where the prayer-halls are distinguished by lofty columns and level roofs (see pp. 42-7).
3. K.A.C. Creswell, *Early Muslim Architecture*, Oxford (1969), part 1, i, pp. 46-8.
4. *ibid.*, ii (1940; reprinted New York, 1979), p. 32.

al-ᶜAyīrī mosque, Burayda ***p. 128***
1. Muḥammad al-ᶜAbūdī, "Burayda, qāᶜida bilād al-Qaṣīm", *al-ᶜArab*, (Dhū'l-Qaᶜda-Dhū'l-Ḥijja 1399/October-November 1979), year 14, parts 5-6, p. 360.

al-Māḍī mosque, Burayda ***p. 129***
1. Muḥammad al-ᶜAbūdī, "Burayda, qā'ida bilād al-Qaṣīm", *al-ᶜArab*, (Dhū'l-Qaᶜda-Dhū'l-Ḥijja 1399/October-November 1979), year 14, parts 5-6, p. 362.

Jāmiᶜ, Riyadh ***p. 156***
1. H.St.J. Philby, *Saᶜudi Arabia*, London (1955; reprinted Beirut, 1968), p. 158.
2. W.G. Palgrave, *Narrative of a year's journey through central and eastern Arabia (1862-63)*, London and Cambridge (1865; reprinted Farnborough, 1969), i, pp. 444-5.
3. H.St.J. Philby, *The Heart of Arabia*, London (1922), i, pp. 73-4 and plate facing p. 72.
4. Ameen Rihani, *Ibn Sa'oud of Arabia. His people and his land*, London (1928), pp. 130-2 and plate facing p. 130.
5. Leopald Mohammed Weiss, "Riadh. Die Stadt des Königs Ibn Sa'ud", *Atlantis*, Berlin (1930), p. 530. I am indebted to Mr Will Facey for drawing this article to my attention.

Southern Nejd ***p. 161***
1. H.St.J. Philby, *Southern Najd: Journey to Kharj, Aflaj, Sulaiyil, and Wadi Dawasir, 1918*, Cairo (1919).
2. Juris Zarins, Mohammad Ibrahim, Daniel Potts and Christopher Edens, "Saudi Arabian Archaeological Reconnaissance 1978: the preliminary report on the third phase of the comprehensive archaeological survey program – the Central Province", *ATLAL*, iii (1399/1979), pp. 9-42.
3. A.R. al-Ansary, *Qaryat al-Fau: A Portrait of Pre-Islamic Civilisation in Saudi Arabia*, London (1982).

al-Kharj ***p. 162***
1. Nāṣir-i Khusraw, *Sefer Nameh, Relation du Voyage de Nassiri Khosrau en Syrie, en Palestine, en Egypte, en Arabie, et en Perse pendant les années de l'hégire 437-444 (1035-1042)*, trans. from the Persian and annotated by C. Schefer, Paris (1881), pp. 223.

al-Aflāj ***p. 166***
1. Nāṣir-i Khusraw, *Sefer Nameh*, trans. from the Persian by C. Schefer, Paris (1881), pp. 221-2. ("We were lodged at the mosque, and as I had a little cinnabar and blue mineral, I drew on the wall a couplet which I bordered with a leafy branch, while another leaf separated the hemistiches. The sight of my picture amazed the people of the castle, who gathered together to see it. They told me, 'If you agree to decorate the *miḥrāb* of the mosque with pictures, we shall give you a hundred *men* of dates.' Such a quantity was, in their eyes, of considerable value.")
2. *ibid.*, p. 222. ("I decorated the *miḥrāb* according to the pledge I had given and received the hundred *men* of dates, which were a great relief to the despair we found ourselves in.")

Jawātha mosque, al-Aḥsā' ***p. 168***
1. F.S. Vidal, *The Oasis of al-Hasa*, Dhahran (1955), pp. 69, 203.

Robert McC. Adam, Peter J. Parr, Muḥammad Ibrāhīm, ᶜAlī al-Mughannum, "Saudi Arabian Archaeological Reconnaissance 1976", *ATLAL, i* (1397/1977), p. 28.

Donald Whitcomb, "The Archaeology of al-Ḥasā' Oasis in the Islamic period", *ATLAL, ii* (1398/1978), pp. 100-1.

Mosque of Ibrāhīm, al-Hufūf ***p. 169***
1. Department of Antiquities, Kingdom of Saudi Arabia, *Muqaddima ᶜan āthār al-Mamlikat al-ᶜArabiyyat al-Suᶜūdiyya*, Riyadh (1395/1975), p. 153/p. ٤٠, gives a date of 974/1558 for the present building. The Ministry of Hajj and Awqāf date the original foundation to 750/1349-50.
2. J.E. Mandaville, "The Ottoman province of al-Hasā in the sixteenth and seventeenth centuries", *Journal of the American Oriental Society*, xc (1970), p. 488.

al-Jabrī mosque, al-Hufūf ***p. 172***
1. I am indebted to H.E. Mr Hussam Khashuqji, Assistant Deputy Minister of Hajj and Awqāf, who communicated this information to me in a letter dated 25 Shaᶜbān 1404, on the basis of the investigations of H.E. The Director of Awqāf of al-Aḥsā' area.

Department of Antiquities, Kingdom of Saudi Arabia, *Muqaddima ᶜan āthār al-Mamlikat al-ᶜArabiyyat al-Suᶜūdiyya*, Riyadh (1395/1975), gives a date of 880/*c.* 1450, referring to it as the "Gobri Mosque" in the English text, p. 151/٤٢.
2. It is possible that the variation of arch and pier type in the Jabrī mosque in part reflects reconstructions or the different date of various parts of the building. More

detailed examination of the mosque would help to establish its structural history.
3. Department of Antiquities, *Muqaddima ^{c}an āthār al-Mamlikat, op. cit.*, p. 151/٤٢.

al-Fātiḥ mosque, al-Hufūf ***p. 174***
1. al-Dibs is a term meaning molasses or syrup obtained from dates, as it was explained to me in al-Hufūf.

al-Sharafiyya mosque, al-Hufūf p. 175
1. J.B. Mackie, "Hasa: an Arabian oasis", *The Geographical Journal* (March 1924), lxiii, no. 3, p. 198 and plate facing p. 196.

Jāmi^{c} of Imām Fayṣal b. Turkī, al-Hufūf ***p. 176***
1. I am most grateful to H.E. Shaykh Muḥammad Mubārak, *imām* of the *jāmi^{c}* of Imām Fayṣal in al-Hufūf, whose great kindness ensured the successful completion of my research in al-Aḥsā'.
2. W.G. Palgrave, *Narrative of a Year's Journey through Central and Eastern Arabia (1862-63)*, London and Cambridge (1865; reprinted Farnborough, 1969), ii, pp. 151-2.

Mosque of Imām Fayṣal b. Turkī, al-Mubarraz ***p. 180***
1. W.G. Palgrave, *Narrative of a Year's Journey through Central and Eastern Arabia (1862-63)*, London and Cambridge (1865; reprinted Farnborough, 1969), ii, p. 172.

al-Rajihiyya mosque, al-Qaṭīf ***p. 180***
1. I express my thanks to Mr Chr. Winterhalter of the Project Department, King Faysal University, for drawing my attention to this interesting mosque. In a communication dated 31 September 1982, Mr Winterhalter kindly provided me with copies of his plans of the al-Qaṭīf mosques.

al-^{c}Uqayr ***p. 182***
1. J.B. Mackie, "Hasa: an Arabian oasis", *The Geographical Journal* (March 1924), lxiii, no. 3, pp. 191-2.

Saudi Arabian mosques and the Islamic architectural tradition ***p. 189***
1. Saad al-Rashid, "Lights on the history and archaeology of al-Rabadhah (locally called Abu Salim)", *Proceedings of the 12th Seminar for Arabian Studies,* ix (1979), pp. 88-101.

idem, "A brief report on the first archaeological excavation at al-Rabadhah", *Proceedings of the 13th Seminar for Arabian Studies*, x (1980), pp. 81-4.

idem, Al-Rabadhah. A portrait of early Islamic civilisation in Saudi Arabia, London (1986).
2. A number of mosques have been recorded at other sites on the Darb Zubayda. Some are mentioned by Dr S.A. al-Rashid, *Darb Zubaydah, The Pilgrim Road from Kufa to Mecca*, Riyadh (1980). Others are recorded as a result of further survey work on the Darb Zubayda:

James Knudstad, "The Darb Zubayda Project: 1396/1976", *ATLAL,* i (1397/1977), pp. 41-68.

Khalil al-Dayel and Salah al-Helwa, "Preliminary Report on the Second Phase of the Darb Zubayda Reconnaissance, 1397/1977", *ATLAL,* ii (1398/1978), pp. 51-64.

Khalil al-Dayel, Salah al-Hilwa and N. Mackenzie, "Preliminary Report on the Third Season of Darb Zubayda Survey, 1978", *ATLAL,* iii (1399/1979), pp. 43-54.

N.D. MacKenzie and Salāh al-Ḥelwah, "Darb Zubayda Architectural Documentation Program: a. Darb Zubayda – 1979, a preliminary report", *ATLAL,* iv (1400/1980), pp. 37-50.

Craig A. Morgan and Salah al-Helwa, "Preliminary Report on the Fifth Phase of Darb Zubayda Reconnaissance, 1400/1980", *ATLAL,* v (1401/1981), pp. 85-107.
3. Ronald Lewcock, *Traditional Architecture in Kuwait and the Northern Gulf*, with an introduction by Zahra Freeth, London (1978), p. 25/١٤٨.
4. R.B. Serjeant and Ronald Lewcock, eds., *Ṣan^{c}ā'. An Arabian Islamic City*, London (1983), p. 331.
5. E.J. Keall, "Zabid and its hinterland: 1982 Report", *Proceedings of the 16th Seminar for Arabian Studies*, xiii (1983), pp. 58-9, 66, fig. 6.

idem, "A preliminary report on the architecture of Zabīd", *Proceedings of the 17th Seminar for Arabian Studies*, xiv (1984), pp. 51-4; 56, fig. 2; 57, fig. 3.
6. K.A.C. Creswell, *Early Muslim Architecture* ii, Oxford (1940), figs. 194, 214 and pp. 268-9.
7. David Whitehouse, *Siraf III, The Congregational Mosque and other mosques from the ninth to the twelfth centuries*, London (1980), pp. 30-57.
8. Joseph Schacht, "Ein archäischer Minaret-typ in Ägypten und Anatolien", *Ars Islamics* 5 (1938), pp. 46-54.
9. The Ottoman style of minaret also established itself elsewhere on the Red Sea coast under the impact of Turkish political and cultural influence (*cf.* Jean-Pierre Greenlaw, *The Coral Buildings of Suakin*, London (1976), pp. 65-70).
10. J. Schacht, "An unknown type of minbar and its historical significance", *Ars Orientalis*, ii (1957), pp. 157-73.

P.S. Garlake, *The Early Islamic Architecture of the East African Coast*, Oxford (1966), pp. 74-5, interestingly, expresses the view that the fixed *minbar* is not indigenous to East Africa. One can reasonably ask if this is in fact an Arabian tradition in Islam which spread to neighbouring Islamic areas of Africa.

G.R. Smith, "A recessed minbar in the mosque of Simambaya", *Azania*, viii (1973), pp. 154-6.

Selected Bibliography of Arabic Sources

Muḥammad al-^{c}Abūdī, "Burayda, qā'ida bilād al-Qaṣīm", *al-^{c}Arab* (Dhū'l-Qa^{c}da–Dhū'l-Ḥijja 1399/Tishrīn, I, II/ October–November 1979), year 14, parts 5, 6, pp. 329-62.
"Madinat ^{c}Unayza", *al-^{c}Arab* (Rajab-Sha^{c}bān 1400/ Hazirān/May-June 1980) year 15, parts 1, 2, pp. 11-40.

^{c}Issam al-^{c}Amād, "Dār ṣinā^{c}a kiswat al-ka^{c}bat al-mushrifa", *Qāfilat al-zayt* (1387/1967), xv, no. 11, pp. 7-12.

Yaḥyā Ibrāhīm al-Alma^{c}ī, *Riḥalāt fī ^{c}Aṣīr*, Jidda (no date).

^{c}Alī al-Muḥammad al-^{c}Amar, "Tabūk", *al-Manhal*, (Rabī^{c}a II 1391/Hazirān/June 1971) year 37, xxxii, part 4, pp. 378-82.

Ṣāliḥ al-^{c}Amri, "Riḥlat ila Wādī'l-Qurrā: āthārhu – madīna dhī'l marwat al-āthāriyya – waṣaf al-marwa – al-ta^{c}rīf bihi", *al-Manhal* (Muḥarram–Ṣafar 1393/March–April 1973), year 39, xxxiv, parts 1, 2, pp. 65-70.

^{c}Abd al-Quddūs al-Anṣāry, *Āthār al-Madina al-Monawarah*, 3rd printing, al-Madina al-Monawarah (1393/ 1973).
"Tawsi^{c}āt al-masjidayn al-sharīfayn bi'l-Madina wa Makkah ^{c}abra al-tā'rīkh", *Qāfilat al-zayt*, (Rajab 1389/ September–October 1969), xvii, no. 7, pp. 7-12.
Bayn al-tā'rīkh wa'l-āthār, 3rd printing, Jidda (1397/ 1977).
Mawsū^{c}a tā'rīkh madīna Judda, 3rd printing, Cairo, (1402/1982).

A.R. al-Anṣāry, A.M. Ghazal and G.R.D. King
Muwāqi^{c} āthāriyya wa suwar min ḥaḍārat al-^{c}arab fī al-mamlikat al-^{c}arabiyyat al-su^{c}ūdiyya: al-^{c}Ulā (Didān), al-Hijr (Madā'in Ṣāliḥ), King Saud University, Riyadh (1404/1984).

Muḥammad b. Aḥmad al-^{c}Aqilī, *al-Āthār al-tā'rīkhiyya fī mantiqa Jāzān*, Riyadh (1399/1979).

Aḥmad ^{c}Abd al-Ghafūr ^{c}Aṭṭār, *al-Ka^{c}ba wa'l-kiswa mundhu arba^{c}t ālāf sinna ḥatā al-yawm*, Makkah al-Mukarramah (1397/1977).

Ibrāhīm b. ^{c}Alī al-^{c}Ayyāshī, *al-Madinah bayn al-māḍī wa'l-ḥāḍir*, al-Madina al-Monawarah (1392/1972).

al-Azraqī, *Akhbār Makkah*, ed. Rushdī al-Ṣāliḥ Malḥas, Makkah al-Mukarramah (1403/1983).

Sayyid ^{c}Abd al-Majīd Bakr, "al-Biqa^{c} al-muqaddisa", *Ashhar al-masājid fī'l-islām*, part 1, Jidda (1400/1980).

al-Balādhūrī, *Kitāb futūḥ al-buldān*, ed. M.J. de Goeje, 2nd ed., Leyden (1968).

Ḥusayn ^{c}Abd Allah Bā Salāma, *Tā'rīkh ^{c}imārat al-masjid al-ḥarām*, 3rd printing, Jidda (1400/1980).
Tā'rīkh al-ka^{c}bat al-ma^{c}aẓẓama, 2nd printing, Jidda (1402/1982).

Ḥassan al-Bāshā, *Madkhal ila al-āthār al-islāmiyya*, Cairo (1979).
"Āthār ^{c}imārat ^{c}Uthmān b. ^{c}Affān fī ^{c}imārat al-masājid", Paper delivered at the *Third International Symposium on Studies in the History of Arabia: Arabia in the Age of the Prophet and the Four Caliphs*, College of Arts, King Saud University, Riyadh (1404/1983).

Abū Zīr ^{c}Umar b. Shibh al-Numayrī al-Baṣrī, *Kitāb tā'rīkh al-Madina al-Monawarah*, Jidda (no date).

^{c}Uthmān b. Bishr, *^{c}Inwān al-majd fī tā'rīkh Najd*, Riyadh (no date).

Department of Antiquities, Kingdom of Saudi Arabia, *Muqaddima ^{c}an āthār al-Mamlikat al-^{c}Arabiyyat al-Su^{c}ūdiyya*, Riyadh (1395/1975).

Muḥammad Maḥmūd al-Dīb, "Nasha't al-Madina al-Monawarah wa qiyām al-masājid fīha", part 1, *al-Manhal* (Rabī^{c}a II–Jumāda I 1395/May–June 1975), year 41, xxxvi, parts 4-5, pp. 360-4; part 2, *al-Manhal* (Sha^{c}bān 1395/ August 1975), year 41, xxxvi, part 8, pp. 569-72.

Aḥmad b. Ḥanbal, *Musnad*, Beirut (no date).

^{c}Uthmān Ḥāfiẓ, *"Ma thār al-Madina"*, *Qāfilat al-zayt*, (Ṣafar 1385/June 1965) xiii, no. 2 pp. 2-6.

Ḥikmat Ḥassan, "al-Ṭā'if: yāqūta mu^{c}allaqa fawq qimam al-jibāl", *Qāfilat al-zayt* (Rabī^{c}a II 1389/June–July 1969), xvii, no. 4, pp. 25-34.
"al-Madina al-Monawarah, māḍīha wa ḥāḍirha", *Qāfilat al-zayt*, (Ramadān 1387/December 1967), xv, no. 9 pp. 5-14.

Ibn Hishām, *al-Sīrat al-nabawiyya*, ed. A. al-Saqqa, Cairo (1399/1979).

^{c}Iṣṣam al-^{c}Imād, "al-Aḥsā' aw wāḥatu'l-mazdūja", *Qāfilat al-zayt* (Rajab 1388/September–October 1968), xvi, no. 7, pp. 25-34.

Ḥamad al-Jāsir, *Fi shimāl gharb al-jazīra*, 2nd printing, Riyadh (1401/1981).

^{c}Abd Allah b. Muḥammad b. Khamīs, *al-Dir^{c}iyya*, Riyadh (1402/1982).

Aḥmad al-Khayārī, "Tā'rīkh masājid al-Madina al-Monawarah qadīman wa ḥadīthan", part 1, *al-Manhal*, special ed., (Dhū'l-Qaᶜda 1379/May 1960), year 15, pp. 622-4; part 2, *al-Manhal* (Muḥarram–Ṣafar 1380/July–August 1960), year 16, pp. 69-71.

Fawziyya Ḥusayn Maṭar, *Tā'rīkh ᶜimārat al-ḥarām al-Makkah al-sharīf,* Jidda (1402/1982).

Suᶜād Māhir Muḥammad, "al-Ṭā'if wa Waj wa mā bihā min āthār al-Nabī, (ṣalā Allah ᶜalayhi wa salam) wa'l-masājid al-āthāriyya", *al-Dāra* (Jumāda II 1401/April 1981), year 6, no. 3, pp. 36-56.

Ibrāhīm Rifaᶜāt Pāshā, *Mir'āt al-ḥaramayn*, Cairo (1344/1925).

Saᶜd al-Rāshid, "Darb Zubayda fī'l-ᶜāṣr al-ᶜabbāsī: dirāsa tā'rīkhiyya wa āthāriyya", *al-Dāra* (Rabīᶜa II 1398/March 1978) year 4, no. 1, pp, 8-31.

Ibn Saᶜd, *Kitāb al-ṭabaqāt al-kabīr,* eds. E. Mittwoch and E. Sachau, 9 vols, Leyden (1904-17).

al-Samhūdī, *Wafā' al-wafā,* ed. M. M. ᶜAbd al-Ḥamīd, Cairo (1373/1954).

Farīd Maḥmūd al-Shāfᶜī, *al-ᶜImārat al-ᶜarabiyyat al-islāmiyya,* Riyadh (1402/1982).

ᶜAbd al-Raḥmān Ṣādiq al-Sharīf, "Dirāsāt fī jughrāfiyyat al-Mamlikat al-ᶜArabiyyat al-Suᶜūdiyya: Juzā'ir Farasān", *Majallat kullīyat al-ādab,* King Saud University, Riyadh, vii, (1980) pp. 3-35.

Shaykh ᶜAbd al-Raḥmān b. ᶜAbd al-Laṭīf Al al-Shaykh, "Shaykh Muḥammad b. ᶜAbd al-Wahhāb", *al-Dāra* 4 (Rajab 1396/July 1976), year 2, no.2, pp. 16-27.

al-Ṭabarī, *Annales quos scripsit at-Tabari,* ed. M.J. de Goeje, *et al,* Leyden (1879-1901).

al-Yaᶜqūbī, *Ibn Wādhih qui dicitur Al-Jaᶜqubī, Historiae,* ed. Th. Houtsma, Leyden (1883; reprinted 1969).

Anon, "Bilād Ghāmid wa Zahrān", *Qāfilat al-zayt* (Rabīᶜa I 1388/May–June 1968), xvi, no. 3, pp. 45-50.

Selected Bibliography of non-Arabic Sources

Robert McC.Adam, Peter Parr, Muḥammad Ibrāhīm, ᶜAlī al-Mughannum, "Saudi Arabian Archaeological Reconnaissance 1976", *ATLAL,* i (1397/1977), pp. 21-40.

Ali Bey (Domenico Badia y Leblich), *Travels of Ali Bey in Morocco, Tripoli, Cyprus, Egypt, Arabia, Syria and Turkey, between the years 1803 and 1807,* London (1816; reprinted Farnborough, 1970).

S.M. Amin, *The Holy Journey to Mecca,* London (1976).

Saleh Muhammad al-Amr, *The Hijaz under Ottoman Rule 1869-1914: Ottoman Vali, the Sharif of Mecca, and the Growth of British Influence,* Riyadh (1978).

A.R. Al-Ansary, *Qaryat al-Fau: A Portrait of a Pre-Islamic Civilisation in Saudi Arabia*, London (1982).

Ibn Baṭṭūṭah, *The Travels of Ibn Baṭṭūṭah,* trans. from the Arabic by H.A.R. Gibb, Cambridge (1962).

Ghazi Izzeddin Bisheh, *The Mosque of the Prophet at Madinah throughout the first century* A.H. *with special emphasis on the Umayyad Mosque,* University Microfilms International (1979).

John Lewis Burckhardt, *Travels in Arabia*, London (1829; reprinted 1968).

Richard F. Burton, *Personal Narrative of a Pilgrimage to el-Medinah and Meccah,* 2nd ed., London (1857).

Kinahan Cornwallis, *Asir before World War I: a handbook* (1916; reprinted London, 1976).

K.A.C. Creswell, *Early Muslim Architecture,* Oxford (1969), i, part 1.

Khalil al-Dayel and Salah al-Helwa, "Preliminary Report on the Second Phase of the Darb Zubayda Reconnaissance, 1397/1977", *ATLAL,* ii (1398/1978) pp.51-64.

Khalil al-Dayel, Salah al-Hilwa, N. MacKenzie, "Preliminary Report on the Third Season of the Darb Zubayda Survey, 1978", *ATLAL,* iii (1399/1979) pp.43-54.

Charles Doughty, *Travels in Arabia Deserta,* London (1923).

Encyclopaedia of Islam, old ed., Leyden (1913–42); new ed., London and Leyden (1960-).

Emel Esin, *Mecca the Blessed, Madinah the Radiant,* London (1963).

Barbara Finster, "Die Freitagsmoschee von Ṣanᶜā', Vorläufiger Bericht, 1.", *Baghdader Mitteilungen,* ix, (1978) pp. 92-133.
"Die Freitagsmoschee von Šibām-Kaukabān", *Baghdader Mitteilungen,* x, (1979) pp. 193-228.
"Die Moschee von Ṣarḥa", *Baghdader Mitteilungen,* x, (1979) pp. 229-42.
"Die Moschee von Hāu", *Baghdader Mitteilungen,* x

(1979) pp. 246-8.
with Jürgen Schmidt "Die Freitagsmoschee von Ṣanᶜā', Vorläufiger Bericht, 2. Der Ostriwāq", *Baghdader Mitteilungen*, x, (1979) pp. 179-92.

P.S. Garlake, *The Early Islamic Architecture of the East African Coast,* Oxford (1966).

Jean-Pierre Greenlaw, *The Coral Buildings of Suakin,* London (1976).

Carlo Guarmani, *Northern Najd. A journey from Jerusalem to Anaiza ain Qasim,* trans. from the Italian by Lady Capel-Cure; introduction and notes by Douglas Carruthers, London (1938).

Muhammad Hamidullah, *The Battlefields of the Prophet Muhammad,* Hyderabad (1392/1973).

David G. Hogarth, *Hejaz before World War I: a handbook,* 2nd ed., London (1917; new ed. with introduction by R.L. Bidwell, 1978).
"Gertrude Bell's Journey to Hayil", *The Geographical Journal* (July 1927), lxx, no. 1, pp. 1-21.

C. Snouck Hurgronje, *Mekka,* 2 vols, with *Atlas,* The Hague (1888-9).
Mekka in the latter part of the 19th century, trans. from the German by J.H. Monahan, Leyden and London (1931).

A. Jaussen and F. Savignac, *Mission Archéologoique en Arabie (mars-mai 1907) de Jérusalem au Hedjaz, Médain Salih,* Paris (1909); *Atlas,* Paris (1914).

Ibn Jubayr, *The Travels of Ibn Jubayr,* trans. from the Arabic by R.J.C. Broadhurst, London (1952).

Hamza Kaïdi, with Nadjm oud-Dine Bammat and El Hachemi Tidjani, *La Mecque et Médine aujourd'hui,* Paris (1980).

E.J. Keall, "Zabid and its hinterland: 1982 Report", *Proceedings of the 16th Seminar for Arabian Studies,* xiii (1983), pp. 53-69.
"A preliminary report on the architecture of Zabīd", *Proceedings of the 17th Seminar for Arabian Studies,* xiv (1984), pp. 51-65.

G.R.D. King, "Some observations on the architecture of south west Saudi Arabia", *Architectural Association Quarterly*, viii, no. 1, (1976), pp. 20-9.
"Traditional Architecture in Najd, Saudi Arabia", *Proceedings of the 10th Seminar for Arabian Studies*, vii (1977), pp. 90-100.
"Islamic Architecture in Eastern Arabia", *Proceedings of the 11th Seminar for Arabian Studies*, viii (1978), pp. 15-28.
"Some examples of the secular architecture of Najd", *Arabian Studies*, vi, (1982) pp. 113-42.
"A mosque attributed to ᶜUmar b. al-Khaṭṭāb in Dūmat al-Jandal in al-Jawf, Saudi Arabia", *Journal of the Royal Asiatic Society,* no. 2 (1978), pp. 109-23.
"Traditional Najdī Mosques", *Bulletin of the School of Oriental and African Studies,* xli, part 3 (1978), pp. 464-98
"Notes on some mosques in eastern and western Saudi Arabia", *Bulletin of the School of Oriental and African Studies,* xliii, part 2 (1980), pp. 251-76.

James Knudstead, "The Darb Zubayda Project: 1396/1976", *ATLAL,* i (1397/1977), pp. 41-68.

Ronald Lewcock, *Traditional architecture in Kuwait and the Northern Gulf,* with introduction by Zahra Freeth, London (1978).

Ronald Lewcock and G.R. Smith, "Two early mosques in the Yemen: a preliminary report", *Art and Archaeology Research Papers (AARP)* (December 1973), pp. 117-30.
"Three medieval mosques in the Yemen", *Oriental Art,* xx (1974), no. 1, pp. 75-86; no. 2, pp. 192-203.

J.G. Lorimer, *Gazetteer of the Persian Gulf, ᶜOmān, and Central Arabia,* Calcutta (1908), IIA, IIB.

N.D. MacKenzie and Salāh al-Ḥelwah, "Darb Zubayda Architectural Documentation Program: a. Darb Zubayda-1979, a preliminary report", *ATLAL,* iv (1400/1980) pp. 37-50.

J.B. Mackie, "Hasa: an Arabian oasis", *The Geographical Journal,* lxiii, no. 3 (March 1924), pp. 189-207.

M.S. Makki, *Medina, Saudi Arabia,* Avebury (1982).

J.E. Mandaville, "The Ottoman province of al-Hasā in the sixteenth and seventeenth centuries", *Journal of the Americal Oriental Society,* xc (1970), pp. 486-513.

al-Masᶜūdi, *Murūj al-dhahab*, trans. from the Arabic by C. Barbier de Meynard, Paris (1869).

Ministry of Information, Kingdom of Saudi Arabia, *The Holy Places,* London (no date).

Tchekof Minosa, *Najran, Desert Garden of Arabia,* Paris (1983).

Craig Morgan and Salah al-Helwa, "Preliminary Report on the Fifth Phase of Darb Zubayda Reconnaissance, 1400/1980", *ATLAL,* v (1401/1981) pp.85-107.

M.S. Mousalli, F.A. Shaker, and O.A. Mandily, *An introduction to urban patterns in Saudi Arabia: the central region,* London (1977).

Carlo Alfonso Nallino, "L'Arabia Saᶜūdiana", *Raccolta di Scritti Editi e Inediti,* ed. Maria Nallino, Rome (1939), i.

A.N. Nasif, *An historical and archaeological survey of al-ᶜUla with special reference to its irrigation system,* Unpublished doctoral thesis, Manchester University (1981).

Nāṣir-i Khusraw, *Sefer Nameh, Relation du Voyage de Nassiri Khosrau en Syrie, en Palestine, en Egypte, en Arabie et en Perse pendant les années de l'Hégire 437-444 (1035-1042),* trans. from the Persian and annotated by Charles Schefer, Paris (1881).

Carsten Niebuhr, *Travels through Arabia and other Countries in the East,* trans. from the German by Robert Heron, Edinburgh (1792; reprinted Beirut, no date).

William Gifford Palgrave, *Narrative of a Year's Journey through Central and Eastern Arabia (1862-63),* London and Cambridge (1865; reprinted Farnborough, 1969).

Angelo Pesce, *Jiddah, Portrait of an Arabian City,* revised ed., London (1976).

H.St.J. Philby, *The Heart of Arabia,* London (1922).
Arabia of the Wahhabis, London (1928).
Arabian Highlands, Ithaca, New York (1952).
Saᶜudi Arabia, London (1955; reprinted Beirut, 1968).
The Land of Midian, London (1957).

Saad A. al-Rashid, "Darb Zubaydah in the ᶜAbbāsid Period: historical and archaeological aspects", *Proceedings of the 11th Seminar for Arabian Studies,* viii (1978) pp. 33-45.
"Lights on the history and archaeology of Al-Rabadhah (Locally called Abu Salim)", *Proceedings of the 12th Seminar for Arabian Studies,* ix (1979) pp.88-101.
Darb Zubaydah. The Pilgrim Road from Kufa to Mecca, Riyadh (1980).
"A brief report on the first archaeological excavation at al-Rabadhah", *Proceedings of the 13th Seminar for Arabian Studies,* x, (1980) pp.81-4.
Al-Rabadhah. A portrait of early Islamic civilisation in Saudi Arabia, London (1986).

Ameen Rihani, *Ibn Sa'oud of Arabia. His People and his Land*, London (1928).
Around the Coasts of Arabia, London (1930).

Royal Navy (Naval Intelligence Division), *Western Arabia and the Red Sea,* BR 527 (June 1946).

Eldon Rutter, *The Holy Cities of Arabia*, London and New York (1928).

G.F. Sadleir, *Diary of a Journey Across Arabia (1819),* London (1866; reprinted Cambridge, 1977).

Jean Sauvaget, *La Mosquée Omeyyade de Médine,* Paris (1947)

Joseph Schacht, "Ein archäischer Minaret-Typ in Ägypten und Anatolien", *Ars Islamica,* v, part 1 (1938), pp. 46-54.
"An unknown type of minbar and its historical significance", *Ars Orientalis,* ii (1957), pp. 149-173.

Jürgen Schmidt, ed., *Archäologische Berichte aus dem Yemen,* Deutsches Archäologisches Institut Ṣanaᶜā', Mainz am Rhein (1982), i.

R.B. Serjeant and Ronald Lewcock, eds., *Ṣanᶜā', An Arabian Islamic City,* London (1983).

G.R. Smith, "A recessed minbar in the mosque of Simambaya", *Azania,* viii (1973), pp. 154-6.

Stacey International, *Jedda Old and New,* London (1980).

Vicenzo Strika, "Studi saudiani. 1. Le moschee di Gedda. 2. Aspetti giuridici delle attività archeologiche", *Annali, Istituto Orientale di Napoli,* xxxv, new series, xxv, part 4 (1975), pp. 555-85.
"A Kaᶜbah picture in the Iraq Museum", *Sumer*, xxxii (1976), pp. 195-201.
"A Kaᶜbah picture from Mosul", *Studies in the History of Arabia, I; Sources for the History of Arabia,* part 1, Riyadh (1399/1979), pp. 145-8.

Maurice Tamisier, *Voyage en Arabie. Séjour dans le Hedjaz – Campagne d'Assir,* Paris (1840).

Fernando Varanda, *The Art of Building in Yemen,* London and Cambridge, Mass. (1982).

F.S. Vidal, *The Oasis of al-Hasa,* Dhahran (1955).

G. Wallin, "Narrative of a Journey from Cairo to Madina and Mecca by Suez, Arabá, Tawilá, al-Jauf, Jubbé, Háil and Nejd, in 1845", *Journal of the Royal Geographical Society*, xxiv (1854), pp. 115-207.

Leopold Mohammad Weiss, "Riadh, Die Stadt des Königs ibn Sa'ud", *Atlantis,* Berlin–Zurich (1930), pp. 522-30.

Donald Whitcomb, "The Archaeology of al-Ḥasā' Oasis in the Islamic period", *ATLAL,* ii (1398/1978), pp. 95-113.

David Whitehouse, *Siraf III. The Congregational Mosque and other Mosques from the Ninth to the Twelfth Centuries,* British Institute of Persian Studies, London (1980).

Abdullah al-Wohaibi, *The Northern Hijaz in the Writings of the Arab Geographers, 800-1150,* Beirut (1973).

E. von Zambaur, *Manuel de Généalogie et de Chronologie pour l'histoire de l'Islam*, Hanover (1927).

Juris Zarins, Mohammad Ibrahim, Daniel Potts and Christopher Edens, "Saudi Arabian Archaeological Reconnaissance 1978: The preliminary report on the third phase of the comprehensive archaeological survey program – the Central Province", *ATLAL,* iii (1399/1979), pp. 9-42.

Glossary of Arabic terms

adhān: Call to prayer.

ḥaramayn: Two Holy Cities of Islam, Makkah al-Mukarramah and al-Madina al-Monawarah.

hilāl: Crescent.

ibrīq: Ewer, used for ablutions (*wuḍū'*).

imām: Individual who leads the Islamic community in prayer.

jāmiᶜ: Congregational mosque used for Friday prayers, having a *minbar*.

khalwa: Lower or covered prayer-hall.

khuṭba: Religious address to the Islamic community during Friday congregational prayers.

madrasa: School. Teaching institutions are found attached to many major historical mosques in the Islamic world.

manāra: Minaret. The tower in a mosque from which the call to prayer is made.

maqṣūra: Enclosed or otherwise specially defined area in the foremost place in the mosque, before the *miḥrāb* or the *qibla* wall.

marūsa: System of plastered water receptacles and water channels for ablutions prior to prayer.

masjid: Mosque.

maṣṭaba: Stone bench built against a wall.

maṭāhir: Walled facilities providing privacy for those performing ablutions before prayer.

mi'dhana: Minaret. Tower in a mosque from which the call to prayer is made.

miḥrāb: Indicates the direction of the Kaᶜba in Makkah al-Mukarramah. It may be a flat panel or a recess, curved or square.

minbar: Raised or stepped position in the mosque from which the *imām* delivers the *khuṭba*. The first *minbar* in Islam was that used by the Prophet Muḥammad (ṣ) in his mosque in al-Madina al-Monawarah.

mu'adhdhin: Individual who gives the call to prayer.

muqarnas: Decorative moulding of blind arches forming stalactite-like ornament, much favoured in the Islamic world.

muẓalla: Roofed area in the mosque which provides shade.

qibla: Direction of the Kaᶜba in Makkah al-Mukarramah towards which all Muslims turn in prayer wherever they may be on earth. The ascertaining of the precise *qibla* is extremely important in the building of a mosque.

raḥba: Open space or public area.

riwāq: Portico.

quḍāḍ: Hard waterproof plaster used in ᶜAsīr and Yemen.

ṣaḥn: Open courtyard preceding the prayer-hall.

shurfa: Balcony around the minaret shaft.

suffa: Covered area for study and rest within the mosque.

wuḍū': Ablution before prayer.

Index

ʿAbbās mosque, Abū ʿArīsh 57, 60-1, 62
ʿAbbāsid Caliphs: architectural style 190; building style and activity 23, 24, 25, 32, 41, 128, 174
ʿAbd Allāh b. ʿAbbās, mosque of 41
ʿAbd Allah b. Ibrāhīm b. Sayf Al Sayf, Shaykh 134-5
ʿAbd Allah b. Saʿūd 15
ʿAbd al-ʿAzīz b. ʿAbd al-Raḥmān Al Saʿūd, King 16, 26, 33, 34, 42, 51, 156, 160-1, 182
al-ʿAbd al-Karīm Al Isā, ʿIsā 125
ʿAbd al-Majīd I, Sultan 32, 33
ʿAbd al-Malik b. Marwān 23
ʿAbd al-Muṭṭalib 20
ʿAbd al-Raḥmān Pasha 48
Abhā, mosques 82, 190
Abī Waṭbān, Mūḍī bint 14
ablutions, provisions for: ʿAsīr 84-5, 89, 94-7; Farasān 65, 68, 72; Nejd 139; Red Sea coast 45; Tihāmat ʿAsīr 57, 60; Tihāma mountains 78-9; *see also* *matāhir*
Abū ʿArīsh 14, 18, 56-7, 74, 89; *see also* ʿAbbās mosque; Masjid ʿUthmān Rifaʿī; Old Mosque; Wāfiʿ mosque
Abū Bakr al-Ṣiddīq 22, 30
Abū Mismār, Ḥamūd 63
al-Aflāj 13; mosque 161, 166
Aḥad Rufayda, ʿAsir, *jāmiʿ* 98-9
Aḥmad b. Ṭūlūn, Egypt, mosque 189
al-Aḥsā' 175, 177-8, 189; control of 13-14, 15-16; *see also* Jawātha mosque
ʿAjāba mosque 34
ʿAlāwiyya mosque, Ṣabyā 56-8
ʿAlawiyya, Zilfī, mosque 134
ʿAlī Bey 25
ʿAlī ʿIsā, *Imām* 47
ʿAlī, al-Khwājā Muḥammad 38
ʿAli Pasha, Muḥammad 15, 16, 26, 34, 41, 42
al-ʿAlī al-Rashūdī, Fahad 126
ʿAlī Sālim Maslūm mosque 113-14
ʿAmr b. al-ʿĀṣ, mosque 44, 189, 190
ʿAnjār, Lebanon, mosque 189
al-Anṣary, ʿAbd al-Quddūs 27, 28, 32; on Jidda mosques 34, 37, 38, 39
al-ʿAqīlī, Muḥammad Aḥmad 63-4
al-Aqṣā mosque, Jerusalem 44
arches: blind 35, 37-9, 42-3, 46, 68, 71-2, 90, 97, 177, 179, 180, 185; keel 88, 135, 136, 138-43, 147, 149, 151, 153-4, 156, 160, 164-6, 169, 172; lobed 37, 38-9, 42, 46, 68, 169, 173, 179, 180, 185; pointed 38-9, 57, 61, 64, 66, 73, 92, 97-8, 169, 172-4, 180, 185, 187-8; rounded 38, 43, 46, 59, 71, 90, 177, 183; trefoil 37, 38-9, 174
architecture, domestic: highland 89; "Red Sea" style 42; traditional 65, 98, 116, 141, 174, 184
architecture, mosque: diversity 189; early 13, 189; Eastern Arabian 176, 177-8; Egyptian influence 16, 24-5, 32, 37, 42; external influences 13, 19, 42, 56, 189; Gulf coast 180, 182, 184-5, 187-8; Ottoman influence 14, 16, 25, 34, 41-2, 50, 82, 169, 171, 175, 190; "Red Sea" style 34; second Saudi state 16; traditional, regional 11, 13, 16, 28, 34, 39, 41, 63-5, 74, 75-6, 110, 116, 122, 125, 127, 130, 132, 135-6, 141, 148, 151, 154, 162, 189-91
al-ʿArīnī, Muḥammad b. Suwailam 14
ʿArqa: old *jāmiʿ* 154-5
al-Asfal, Masqī, ʿAsīr, mosque 93-6, 98
Ashrāf mosque, Abū ʿArīsh, *see* Masjid ʿUthmān Rifaʿī
Ashrāf mosque, al-Wahj 39, 43-4, 45-6, 199n.
ʿAsīr region 82, 83-99; control of 15-16, 41; geography 18
al-ʿAwda, *jāmiʿ* 141, 142
al ʿAyīrī, Burayda, mosque 128-9
Ayyūbids 13

Baghdad, *jāmiʿ* 128, 189
al-Bāha, mosque 82
Bakr Basha 39
Banī Khālid tribe 14, 15
Barsbay, Sultan al-Ashraf 25, 32, 34
al-Bāshā mosque, Jidda 39-41
al-Batrā', *jāmiʿ* 130-1
Bell, Gertrude 120
Bilād Banī Salmān, Bilād Banī ʿAlī mosque 110-12
Bilād Zahrān mosque 83
al-Birk, mosque 57
Budaywī al-Shaḥāta mosque 39, 43, 44, 45-7, 67, 199n.
al-Bunduqdārī, al-Ẓāhir Baybars 32
Burayda 131, 134, 189; *see also* al-ʿAyīrī mosque; al-Ḥuwayza mosque; al-Mādī mosque; al-Mushayqah mosque
Burckhardt, J.L. 25, 26, 32-3, 41, 82, 195n.
Burton, Richard 33, 42
buttresses 37, 38, 40; Eastern Province 169, 172; Farasān 73; Najrān 106

climate 18, 41, 56, 116, 168, 182
colonnades: Eastern Province 169, 174-5; Farasān 73; Holy Mosque 23, 25-6; Mosque of the Prophet 31, 32-3; Nejd 125, 127, 131, 134, 146-7, 154, 156-8; Tihāmat ʿAsīr 59, 64; as typical design feature 189-90; *see also* piers
Cornwallis, Kinahan 59
crenellation 39, 40; ʿAsīr region 86, 93, 96; Eastern Province 178; Hejaz 54; Najrān 99-100, 102, 105, 108-9, 112, 114; Nejd 120, 124, 125, 129, 131; Muḥāyil 65; Tihāma mountains 76, 80

Dahdha al-Ṣuqūr, Najrān North Mosque 101-3; South Mosque 99-101; *see also* ʿAlī Sālim Maslūm mosque; Bilād Banī Salmān mosque; Muḥammad Manṣūr mosque; Muḥammad Ṣāliḥ Azaʿjūr mosque; Shaʿb Burān al-Ḥārith mosque
Damascus, Great Mosque: colonnades 44, 189; mosaics 23, 31
Darb Zubayda, early mosques 11, 189
decoration 23, 30-3, 66; ʿAsīr 85-6, 97; Eastern Province 180-1, 186; Farasān 69-73; Ḥā'il 121; Jidda 37-40; low relief 37, 86, 125, 128-9, 136, 141-2; Najrān 102, 112; Persian influence 36; *see also* gold; marble; mosaic; *muqarnas*; plaster
design, *see* architecture
al-Dirʿiyya area 14, 149-53, 161; *see also* Imām Muḥammad b. Saʿūd mosque; Saʿd mosque; Wādī'l-Ḥanīfa mosque
domes: Eastern Provinces 169, 171; Farasān 67, 73, 74; Tihāmat ʿAsīr 57, 60-61, 62-4
doorways: ʿAsīr 84-6, 88-9, 94, 96-7, 99; Eastern coast 182, 185; Eastern Province 171, 172, 174, 180; Farasān 66, 68, 70-1, 74; Hejaz 52; Najrān 102, 105, 106, 108-9, 112, Nejd 121-2, 124, 125, 129-32, 134, 143-4, 163; Red Sea coast 38-9, 43, 45-6; Tihāma mountains 75-6, 78-81
Doughty, Charles 196n.
drainways, plaster-lined 91-2, 116, 125, 138
Dūmat al-Jandal 13, 15, 50, 117-20, 189

Eastern Province 168-90
Ebony (Ābanūs) Mosque (mosque of ʿUthman b. ʿAffān) 34
Egyptian influence 13-16, 24-5, 26, 32, 34, 42

Fahad b. ʿAbd al-ʿAzīz Al Saʿūd, King 27, 33
Fakhrī Pasha 32
Farasān islands 18, 60, 63, 65-74
al-Fatḥ, mosques of 34
al-Fātiḥ mosque 174-5
al-Faw 161
Fayṣal b. ʿAbd al-ʿAzīz Al Saʿūd, King 27, 33, 48, 92

al-Ghasība mosque 153
Ghat Ghat, mosque 160-1
glass, use of 33; *see also* windows
gold as decoration 23-4, 26, 30, 32
Guarmani, Carlo 120

Ḥā'il 16, 142, 190; *jāmiʿ* 120; *see also* Al Rashīd mosque; Ḥarta al-Zubāra mosque; al-Wāsiṭ mosque
al-Hajjāj at al-Wāsiṭ, *jāmiʿ* 172, 189
al-Ḥamawī, Yāqūt 143
al-Ḥanīfī (Abu Ḥanīfa) mosque 36-8, 39, 40
Harrān, Turkey, mosque 190
Ḥarta al-Zubāra, Ḥāʿil, mosque 120-2
Ḥassan, Sultan, mosque of 39
ḥatim (Honourable Kaʿba) 20
al-Ḥawṭa/al-Ḥilwa, mosque near 64
al-Ḥawṭa mosque 165
Hazwa, mosque 149
Hejaz region 18, 54; architecture 25, 42, 190; control 13-14, 15-16, 42; geography 18; southern Hejaz 82-99
hijras 16, 160
hilāl (crescent) 67, 173, 175
ḥiṣn Marḥab, Khaybar, mosque of 51, 53-4
Hogarth, D.G. 42
Holy Mosque (Ḥarām Mosque), Makkah al-Mukarramah 11, 13, 19-26, 190; decoration 23; descriptions 24-6; flooding 18, 25; minarets 23, 24-5; *minbar* 25; reconstruction and enlargements 23-4, 25-6
Honourable Kaʿba 19-26; Black Stone, decoration 23; first Kaʿba 19-20; flooding 18, 20, 22, 25; interior 24; *kiswa* 23; Mizāb al-Raḥma 23; rebuilding and restorations 20, 23, 25
al-Hufūf: *see* al-Fātiḥ mosque; Ibrāhīm, mosque of; Imām Fayṣal b. Turkī, mosque of; al-Jabrī mosque; al-Sharafiyya mosque
Hunūd, mosque of the 41
Ḥuraymilā' 14; old *jāmiʿ* 137, 139, 144-6, 147
Hurgronje, Snouck 26
al-Hussayni, Sharīf Abū Yaʿlī 27
al-Ḥuwayza, Burayda, mosque 125, 126-8, 129-30

Ibn ʿAbd al-ʿAzīz b. Muḥammad b. Saʿūd, Imām Saʿūd 92
Ibn ʿAbd al-ʿAzīz, ʿUmar 27, 30
Ibn ʿAbd al-Majīd, ʿAbd al-Ḥamīd II, Sultan 48
Ibn Abī Ṭālib, ʿAlī, Caliph 51
Ibn ʿAffān, ʿUthmān 23, 27, 30, 34; mosque of 34
Ibn ʿAjlān, Sharīf Ḥusayn 38
Ibn ʿAlī, Sharīf Ḥusayn 34
Ibn ʿAlī al-ʿAyīrī Aḥmad 128
Ibn ʿAwn, Ghālib 25, 34
Ibn Barqūq, Sultan Faraj 25

Ibn Battuta 34
Ibn Bijād, Sultān 160
Ibn Bishr, ᶜUthmān, historian 14, 136
Ibn al-Hadramī, al-ᶜAlā' 168
Ibn Hamūd al-Mushayqah, ᶜAbd al-ᶜAzīz 125
Ibn Jarrāh al-Thawri, Zuhrī' 122
Ibn Jubayr, traveller 24, 31-2, 34, 189
Ibn al-Khattāb, ᶜUmar 13-14, 30, 34, 38, 117, 120
Ibn al-Khattāb, Zayd, tomb of 14
Ibn Kilāb, Qusayy 20
Ibn Muᶜammar, ᶜUthmān b. Hamad 14
Ibn Nāsir Muhammad, Sultan Hasan 32
Ibn Qalā'ūn, Sultan al-Nāsir Muhammad 25
Ibn Qatāda 14
Ibn Saᶜūd, Muhammad 14, 149-51, 156
Ibn Shaᶜbān, Sultan al-Mansur ᶜAlī 25
Ibn Taymiyya, jurist 14
Ibn Turkī, Imām Faysal 15-16, 156, 158, 161
Ibn al-Walīd, Khālid 48
Ibn Yūsuf, al-Hajjāj 23, 189
Ibn al-Zubayr, ᶜAbd Allah 23
Ibrāhīm, mosque of, al-Hufūf 169-72, 173, 179, 186
Ibrahīm Pasha 15, 150-2, 154, 156, 161
imām, entrance for 135, 147, 153
Imām Faysal b. Turkī, mosque of, al-Hufūf 16, 176
Imām Faysal b. Turkī, mosque of al-Mubarraz 16, 176-7
Imām Muhammad b. Saᶜūd, al-Dirᶜiyya, mosque 150-1
inscriptions 112, ancient 50; dated 37, 43, 65, 83, 91-2, 97, 175; in Holy Mosque 24; Jidda mosques 37-38 in Mosque of the Prophet 33; Tabūk 48; Turkish 37
Ismaᶜīl, Burayda, mosque 199n.

al-Jabrī, al-Hufūf, mosque 172-3, 186
al-Jafr, al-Ahsā', mosque 178
Jalājil: disused mosque 139-40; new *jāmiᶜ* 122, 136-137; old *jāmiᶜ* 136-7, 146; small mosques 138-9
Jamal, ᶜAsīr: old mosque 88-9; small mosque 87-8
al-Jāsir, Hamad, Shaykh 120
al-Jāsir mosque, al-Zilfī 127, 133-4
Jaussen, A. 48
al-Jawād, Jamāl al-Dīn al-Isfahānī 24
Jidda: architectural styles 16, 18-19, 25; mosques 34, 36, 38, 39, 189-90; *see also* al-Bāshā mosque; al-Hanīfī mosque; al-Miᶜmār mosque; al-Shāfiᶜī mosque
Jīzān 18, 56, 60, 72, 74
al-Jubayl 168, 189; newer mosque 187; old *jāmiᶜ* 173, 184-6, 188, 197n.; old mosque 187; seashore mosque 188
al-Jubayla, tomb at 14
Jumaᶜ mosque, al Madina al-Monawarah 34
Juwāthā, early mosque 13, 168-9

al-Khabza, Masjid 41
Khādim Pasha 48
Khalīd b. ᶜAbd al-ᶜAzīz, Al Saᶜūd, King 26
khalwa (underground mosque) 125, 127, 130, 139-40, 146, 151, 156-8
al-Kharj, old mosque 162
al-Khattāb., ᶜUmar b, mosque of 13, 22, 30, 34, 117-120
Khaybar 51-4; early mosque 13, 51-2, 53, 189; *see also* ᶜAlī mosque; *hisn* Marhab Khaybar
Khirbat al-Mafjar, Palestine, mosque 189
Khusraw, Nāsir-i, traveller 13, 24, 34, 41, 162, 166
Kirk, Rupert 55, 56, 197n.
al-Kūᶜ, Masjid 41
Kufa, Iraq, *jāmiᶜ* 127-8, 189
Kuwayt, mosques 189

Layla, mosque 166
lock, wooden 121, 134

Mackie, J.B. 175
al-Mādī, Burayda, mosque 129-30
al-Mādī, Mādī 129
al-Madina al-Monawarah: architectural style 25, 127; mosques 34, 189; *see also* Prophet, Mosque of; Qubā', mosque of
madrasa (school) 41
Maghlūth mosque, al-Mubarraz 175, 177
al-Mahdī, Caliph 23, 31
Mahmūd II, Sultan 27, 32
Majmaᶜa, *jāmiᶜ* 134-6
Makkah al-Mukarramah: mosques of 26, 189; Prophet in 20-2; siege of 23; *see also* Holy Mosque; Honourable Kaᶜba
Malham, mosque 143-4
Manādhir, *jāmiᶜ* 82
al-Mansūr, Caliph Abū Jaᶜfar 23-4, 128, 189
Maqām Ibrāhīm 20, 22
maqsūra 30, 31-2
marble as decoration 23-4, 25, 30, 32-3
al-Marmār, Fayfā', *jāmiᶜ* 80-2
marūsa 85, 96-7
Masjid ᶜUthmān Rifaᶜī, Abū ᶜArīsh (Ashrāf mosque) 63-4
mastaba (stone bench): Khaybar 52; Tihāma mountains 78, 81
matāhir 78, 85, 94, 96; *see also* ablutions, facilities for, materials, building: baked brick: Eastern Province 169; Tihāmat ᶜAsīr 56, 59-60, 64; basalt 18, 51, 56, 59-60, 64; concrete 16, 54, 74, 93, 116, 132; coral 18, 34, 43, 45, 47; Eastern Province 168, 180, 182, 184, 187-8; Tihāmat ᶜAsīr 56, 65, 68, 74; mud 18, 99-100, 104, 109, 114, 116, 168; mud-brick: Hejaz 51; Najrān 100, 101, 104, 106, 110, 114; Nejd 28, 120, 122, 124, 126, 128-9, 130, 134-6, 138, 141-4, 151, 153-4, 156, 160, 162-4; stone 18, 41, 42, 50, 53, 65; ᶜAsīr 83, 87, 89, 92, 94, 96; Eastern Province 172, 175, 178; Nejd 116, 117, 122, 124, 129, 141, 153, 156, 164; Tihāma mountains 75-6, 78-80; wood 34-5, 96, 116, 127, 156, 160, 184; *see also* plaster, use of
merlons: ᶜAsīr 86, 91, 96; Holy Mosque 24; Najrān 100, 101-2, 106, 109, 111-12, 114; Nejd 131, 134; Tihāma mountains 77, 82
mihrāb 27, 36, 189; arched 182; curved 44, 52-4, 57, 59, 82-3, 88, 96, 99-100, 106, 122-3, 126-7, 131-2, 139-41, 146-7, 149, 151-4, 163-4, 169, 172, 174-5, 186-7, 190;
rectangular 47, 64, 67, 72, 74, 76-9, 90, 92, 98, 108-9, 111, 128, 164, 166, 169, 172-3, 177-9, 190;
six-sided 64; square 80, 102, 114, 165, 166;
tapering 65, 139, 141, 160-1;
three-faceted projection 38, 137;
see also Prophet, Mosque of
al-Miᶜmār mosque 34-6, 39, 67;
minaret 39, 40-1
Miᶜmar Pasha, Mustafa 34
minarets: circular 50, 82, 120, 124, 128-9, 134, 136-7, 141-2, 171, 173, 175, 177, 190, 199n.; early 23, 27, 38; Egyptian style 32; free-standing 123, 125, 136, 141-2, 162; Huraymilā' 145; octagonal 36-7, 39-42, 44-5, 69, 190; Ottoman style 25, 34, 41-2, 44-5, 50, 69, 190; positioning of 37, 39, 41; rectangular 52, 54, 64, 83, 86, 118, 131, 132, 148, 162, 177, 190, 199n.; square 37, 45, 56, 61, 86, 98-9, 127, 132, 154, 158, 166, 178; *see also* Holy Mosque; Prophet, Mosque of; staircase: to minaret
minbar 99; early 30, 189; fixed 39, 50, 52-4, 82, 118, 147, 149, 172-3, 190-1; *see also* Holy Mosque
mosaic as decoration 23-4, 30-3
mu'adhdhin, room for 69, 104-5

al-Mubarraz: *see* Imām Faysal b. Turkī, mosque of, al-Mubarraz; Maghlūth mosque
Muhammad IV, Sultan 48
Muhammad Mansūr mosque, Dahdha al-Suqūr 104-6, 111
Muhammad Sālih Azaᶜjūr mosque 106-8
Muhammad Saᶜūd b. ᶜAbd al-ᶜAzīz 25
Muhāyil mosque 65
al-Munayzila, al-Ahsā', mosque 177-8
al-Muqanda mosque 75-7, 80
muqarnas moulding 37, 38-40, 42, 171-2
Murād IV, Sultan 25
al-Mushayqah, Burayda, mosque 125-6, 129
al-Mustansir Bi'llāh, Caliph Abū-Jaᶜfar 25
al-Mustaᶜsim, Caliph 32
al-Muᶜtamid, Caliph 24
al-Mutawakkil, Caliph 31, 189
Mutawiᶜ, Burayda, mosque 199n.
al-Muzaffar, al-Malik 25, 32, 38
muzalla 80

Na'ām, mosque 166
Najrān, mosques 99-114, 190
al-Nāsir Muhammad, Sultan 32
Nejd region: architectural styles 14, 39, 189-90
Nejd, Central 133-61, 190
Nejd, Northern 117-30
Nejd, Southern 161-6, 190
Nejd, Western 130-3
al-Nejdī, Farasān, mosque 67, 68-73, 74
al-Nejdī al-Tamīmī, Ibrāhīm 68, 72
al-Nejdī al-Tamīmī, Yahyā 197
Nīd al-Haqū, mosque 78-9
Niebuhr, Carsten 15, 55-6
North Mosque, Dahdha al-Suqūr 101-3

Old Mosque, Abū ᶜArīsh 60, 61, 64
Old Mosque, Sabyā 59
Ottoman empire: building activity 27, 32, 38; in Arabia 13-14, 15-16, 25-6, 34, 168; influence on al-Wajh 42, 44-6, 190; *see also* architecture

Palgrave, W.G. 16, 120, 156, 158, 161, 176-7
Pelley, Lewis 156
Pesce, Angelo 34, 39, 41
Philby, H.St.J. 48, 51, 56, 59, 63-4, 78, 82, 156, 158, 161, 198n., 199n.
piers: octagonal 59; rectangular 44-5, 52-3, 67, 71, 106, 114, 118, 120-1, 172-3, 184, 186-7; rounded 85, 172-3, 179; *see also* colonnades
pilgrimage, provision for 13
plaster, use of: carved 66, 71-2, 168, 171-2, 178-9, 184; grey 47, 135, 153; mud plaster: Hejaz 51, 53; Najrān 99, 101, 102, 104-6, 108, 112; Nejd 122, 125, 129-30, 134, 136, 139, 142-3, 146-7, 151, 153-4, 156-8, 163-4; ochre 59, 64, 68, 80, 98, 127, 128, 172-3; waterproof 18, 85, 94, 96, 125; white ᶜAsīr 83, 89, 92, 96-8; Eastern Province 169, 173-5, 187; Farasān 68-71; Hejaz 41-2, 50-1, 53; Mosque of the Prophet 31-2; Najrān 101-2, 106, 109, 112; Nejd 118, 125, 129, 131, 139-40, 143-4, 146-8, 153; Red Sea coast 37-8, 43, 45; Tihāmat ᶜAsīr 57-8, 60; Tihāma mountains 76, 78-80
porch: ᶜAsīr 96-7; Red Sea coast 39
Prochazka, Theodore Jr. 56
Prophet, Muhammad (S), Mosque of, al-Madina al-Monawarah 11, 13, 27-33, 127, 190; decoration 30-2; descriptions 31-3; early building 28-30, 189; enlargements 23, 30-1; fires and restoration 32; influence on architecture 28, 189; interior 33; *mihrāb* 30, 31, 32, 33, 190; minarets 30, 32-3; *minbar* 30, 32; modern construction work 33; Noble *hujra* 30, 32, 33
Prophet Muhammad (S), Mosque of,

Tabūk 13, 48-9

al-Qahaba mosque 77-8, 81
Qalā'ūn, Sultan 32
al-Qānuni, Sulaymān II ("the Magnificent") 25
al-Qāra, mosque 178-9, 181
al-Qasīm area 116, 120, 122-31, 134, 141-2, 190
Qaṣr al-Hayr al-Sharqī, Syria, mosque 189
Qaṣr Mārid 117
Qaṣr al-Minyā, Tiberias, mosque 189
Qaṣr Saᶜd 151
Qaṣr al-Ukhaydir, Iraq, mosque 190
Qaṣr Zurayb, 42
al-Qaṭīf 168, 189; control 14; oasis mosque 181-2; al-Rajihiyya mosque 180-1, 182
Qayt Bay, Sultan 25, 29, 32-3
Qiblatayn mosque 34
Qubā', mosque of 27
quḍāḍ (plaster) 85, 94, 96
al-Qunfudha mosque 18, 55-6

al-Rabadha excavations 11, 13, 189
raḥaba 27, 33
al-Rajihiyya mosque, al-Qaṭīf 180-1, 182
Al Rashīd, Hā'il, mosque 120
al-Rashīd, Harūn, Caliph 13, 34
al-Rawda, Sudayr, *jāmiᶜ* 141-2
al-Rawḍa, Western Nejd, *jāmiᶜ* 130-1
Rihani, Ameen 42, 156, 158
riwāqs: ᶜAsīr 83-5; Eastern Province 172-3; Holy Mosque 23; al-Madina al-Monawarah 27, 30, 32, 33; Nejd 120-1, 122, 127-8, 145-6, 158; Red Sea coast 39; Tihāma mountains 77, 80
al-Riyadh 156; old *jāmiᶜ* 122, 137, 144, 146, 156-9
roof, flat: ᶜAsīr 89, 96; Eastern Province 177-9, 183-8; Hejaz 50, 54; Nejd 127-8, 130, 134-5, 138-41, 142-3, 154, 156, 162-5; Red Sea coast 39, 43-4; Tihāmat ᶜAsīr 59; Tihāma mountains 78-80; as typical design feature 189-90; *see also* domes
Rutter, Eldon 33, 56, 57

Sabyā, mosques 18, 56-9, 60, 63, 72, 74, 89
Saᶜd, al-Dirᶜiyya, mosque 146, 151-2
Sadleir, G.F. 15
al-Ṣahanā': old *jāmiᶜ* 162-3; small mosques 163-4, 166
Salīm II, Sultan 25, 32
Sāmarrā', *jāmiᶜ* 189, 190
Sanᶜā', *jāmiᶜ* 23, 189
Al Saᶜūd: first state 14-15, 25-6, 34, 92, 149-50; and mosque building 14, 16; and Ottoman rule 15; second state 15-16, 156, 177; third state 16, 33
Saᶜūd b. ᶜAbd al-ᶜAzīz b. Muḥammad b. Saᶜūd, Imām 25
Sauvaget, Jean 32
Savignac, F. 48
Schacht, Joseph 190
Shaᶜb Burān al-Ḥarith mosque 108-9, 112
al-Shāfiᶜī (al-Jāmiᶜal-Atīq) mosque 34, 38-9, 41
al-Shahīr, Masqī, mosque 94, 96-8
al-Shanāna, tower 199n.
Shaqrān, mosque 132-3
al-Sharafiyya mosque, al-Hufūf 175-6, 177
Sharama, ᶜAsīr, mosque 89-91
Al Shaykh 14-15
shurfa (balcony) 37, 39; Eastern Province 171; Hejaz 82; Jidda mosques 36, 37, 39, 40; al-ᶜUlā 50; al-Wajh mosques 44, 45
Sirāf, Iran, mosques 190
South Mosque, Dahdha al-Suqūr, 88-100, staircase: to minaret 52, 54, 60-1, 64, 86, 99, 118, 131, 136, 147, 190; palm-trunk 100, 102, 105, 106, 111, 113-14; to platform 57, 60, 89, 94, 98; to roof 64, 90, 99-100, 102-3, 106, 114, 122, 125, 127-8, 130, 134, 138-42, 143, 145, 148-9, 152, 158, 162, 165-6, 186, 190
Strika, V. 36, 38, 39, 41
Sudayr mosques 134, 142
Sudūs, *jāmiᶜ* 50, 146, 149
Sulayman II, al-Qamūnī, Sultan 25, 32
sūq, close to mosque 120, 135, 156
Sūq al-Khamīs, Bahrayn, mosque 189
al-Suqā', ᶜAsīr, *jāmiᶜ* 83-7, 96

Ṭabab, ᶜAsīr, *jāmiᶜ* 91-3
Tabūk mosques 47-9; early mosque 13, 48, 189
al-Ṭā'if 18, 41-2; architectural styles 16, 19, 25; early mosque 13
Tamisier, Maurice 34, 39, 41, 56, 82
al-Thamad mosques 54-5, 132
Tihāma area: architecture 55-6, 189; control of 14; geography 18
Tihāma mountains 75-82
Tihāmat ᶜAsīr area 15, 56-65, 190
tomb of the Prophet 30, 32, 33
Turkī b. ᶜAbd Allah b. Muḥammad b. Saᶜūd, *Imām* 15, 122, 137, 144, 146, 154, 156, 161
Ṭūsūn Pasha, Aḥmad 15
tympanum: Eastern coast 185; Eastern Province 180; Farasān 68, 70; Red Sea coast 37-9; Tihāmat ᶜAsīr 62

al-ᶜUlā: architectural styles 25, 39; mosque 50, 190
ᶜUmar II, Caliph (ᶜUmar b. ᶜAbd al-ᶜAzīz) 27, 120
ᶜUmar b. al-Khaṭṭāb, Dūmat al-Jandal mosque 117-20
Umayyad Caliphs: architectural style 44, 189-90; building activity 23, 27, 30-31, 127-8
Umm Farasān 65-74; *jāmiᶜ* 65-7, 74; mosque 74; *see also* al-Nejdī mosque
ᶜUnayza: *jāmiᶜ* 122-4, 146; small mosque 124
Unitarianism reform movement 14, 15, 16
al-ᶜUqayr, mosque 168, 179, 182-3
Uqlat al-Ṣuqūr, mosque 132
Usayliya, mosque 166
al-ᶜUyayna 14

ventilation 18; Eastern coast 181, 184-185; Eastern Province 168, 178; Farasān 67; Hejaz 52; Red Sea coast 35, 44

Wādī Najrān area 99-114
Wādī-Hanīfa mosque 152-3
Wādī'l-Qurā', mosque 48, 50
Wāfi' mosque, Abū ᶜArīsh 62
al-Wahhāb, Muḥammad b. ᶜAbd, Shaykh 14-15, 134-5, 144, 149-50, 152
al-Wajh 42-7; architectural styles 16, 18-19, 25, 42, 69, 189, 190, 199n; *see also* al-Ashrāf mosque, al-Wajh; al-Budaywī mosque
al-Walīd I, Caliph 23, 27, 30-1, 189
Wallin, Georg Augustus 120
al-Wāṣit, near Hā'il, 120
al-Wāṣiṭ, al-Hajjāj, mosque 172, 189
whitewash: Eastern Province 178; Farasān 66, 74, Hejaz 54; Mosque of the Prophet 32; Tihāma 56; Tihāmat ᶜAsīr 62; Tihāma mountains 76, 78, 79, 80
windows: ᶜAsīr 86, 99; Eastern coast 181-3, 185-6, 188; Eastern Province 171-2, 174, 177-8; Farasān 67, 70, 72; Hejaz 52, 54; lobed 174; Mosque of the Prophet 33; Najrān 100, 102, 106, 108, 112, 114; Nejd 123, 124, 128, 131, 132, 138-9, 148, 162-4, 166; Red Sea coast 35-9, 41, 44, 46-7; Tihāma mountains 80, 81; *see also* glass
al-Wushr, *jāmiᶜ* 79-80

al-Yamāma, mosque 162
Yemen: architectural influence 38-9; control 15-16

Zabīd, mosque 189
al-Ẓāhir Jaqmaq, Sultan al-Malik 25
Zamzam, Well of 20
al-Zilfī 189; *see also* ᶜAlawiyya mosque; al-Jāsir mosque
Zubayda, Lady 13